EUR0MENU

EUROMENU

Marianne Wachholz and Gretel Weiss

DEUTSCHER FACHVERLAG

Distributor to the book trade in the United States and Canada:

Rizzoli International Publications Inc.
300 Park Avenue South
New York, NY 10010

Distributor to the art trade in the United States and Canada:

PBC International, Inc.
One School Street
Glen Cove, NY 11542
1-800-527-2826
Within New York State
call 516-676-2727
Fax 516-676-2738

Distributor throughout the rest of the world (excluding Europe):

Hearst Books International
1350 Avenue of the Americas
New York, NY 10019

Library of Congress Cataloging-in-Publication Data

Wachholz, Marianne.
   [Speisekarten Design. English]
   Euromenu / Marianne Wachholz and Gretel Weiss.
       p.   cm.
   Includes index.
   ISBN 0-86636-246-0   ISBN 0-86636-247-9 (pbk)
   1. Menu design. 2. Graphic arts. I. Weiss, Gretel. II. Title.
III. Title: Euro menu.
NC1002.M4W2313   1993
741.6--dc20
                                                                              93-3312
                                                                              CIP

CAVEAT—Information in this text is believed accurate, and will pose no problem for the student or casual
reader. However, the authors were often constrained by information contained in signed release forms,
information that could have been in error or not included at all. Any misinformation (or lack of information)
is the result of failure in these attestations. The authors have done whatever is possible to insure accuracy.

Color separation, printing and binding by
Toppan Printing Co.

Typography by
TypeLink, Inc.

Printed in Hong Kong

10 9 8 7 6 5 4 3 2 1

CONTENTS

Introduction

The idea for this book was born right in the middle of the food-service editorial staff's everyday work, in a gastronomical trade magazine's mental consideration of the development and happenings in an increasingly professionalizing business.

Two instances provided decisive impulses: on one hand the fact that consumers in the highly-technicized wealthy nations react to visual impulses to an extent not known hitherto, a finding not only relevant in this branch. We have all been spoiled by designing, we live in the midst of colourful picture worlds and can only be visually impressed by the extraordinary. The stimulus threshold is climbing higher and higher .... This era is marked by visual perception, something not only the advertising media have come to realize.

On the other hand is the quest for improvement opportunities and progress; the search for new ways of success for the restaurant business is the focus of editorial work of food-service. And there is no doubt that opportunities of profiling, sales and thus success in the sphere of menu-card design all too often are neglected.

The preliminary work for this book confirmed that estimation: it's almost depressing to see how little menu-cards are consequently and offensively used as marketing instrument activating all dimensions of effect. It's almost frightening how often one encounters dull imitation leather covers with unimaginative and terribly boring price lists, menu-cards with minimal recollection value, without courage and without character. The creative exceptions are reckoned in per thousands instead of per cent.

An unpleasant balance, as the menu-card from a strategical standpoint of view plays the role of a protagonist in all kinds of restaurants, with the exception of self-service outlets. The menu-card is the key to successful marketing. As soon as the guest enters the premises, the card joins in the sales spiel: it to a large extent is responsible for what the customer orders, how much he spends and what impression he has of the businesses' entire service offer.

The menu-card is the most important means of communication, selling and image-promotion for direct approach to guests on the premises. Their marketing function accordingly reaches far beyond that of simply listing the offer and prices.

If successful selling today in an environment characterized by general affluence and dominance of optical impulses is increasingly a matter of visual approach, that must have consequences for the menu-card design. Ultimately it might even be stated that those conceptions totally doing without the card as mediator and instead opting for the impulse effect of direct product presentation today have the best sales chances; leader of the pack here are the open-market type restaurants. They have set irrevocable standards in the sales animation sphere, against which the service conceptions with their menu-card design must stand.

As a general rule, it can be stated that the card's overall impression manifests the character of the gastronomical enterprise for the guest, and that in a very complex manner.

That's precisely why the non-lingual communication facility of the card not solely aiming at the ratio is so important. Experienced restaurant operators know very well that food and beverages are decreasing in importance as motive for their guests to visit a certain establishment.

Other immaterial moments are involved, occasionally even predominant.

They become evident in the structure of offers as well as in the ambiance, service style, atmospherical statement – and, symbolically intensified, in the appearance of the card.

That also implies that the menu-card must be seen as one of many elements in the entire network of gastronomical success factors. Anybody furnishing his menu-card with a flippy shrill design will bewilder his guests with simple home-style cooking or starchy table service. The card may not and should not stand isolated without any context or even in opposition to the remaining concept elements. Congruence – this rule certainly applies to the main menu-card, which in the ideal case is designed to reveal the conceptional core to the guest. Not that extravagant appearances are prohibited, but radical divergence from the overall line is at the most permissible for special cards.

There accordingly is a direct connection between the conceptional orientation of a restaurant and menu-card design – which therefore is not a matter the restaurant operator may exclusively leave to the designer, the agency or the graphic artist.

Consciously planned menu-card design implies that the operator considers matters from the guests' standpoint of view, i.e. sales oriented and not product oriented: the classical marketing approach.

It's no wonder that the crop of menu-cards with distinct design in the sector of nondescript traditional independent restaurants is very meager indeed, and that not necessarily for monetary reasons. More likely it has something to do with the fundamental profilic weakness of this kind of restaurant. To state it very sharply: only unique conceptions can generate unique menu-cards. Looked at from the other side, the subjective disregard of the medium ultimately is only the last consequence of conceptional anemia.

On the long run, the restaurant business will not be able to survive without professional marketing strategies; and menu-card design is the last leg on the mental road of gastronomical marketing considerations.

Inspite of the necessary concentration on its real topic i.e. design, this book at all times endeavours to make this context visible by presenting five exemplary comprehensive case studies which show the relation between menu-card, corporate design and the overall gastronomical conception.

Focuspoint of this book is the documentation of current examples of successful menu-card design. The itinerary leads through the German and Middle European gastronomical world, including excursions to the continent's north, and right across the spectrum of market segments and business types. About 80 catering businesses are introduced along with their most important front, their calling card of self-image, in several cases also with the related means of communication.

This collection considers itself a show-case for exemplary design solutions, exemplary in the sense of creative independence and comprehensive marketing-oriented thinking. It aspires to provide a representative survey on how multifarious, creative and varied European menu-card design today presents itself on its most advanced development level.

Presentation of the card material frequently is concentrated on the cover solution, and this for good reason, as the cover's designing standards aren't always adhered to in the menu-card's interior. Normal type faces very often are employed here, not the least due to cost considerations.

And then there also is a pragmatical aspect. This book doesn't aspire to provide instructions on how to structure the content of a menu-card. Questions of price-policies, verbalization, structure and scope of offer, and also technical aspects of card manufacturing – all this is quite a different matter. The approach chosen here is primarily targeted at the visual dimension. Expert support is provided in form of fundamental statements by three guest authors, each one an absolute pro in his/her field, on this topic from an entrepreneur's, a designer's and a marketing expert's view.

In respect of selection of menu-card examples, the decisive feature wasn't beauty per se, hardly something to be objectivized anyway. Visual power and the appropriateness of design in relation to the overall scheme were much more important. The composition reflects comtemporary taste, the key note is urban, cosmopolitian and not romantic or backward faced. Inspite of intensive month-long research, quite a few presentable examples will have remained undiscovered, but such a project must live with this kind of imperfectness if it is to brought to a conclusion at all.

That also implies that in a very few cases the businesses whose cards are presented here are no longer existent. High fluctuation is grim reality in this branch. That, however, was no reason not to feature them in this book – the design-related quality of a menu-card ranks above the criteria of economic success.

Today, design can only be understood as multicultural phenomenon. Design trends surpass lingual or political borders without any trouble at all; the international viewpoint of this book is to take that into account. This applies to the presented examples, but also to the topic's range: experts in other parts of Europe are also confronted with it. That's why this book is bilingual – in the interest of its useability outside of Germany resp. the German-speaking region.

A pointer on structure of the documentary section: in order to show similarities in the marketing approach as well as the variety of solutions found, the subdivision in the widest sense mixes business-type-related and function-related categories. This subdivision must be understood as loose framework and lays no claim to a strict categorization without overlapping. Some of the examples can be allocated to than one category anyway. In any case, the order in general as well as that in the subsections is in no way to be understood as classification.

Beverage cards are not represented with an own section, the reason being simply that only minimal design-related attention is directed at separate beverage cards – with a few notable exceptions proving the rule. Table and tray sets are a totally different story. Even though they are only partially used as menu-card equivalent, they provide such massed illustrative material in respect of attractive and sales-promoting design that their presence in this book is an absolute enrichment.

Anybody browsing through the book will soon find that chain-affiliated restaurants with their cards are overproportionally represented. That is in fact only logical. Due to their business and material volume, restaurant chains have a much better financial punch than independent operators, and the value of marketing isn't even argued about any more.

The end of the collection phase for this book saw a totally polarized picture: the best results in respect of design were found among the chain restaurants and among the absolute élite gourmet restaurants.

And here's where covers often are designed by artists, frequently resulting from a personal relationship between the restaurant operator and the artist, resp. the specific affinity of the owner to this creative sphere. This exploitation of art is surprisingly wide-spread among outside the top-notch restaurant sphere, too. And that's the way it should be: nobody really likes art locked up and isolated in museums and galleries.

And something else was worth noticing, too: nowhere else in Europe has the world of menu-card design reached a similarly high and wide-spread creative level as in Switzerland. This is the more true for table sets. Volume, professional level, and design quality of the examples put to shame everything offered outside the Swiss borders. A genuine table set culture has blossomed here; without any doubt supported by the altogether favourable conditions and advanced by the engagement of the industry behind it.

From this view-point, it is indeed appropriate that the Swiss company Mövenpick is overproportionally represented in this book. But above all that reflects the company's absolute trailblazing facility for the development of the business all over Central Europe. And that on the conceptional level as well as consequently the level of menu-card design. This company with its high degree of affinity to the field of marketing has not only started things moving internally: in respect of its innovative radiation of this pioneer role, the creative input initiated by Mövenpick for the entire Central European gastronomy is comparable to that T.G.I. Friday's had in the US during the early 1980's.

To awaken the courage and desire to innovation is one of the main intents of this book. It wants to initiate and motivate more and new attention being paid to the menu-card as instance of gastronomical professionalism. It's addressed at all those interested in this field, be it for professional or more affectionate reasons: entrepreneurs in the business, their marketing experts, and the relevant service providers: designers and photographs, graphic artists, printing companies and agencies.

This was and is the real legitimation for us to dare and venture on this book project: stimulation and sensual inspiration in order to provide the menu-card as the classical marketing instrument in the restaurant business with new and increased importance, creativity, and utilization, and thus to further advance professionalization in this branch.

This book could never have been compiled without the help of many restaurant operators in Germany and the neighbouring countries. We owe a lot to these and all others who provided us with information and hints, who actively helped us along and were willing to contribute material, time and knowledge. Special thanks goes out to the three experts Ueli Prager (Mövenpick), Ursula Hild (Wienerwald) and Dieter Dreesen (Dreesen Design), who gave the topic its general theoretical background with their very competent articles. And last but not least, we are indebted to the photographer, the translator, the producer as well as the sponsoring editor for their committed and productive cooperation.

And that's enough introductory words; design is after all a visual discipline.

Fundamental Dimensions of Menu-Card Design

Three professionals state their opinions

Menu-cards are applied art

Most readers will probably think that for me to write about something I have dealt with in 50 years of professional life shouldn't be all too difficult.

However, the more I concern myself with this sphere in depth, the larger my doubts grow. Doubts about the correctness of statements which appear to be self-evident only on first sight, and doubts whether things that appear to be right for me must also be right for others.

Let me start at the very beginning with the gastronomer, the restaurant operator. The young restaurant owner opening his business as pioneer feat believes in his mission, or else he wouldn't be a pioneer. He knows how to transmit to other people, to find forms of expression for his thoughts, in other case he wouldn't be successful in his profession. And he knows how to communicate, or else he wouldn't be in the restaurant business.

His menu-card and selection are his form of communication. They reflect personality – that of the business and, if things are the way they should be, also that of the restaurant owner. Committed work in this sector should make visible the person behind all this work in all dimensions: the menu-card design, the nature of presentation, the food and the language these foods are offered in. Matching his talents, his personnal wishful thinking as well as the esprit of the establishment and the location – if these don't fit in with the entrepreneurial intention, they have been badly chosen anyway.

Card and offer should, in fact they must speak the gastronomer's language.

Regardless of whether the card is very simply designed or is just a slate, whether it is plastered full of paper slips – chaotic and nonconformistic, like my Mövenpick card

which made gastronomiocal history between the late 40's and the mid 50's, or whether it is made up of artful photographies of the dishes/products coming up – like when the phase of the attached slips of paper was replaced by the era of artistic-aesthetic colorful photographies in menu-card design, whether it features copies of impressionists or design by a modern abstract painter or graphic artists favoring the 'art primitive', the card should always be marked by the gastronomer's system of values, by his character.

I believe that the design of menu cards has been developed as new art trend in the past three decades.

Menu cards produced in the first half of this century usually were accurately-made printed matters decently type-set by compositors, if things went alright. Graphic art, color photography, awareness of the effect of color, writing and pictures in everyday use – these are the milestones of the phantastic development in menu-card design in the past decades. Since then, restaurants and their offer have fascinated and fired the artistic imagination of thousands of adepts. Wonderful.

However, if the innovative advertiser, or the advisor dedicated to a certain art trend, or a centralized marketing department come up with a ivory-tower creation which serves more to satisfy the designer's wishes than it does to serve the sales cause, then it has simply fallen short of its objective.

Menu-card design is not l'art pour l'art, is not art per se. Menu-card design is applied art. This kind of art must pursue an objective not enveloped by aesthetics; it must capture and graphically represent what the gastronomer wants to achieve with his work.

The menu-card designer must capture his customer and the genius loci like a portraitist. If the guest believes to have recognized the gastronomer while browsing through and reading the menu card, the portraitist, i.e. the menu-card designer has done his job well. However, anybody looking for

appreciation by the small group of art directors or graphical purists, has badly invested his client's money. The designer's job is of an interpreting nature. His primary function is to find a form of expression which reflects what the business and the people in charge are capable of performing in gastronomical respects, what they are willing to perform, and what they are able to fulfill with the help of the staff members.

Keeping in line with this doctrine, one of my intentions was to try and present one product in depth with my sales promotion cards. My idea was to present an entire range of different meals at various prices and prepared with different recipies based upon one product. It was not only necessary to depict the raw product in an alluring and appetizing manner, it also was a matter of generating the product-specific aura through artistically perfect color photographies.

* The mysteriously dark smoking room for smoked salmon, sprats and mackerels.
* Artic freshness for lobster or halibut on blue shimmering ice.
* The exotic erotic flair for the creamy honeysweet walnut ice-cream.
* The rustic down-to-earth background for sauerkraut and cabbage dishes.
* The wild and romantic Marlboro style for American steaks.
* And finally: Bella Italia for pasta foods.

These and all other Mövenpick cards are at the same time embodiment of my basic gastronomical convictions. Eating and drinking are supposed to be some of the small everyday pleasures. Whoever visited my restaurant, my Mövenpick, was there to enjoy, to enjoy and relax.

With small or big appetite.
With small or big wallet.

At mealtime or any other time of the day.

Enjoying isn't bound to any time and to any rules. The German poet and writer Goethe had his character Tasso declare: "Everything enjoyable is permissible."

I wanted to be just right for those interested in culinary surprises, for the lover of small and exquisite delights as well as for the hearty eater. For those without chronological restrictions, who prefer to sit down at the table at 3 p.m. or after a theater performance, as well as for those who prefer to adhere to the traditional mealtimes.

Quality in vivid variety, that was my motto; exacting demands for everything served in a glass or on a plate.

All those things that only cost money and didn't actually contribute to enjoyment had to be omitted. The design of cards had to adhere to this principle, too.

The proper catchword to be introduced here is honesty.

If the menu card promises more or something else than what is served on the plate, in the glass, or as overall service, then false expectations are evoked. Disappointed expectations, however, lead to disillusionment and ultimately to rejection. Here's where the guest turns away with a shudder . . .

If the selection is only mediocre, then the card should also only reflect normal matter-of-fact everyday life, and of course also the prices. Luxury, the refined sophisticated life style must be understood, interpreted and celebrated by those demanding the corresponding prices.

We live in an honest time. Simplicity is in demand, authenticity is expected. Stand by what you are and what you can do. Plagiarism is looked down upon, anybody simply imitating another won't gain a profile, and only profiles are in demand today – even if they are occasionally have sharp edges. We at Mövenpick consider that to be one of our guiding principles – a phrase quickly spoken but which only can entirely be understood and lived by mature people.

To be yourself, that's what it's all about. "Know thyself" is an inscription on the temple of Apollo in Delphi. Nothing less, I believe, is the most important demand upon the gastronomer at the time he undertakes to detemine his selection and design his menu card.

Be critical with yourself, see through yourself, recognize your position. Accept your faults and weaknesses, strengthen your virtues. This kind of mental attitude will allow production of a genuine, credible menu card. The customer will notice this, success will come about.

Should I 'be myself', that's what I also asked myself when I sat down to write this article. Was I to uncritically and unalloyed praise all the beautiful pictures to which we also contributed our share? Or was I also to write about what I found to criticize even about the most beautiful of cards. Was I, under the risk of being misunderstood, to insist that aesthetics shouldn't be achieved at the expense of authenticity of a card?

I want to remain honest, and I admit that I often view artistically perfect cards made to meet all marketing requirements with critical eyes, because I don't consider them to sufficiently represent the people in the front line.

I love to admire a nice-looking card, but it has to fit to what I experience – the restaurant's ambiance, the staff's and its chef's style, simply all that is being offered.

The corporate design, which possibly becomes visible in a color, in a logo or an artistic character, at first is only a form of outward appearance. It can never replace what has been lived, the esprit you want to encounter in companies where corporate identity is intact.

This perceptible unity between restaurateur, his team in kitchen and service, and the piece of art we know as menu-card is essential. And I want to be able to sense the human beings in every card, every show window, every advertising letter and every newspaper ad. Not the people who created the card, but those who are responsible for and must account for the product, the atmosphere, in brief all that I experience in a restaurant. That's what I call corporate identity.

*Ueli **Prager** (Zurich) is founder of the Mövenpick Restaurants and Hotels; he is in fact one of Europe's outstanding gastronomical pioneers. The Swiss entrepreneur has been active in this business for almost five decades and in this time has set milestones, among other things also in the field of placative, effective menu cards.*

Whole generations of chefs, waiters, and restaurant experts in general have learned from him and have later carried their expertise into the entire business.

Prager incidentally was one of the first entrepreneurs in the field of food and beverages to introduce ideas and trends from the New World to the old one. A fanatic for conceptions and details.

Culmination of conceptional statements

A big discussion most probably is due in restaurant chain's marketing departments everytime a new menu card is to be printed as to whether all this dealing with graphs, colours, type size, selection of pictures, paper strength, etc. is necessary in addition to the already quite difficult work concerning contents. Can't our service staff patiently, courteously and competently present the selection? Or why don't we simply provide the restaurants with blackboards, a text manuscript and chalk? That way we could rid ourselves of all the trouble. Or we can exhibit plastic imitations of our offer like they do in Japan; we'd only have to worry about placement of price tags ...

These Japanese food plastics are not something just to be smiled about. They reflect the correct idea that visual impression is a more reliable sales aid than the spoken or written word.

In this respect self-service conceptions are in a situation to be envied. They can totally rely on the immediacy of the experience, which has advantages concerning buying incentive as well as communication. Misunderstanding, disappointments are practically excluded: where products are shown, everybody knows much better what to expect than if they were only listed in the menu.

However, the basic conceptional decision often is made in favor of service. Even if the principle of presentation is made use of as far as possible – integration of self-service counters, look-in kitchens, etc. – the menu-card cannot be omitted as necessary instrument here. And most certainly uncalculable procedures such as oral recommendations or writing tablets aren't adequate for restaurants adhering to a certain system.

Above all, because purposive employment of the menu-card is capable of doing a lot more than just informing on selection and prices.

In lieu of waiter or restaurant owner, a printed menu-card is in charge of communication with the customer. It is a 'mute salesperson' – and thus the most important means of advertisement in the restaurant. But this card not only mediates information related to the selection, the advertising factor comes in on top of this more factual component: attractive pictures and descriptions stimulate and motivate (additional) purchasing.

Over and beyond that, the card represents a restaurant's positioning, profile and atmosphere – the image component. And finally, it allows scattering of sales by targeted product placement – the sales component.

Thus the rank of a menu-card in marketing mix is much higher than that of a simple price list. It is the central marketing instrument effective on-site in all kinds of restaurants.

This assessment is by no means merely academical, it is impressively substantiated by the results of a survey conducted by Wienerwald a few years ago, which came up with the following findings:

* About 90% of the guests have not definitely decided what they want to eat when they enter they restaurant.

* About 85% read the menu-card relatively thoroughly.

* According to own statements, the interviewees concern themselves with the menu-card for approximately 5 minutes. This subjective perception is considerably higher than the time actually spent.

* The time spent with the menu-card in the evenings and on week-ends is longer than that at lunchtime.

* About two thirds are not only interested in dry information on selection and prices, they look for an appetite-whetting design.

* Almost 90% of those questioned enjoy reading the menu-card.

* About two thirds browse through the menu-card after they have made their selection.

* 'Fat' menu-cards are not considered a deterrent.

These findings must be considered an urgent appeal to the restaurant operators to very intensly occupy themselves with the menu-card and its design. The menu-card's key position in respect of a restaurant's sales objectives can hardly be more impressively verified!

When concepting the menu-card, any kind of restaurant business – whether plain cooking, restaurant chain branch or high-class cuisine hot-spot – first of all must ask itself the question: "What do I want to tell my guests?" Mind you, this is not alone a question of the selection. Be it consciously or subconsciously, the menu-cards help guests inform themselves about what kind of restaurant they actually are sitting in. At the latest here's where the customer classifies the business according to subjective standards – popular, expensive, conservative, elegant, trendy, etc.

The card is no less than the culmination point of conceptional statements – advertisement, brand, facades, interior furnishment ultimately can only support the approach, evoke expectations. A businesses' target group approach, services, and marketing conception are visually/linguistically illustrated.

That's why it is extremely important to neatly coordinate all other conceptional levels with the card performance. Starting from the ambiance over service style all the way to price level – discrepancies and ruptures cause irritations and can considerably endanger a conception's success.

The level of contents as well as that of artistic design play a most important role here. "What do I want to tell my guests?" inevitably also includes "How do I tell them?" Design, that implies determination of forms and colors, typography, illustrations – but that also means rivalry for placement. How are the meals, the product groups to be arranged? Conflicts of interest must be solved, criteria such as profile and positioning, aspects of novelty and sales statistics findings in reference of sales as well as profit contribution must be taken into consideration.

This does not only affect the food and beverages card, which we regard as one unit. Wienerwald, for instance, operates with a separate card for across-the-street sales for organizational reasons. There also are special cards for events or special promotions, cash-register cards, display-case cards and a children's card.

To produce beverages or dessert cards, breakfast or children's cards is a question of image and sales targeting. Differentiation of cards in order to distinguish product groups is sensible especially in those cases where the competence profile in certain fringe segments is to be pushed ahead. An important factor here: the more distinct the 'luxury character' of the product group is, for example desserts, the more emotionalized the card presentation should be to make sure the purchase incentive takes effect.

A principle rule is that foods compete with beverages, main dishes with snacks. Naturally we all try to boost hors d'oeuvres – often identical with snacks – by prominent placement catching the eye. But our guests' attention as before at first is turned towards main dishes. About two thirds of those questioned in our survey began reading the card in the main-dishes section – which doesn't imply that the menu card is not considered interesting reading material and pastime after the selection has been made.

Nonetheless, the influencing facilities of placement are not to be underestimated. It's no secret that, depending on the customer's reading habits, the card has a good and an bad side, just as well as the circumstance that our guests avoid extremes in selection habits. An overall psychological phenomenon applies here: the large majority of people feels safe in the middle field, only very few are willing to expose themselves. What does that have to do with design of menu-cards? Quite a lot. The extreme positions in reference to both price and positioning, that is the very beginning and the very end, will practically never be favorites. Experience shows that the demand always balances out in the middle range. This finding is extremely important for sales-related strategical considerations in designing cards, incidentally also useful for the planned price structure.

In an exaggerated form, the question might be: should individual products be employed for sales stimulation and monitoring? If so, which products? Only main products? Profit contribution smashers? The positioning 'star' – in case of Wienerwald accordingly the famous chicken? New products requiring an explanation? This question also should be decided under consideration of the profile-maintaining aspect. In this specific case illustrations are the sales booster per se – illustrations can influence sales by 100 per cent. The more popular a gastronomical conception is, the more true this is. To say it extremely: the perceptional approach of a yellow press reader differs from that of a subscriber to Herald Tribune or The Financial Times. One will react more strongly to graphic impulses, the other will do so in a somewhat moderate form. Depending upon the target group focus, this will play an important role in menu-card design.

Our experience shows that graphic representations at the most are suited for loosening up a menu-card; their appetite appeal is much too low for targeted stimulation.

But what should be depicted? As much as possible? That will hardly be possible if alone for the limited space available and it would also even out all sales-related dramaturgical intentions. And then – which photographical approach? Which decoration, which lighting? Depiction of components or true-to-life illustrations of what the guest actually will find on his plate?

A general rule should be not to overstress the customers' ability to think abstractly. That means the depictions should correspond with reality, at the most with a slight touch of idealisation, as nothing is more fatal for gastronomical success than to disappoint your guests. To the contrary, they must experience the services supplied as being positive: the product on the plate must at least correspond with the developed expectations, better even if they are surpassed. For kitchen and service, working with photographies at the same time implies an educative effect: the pictures are both obligation and incentive.

On the other hand: photographical solutions are expensive, and as consequence frequently not to be realized by single enterprises requiring only low volume card editions. No wonder then that the questioned consumers who were shown four different card versions spontaneously related the illustrated cards with restaurant-chain-type businesses – simply a matter of experience.

And again the customer perspective: concerning the folded form of the menu-card, be it bound or spiral-seam, fan-folded or simple cover, the pros and cons balance each other. Expectation and overall view, the possibility to compare and easy handling – each solution has its advantages.

Here's where the crux of many market research analysis becomes obvious: their results don't provide us with definite clear-cut answers which would simplify making a decision, instead they seem to allow any solution. So it ultimately is a matter of uncalculable factors – vision, instinct, creative competence.

Specifically in larger restaurant chains it's a matter of designing a menu-card in headquarters which is not only accepted and tolerated in the branches, but which is lived. In other words, a card every staff member can identify with. What was developed and produced over months after all is at the same time calling card of each and every one of the chains's restaurants – and at the same time expresses corporate identity. That also includes advancing values which reflect on the overall setting.

Ursula Hild (Munich) *is marketing director of Wienerwald Germany. The graduated national economist has been with this oldest German restaurant chain for a total of more than 15 years. She executed the most recent relaunch and again revitalized the almost 40-year-old chicken scheme.*

Her strong point is the ability to align theoretical and practical aspects, and her profound experience in the sphere of menu cards encompasses design, supply monitoring, price policies and—perhaps most important of all—concrete target group approach. She really knows what it means to advance success through this medium.

Interface between art and function

Design, including that of menu-cards, always obeys two masters; it exists in the polarity between art and function. Design acts as integrating element in the field of tension between both forces; it combines both the aesthetical and the functional motive to a synthesis. Thinking in hierarchies in the line of „Form follows Function" won't lead to any success; the conditions are of a more complex nature. An initial designing idea can indeed be the starting point for the overall development of a menu-card.

If one neglects all creative design-related elements, there is one constant factor: menu-cards are means of communication. However, it is common knowledge that communication is a very complex matter. In this case, there are four levels of communication:

Level I: Information. The factual level.

Level II: Interpretation. The emotional level.

Level III: Animation. The level of action resp. invitation.

Level IV: Projection. The level of imagination.

What's behind all this? Information means explicit, virtual, and factual communication. Designation of offer, price, quality, including technical aspects: opening hours, service pecularities or credit card acceptance.

Interpretation means mediation of a businesses' conception of values, of its philosophy. It can be implicit or explicit, and as any in the widest sense of speaking ethical category aims at emotions and feeling.

Animation means activation, kindling of cravings and wants, provocation of reactions. And this in a very targeted manner, too: monitoring of interests, craving for food, food appeal.

Projection means: mediation of identity, positioning, image pattern. It's a matter of generating an image for the reader, „mind cards" as Gerd Gerken calls them, that are to manifest themselves in the card user's head as elements of interest.

The task of communication increases in complexity in each subsequent phase. And the further away you move from the factual level, the less you can be certain that the guest correctly receives the intended message.

The whole matter becomes even more complicated by the fact that all four levels practically blend and shift one on top of the other in the concrete form of the menu-card.

For this reason, communication between designer and restaurant operator isn't all that easy; and that's why it is so difficult to create good menu-cards. Incidentally, that corresponds with the general communication problem all people have with each other, it's what psychiatrists call „transmission on four frequencies".

The designer's objective accordingly is to harmonize all four aspects with each other. The menu-card admittedly is an extraordinarily important instrument in the sphere of restaurant conception, but one must always remember that it doesn't stand alone. The card is embedded in the ambiance, the service staff's conduct, the restaurant atmosphere, etc..

The menu-card accordingly is element of the entire communication mix and the identity of a restaurant conception. It is an element of corporate design, just as the logo, the facade, architecture, decoration, and the staff's uniform, other printing matters in the business, advertisement and sales promotion means. And accordingly also an element of the entire corporate identity. But that implies that the inner harmony of the menu-card is as important as the exterior one: consonance with all the other design and identity statements. To give a graphic example: a hand-written calligraphic-style menu-card would look kind of foolish in a typical fast-food outlet.

But you don't have to make a dogma of it: intentional disharmonies under certain circumstances can be an adequate designer's means to achieve a certain effect. If specific forms of expression become common property or better, assume the character of a cliché, the individual setting a counterpoint will attract attention. In that case, controversy itself, alienation, deviation from traditional harmony patterns can create identity. Aesthetical standards simply aren't categories inscribed for all times, they are only valid until somebody breaks through them. And here's another relativization: whether the design of a card is successful or not isn't anything to be assessed in isolation. Speaking for myself, I believe that to a very large extent is dependent upon the nature of business and its overall identity.

Three basic elements by harmonizing generate a menu-card's complex visual message:

* material
* text
* graphical means

The choice of material alone, i.e. simply of the mediating means of the text/graphical information, encompasses a design-related intent.

Paper or cardboard is available in a vast array of qualities, sizes, colors, with structured or smooth surfaces, matt, glazed, or glossy, with no regard to the additional possibilities of handling with printing techniques and surface treatment. And those are only the best-selling products, just as well conceivable is the utilization of other media such as wood, textiles, plastic or plexiglass.

The card's text, initially only the mediation of linguistic messages through letters, also has a second dimension effecting the design aspect in addition to its purely lingual function. The manner of type face arrangement, the design and composition of the letters is in itself again a graphic statement. That makes typography yet another of the design-related instruments. Not to forget the language itself, i.e. formulations, choice of words, language structure. They to a large extent transport those informations of the second, third, and fourth degree not situated on the factual level. The designer therefore must always see lingual and graphic dimension of the text as a whole.

The third variable for the creative individual are the graphical means in a narrower sense: depictions, illustrations, the entire layout. Very important here: handling with colors. And then there also is the question of a menu-card's format, size, style, and volume.

Design and composition of the three basic elements constitute the visual appearance of the menu-card, so to speak in the next dimension, and consequently its overall communicative performance.

That actually sounds kind of dry, but the variety of the resulting solutions/statements is almost unbelieveable.

Of course there is a basic differentiation between pure text cards and illustrated cards, but even if text and typography are the only intruments used, the interpretation and projection are totally different depending on whether one and the same text appears

* handwritten on white paper;
* handwritten on a chalkboard in the restaurant;
* typewritten or printed by PC on paper; or
* printed on high-gloss paper.

If illustrations are to be used, it's a matter of weighting. Dominance of text or of illustration? Should only the cover be illustrated or should pictures appear throughout the card? Should the products be shown, or emphasis laid upon lifestyle motives? Drawings or photographies?

The designer's creativity principally operates free of any limitations on the open field of possibilities. It is steered in certain tracks by a number of restricting factors: functional aspects such as cost margins, practical handling and durability requirements, corporate design standards or also sales strategical objectives.

The first thing to do in any case is to define a clear-cut communication-related objective together with the restaurant operator. That also implies determination of which one of the four communication levels is to be emphasized; whether a specific lifestyle is to be stressed or if the menu-card simply is to have an appetite appeal, whether certain target groups are to be addressed through specific designing means, etc …

Something not to forget in this context is the fact that modernity and zeitgeist contents of a menu-card – and consequently of a restaurant conception – are determined by a guest by means of swiftly adapted optical signals, which he more or less subconsciously assimilates, compares with his repertoire of symbols stored at other occasions, and categorizes accordingly.

The consequence is the continuous – and increasingly faster – formation of new visual standards marking entire menu-card generations. A number of cards created in the early '80s clearly show the influence of Memphis Design, in the mid-80s we find layout style and typography influenced by Neville Brody.

Photography is a relatively young, sensible and multi-level means of menu-card design. The specific property of photographies is that several adoption levels are addressed at the same time. For one, there is the real image shown – the factual level. At the same time, one and the same photography evokes associative, interpretative impressions: through the accessories, through action and incidence of light, the visual angle, etc . . .

So to speak the newest fad are computer-technical realizations. Every single restaurant business can directly realize layouts with the help of DTP programs provided by computer resp. software producers; provided there is someone who can handle the equipment! One thing must be understood: a computer is only an instrument, it's a matter of how well one can play it – that goes for the graphics program just as much as it does for the drawing pencil.

There is a large risk of becoming stuck in standardized uniformity and thus becoming entirely comparable with others in respect of restaurant identity.

Every restaurant operator seeking to introduce a new menu-card will of course ask about the costs. Printing is always a problem specifically for individual businesses. Offset printing, the only such method capable of converting photographies, isn't worthwhile for smaller amounts, precisely the problem for individual businesses. Even in case of using the so-called proofing method, which allows production of smaller quantities, the price-per-unit remains relatively high, as the costs for the lithographic production are fully apportioned to the low volume amount.

Yet another production method is silk-screen printing, which does not, however, allow reproduction of photographies. That's why individual businesses often have illustrated menu-cards, as these are relatively easy to produce with the silk-screen method, provided the originals feature pure colors. The more complex and colorful the illustration, the more expensive the production.

A frequently recurring problem is the menu-card changing in daily or weekly intervals. From a designer's point of view, there are only very few outstanding examples on the market in this field. The loose sheet to be exchanged in the menu-card usually is fastened by clips, adhesive or tape. It comes quite naturally that these covers frequently look a mess after only a few months. On the other side, exchanging the menu-cards is an important identity and marketing factor for a number of businesses. To find better and innovative solutions should prove to be a rewarding task for future designers of menu-cards.

Regardless of whether it is extravagant or plain, the menu-card is the centerpiece of communication with the guest. And everybody knows for him or herself how he or she reacts to a well-devised card. And everybody instinctively knows what a good menu-card is! It certainly isn't the only argument for visiting a specific restaurant, but the quality of a menu-card can tip the scale – in either direction.

Dieter Dreesen *(Düsseldorf) is director of a designing agency. Renowned names in the European and Oriental gastronomical business rank among his clients; he is considered a pro in design, creation of brand image, and marketing. His philosophy is to take a look at things in their context, their entirety, and not as isolated objects.*

The studied designer considers himself a stylist, an expert with words and images. His capability of approaching matters analytically without omitting the emotional moment is the basis of his success. Restaurant and hotel business as well as product presentations are his principal domains.

Menu-Card Design—

Center Piece of Comprehensive Image-Promotion

Five exemplary case studies on Corporate Design

Design gone art

Neon pink and garish green: extreme colours set shrill accents in Stuttgart's new Staatsgalerie (state gallery) created by architect James Stirling. Part of this cultural monument opened in 1984, which not only houses works of art but can be considered one itself, has been turned into a restaurant named Fresko.

A museum location, that is, a situation in which culinary enjoyment is only the secondary attraction; what can be made of it in spite of many unpresentable counterparts is aptly demonstrated by this example. A major prerequisite is a separate entrance, so as to be independent of the museum's regular opening hours.

Even though its not only locational proximity to the world of art is already expressed by its name, the Fresko's concept was developed with only one eye cast on the museum's visitors. During the day, the museum's visitors are a major part of the clientele. After closing time, however, there is a complete shift in scenario. At nighttime, the nicely decorated restaurant – replete with table cloths, paperdoilies and candles – is crowded by Fresko-fans. Creative people with an educational background, with a scent of avantgarde. Artists, art-lovers and connoisseurs; and all those who are attracted by this colourful mixture.

Fresko has chosen a location smack in the center of Stuttgart's art world, in more than one sense. Some factors are location and ambiance, also an excellent cuisine. But most important is the personal style of the proprietors – they cultivate a very unique, creatively alive atmosphere.

It unfolds in an ambiance which to a large degree carries the design signature of architect Stirling. The enormous window-front opening onto a terrace was his idea, as well as the unusual bar-counter construction and the classically shaped light-coloured wooden chairs. And – not to be overlooked – the grass-green nubby synthetic floor which serves as a connecting colour element. The proprietors have added their own details: giant mirrors hung with a slant, palmtrees and opulent flower-arrangements, selected accessoires dating from different periods of style. The pictures decorating the walls are exchanged regularly. Light and spacious, above all open, fostering communication, the ambiance does not grab the attention but serves as a backdrop, a platform for a gastronomical production in which both host and guest can play their part.

The customers are encouraged to leave behind their usual passively consuming role and be part of the action. Spontaneity is the key word here. Anybody wanting to can play the piano or turn one of the paper table covers into a canvas: actual art. The Fresko's staff gives an example: they'll use the table cover to mark reservations, to list the bill of fare for a special gathering – or – to present the bill! Here restaurant life can turn into a happening – a little 'off', a little extravagant, a little flippant. This can go all the way to regularly organized performance-evenings: dinner spectacles.

The Fresko's self-image and clientele-focus are based on a close connection between art and cuisine. This is documented in a phenomenally successful way by the restaurant's menu-card.

The menu-card, concipated as loose leaf folder, actually leaves the category of design to become a work of art. The outside is bright green, the inside pink plastic material – the daring colour combination favoured by Stirling was also chosen by the proprietors as the 'house-colours'. Inside there is a veritable firework of ideas, an extremely funny concoction mixed together of all eras of art history, a genuine pleasure to read.

The items classified by three different colours are listed on twelve double pages. Green and pink (how could it be different!) respectlessly combined with blue. As you turn the pages, different categories of products are highlighted: green is reserved for breakfast, rosy shades announce all food items from appetizers to main dishes. And blue is not the mood, but sets the stage for the listing of beverages. The actual information is arranged into beautifully designed tableaus, unabashedly quoting from a variety of styles.

A smartly chaotic mix of surrealism, Dada and pop-art-elements, caricatures, collages and photomontages mingles style-typical images such as the American highway-cruiser of pop-art-fame with 'home baked' interna, insinuations of tales only known to insiders – a special treat for regulars!

Script-image collages in Dada-style, mystifying montages, caricatures and little jokes illustrate the gastronomical main attractions – food and drink.

The dinner show announcements are made up in the same eccentric manner: folded stick-in pages, giving no thought to harmony (of colours). And also the caricature which makes up the Fresko's signature shows a definite tendency towards Dada.

Freedom and nonconformity not only in art – but also as a life-style: by drawing inspiration from a style of art which in its day was meant to be shocking, anti-establishment, critical and witty, as avantgarde as could be, the Fresko-card takes a definite position. It is just as far removed from mainstream thinking as the entire restaurant's concept. The aesthetic values are intellectually flavored and demand quite a bit of cultural literacy in order to be fully appreciated.

In the choreography of design and information, the latter is subject to aesthetic dominance. Bending all rules, readability is not the primary objective here. The handwritten scriblings look improvised, spontaneously thrown in. Functional it is; single pages can be exchanged easily, small changes in the card can be made without causing any breach of style.

This menu-card, which took an entire year of collecting ideas, can not only claim a high entertainment value: the feat is the identity expressed and generated at the same time.

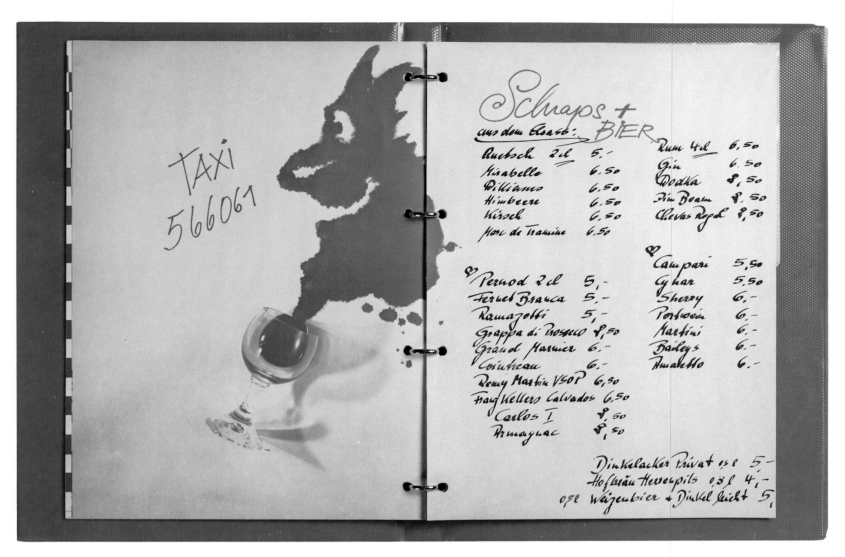

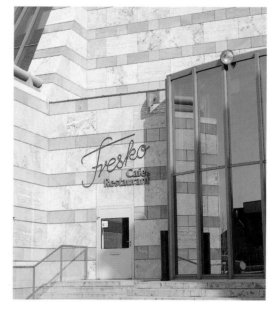

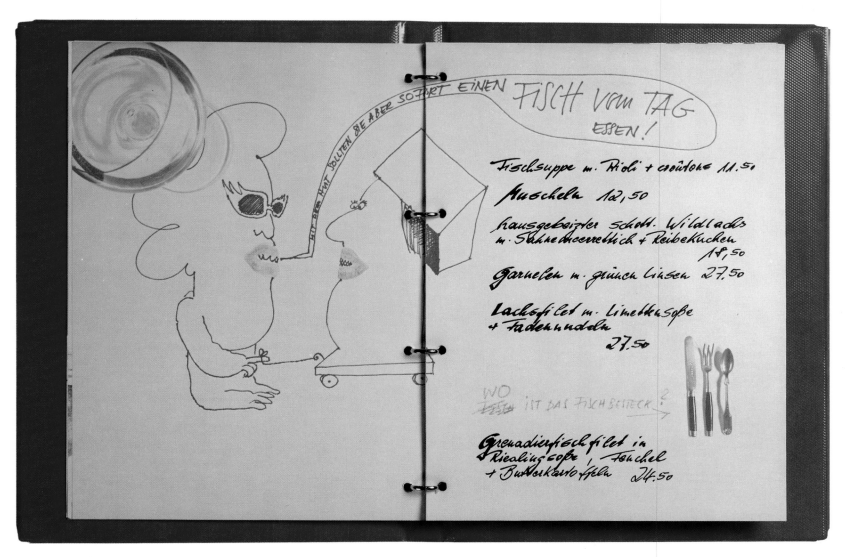

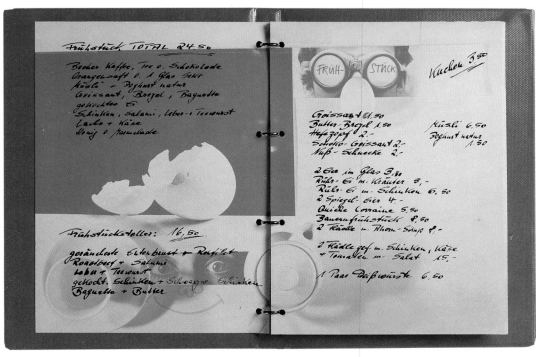

Gastronomen:

Helga Hofmann, Petra Cali, Stuttgart.

Interieur Design:

James Stirling, London.

Logo:

Helga Hofmann, Fresko.

Karte:

Die Künstlerin Gisela Zimmermann, Stuttgart.

Proprietors:

Helga Hofmann, Petra Cali, Stuttgart.

Interior design:

James Stirling, London.

Logo:

Helga Hofmann, Fresko.

Menu-card:

The artist Gisela Zimmermann, Stuttgart.

Dessert + Käse   Eis: Vanille
                        Schokko
                        Pistazie
                        Dalueis
                        Erdbeer
                        Zitrone

3 Bobbl Eis 5,-

Mousse au chocolat 10,50

Joghurtschaum m. fr. Früchten 10,-

Karamelköpfli m. Vanille-Eis
+ Nektarinenspalten 9,50

Rhabarber in Champagnergelee
m. Marzipansoße + Erdbeermark 11,-

Rote Grütze m. Vanilleeis+Sahne 11,-

Erdbeeren m. Sabayon 8,50

Ofenschlupfer m. Vanillesoße 7,50

versch. franz + ital. Käse
m. fr. Obst ab 15,-

DIPLOMATE

Wer ist das?

FRIEDEMANN

Getränke ohne
ALKOHOL

doppel. Espresso 5,-   Tonic Water   } 0,2ℓ
Becher Kaffee 5,-   Ginger Ale   } 3,50
Milch Kaffee 5,-   Bitter Lemon
Becher Schokolade 6,50   Fanta   } 0,2ℓ
Portion Tee   6,50   Coca Cola   } 3,-

SAN BITTER 0,2ℓ 3,50   Teinacher 0,25ℓ 3,-
+ Orangensekt   Teinacher 0,33ℓ 3,50
CHAMP-Fitness 0,33ℓ 4,-

Blutorangennektar 0,25ℓ 3,50
Apfelsaft naturtrüb   3,50
Kirschsaft   3,50
Johannisbeernektar   3,50
Tomatensaft   4,50

Eiskaffee   6,50

nur
INSIDE: Tasse Kaffee 3,-
        + Espresso 3,-

24

Taking a bow to the location

Just a stone's throw away from Vienna's St. Stephan's cathedral, very worldly competition has sprung up for this respectable sacral building: the Haas-Haus, a temple of luxury and consumerism designed by the famous architect Hans Hollein. The restaurant Do & Co is situated on the top floor of this building. Quite a location!

If you've gotten a kick out of the shocking concentration of sacral architecture and the post-modern styling of this very noble shopping passage – just wait until you're inside!

The transparency of the Haas-House's facade opens up to fascinating perspectives of the cathedral – the higher up you get, the more breathtaking they are. The exclusive view, not to be had from down below, secures a unique bonus for Do & Co.

The actual restaurant on the 7th floor – as exclusive as Haas-Haus itself, not to be taken for another example of the 'scenic view' genre – with its open-air terraces is complemented by a bar and a café, which in the evening is often used for 'closed company' functions.

The ambiance is quietly modern, matching the Haas-Haus' architecture without picking up on its postmodern extravagance. The impression is refined, informally elegant and 'with it'. Catching the eye are a small Teppanyaki-area and an open show-kitchen with a presentation counter. Otherwise, the atmospheric strength of the view is allowed to develop without hindrance. The café gets the full benefit of the nearby cathedral and the evening panorama is even more breathtaking.

Logo and menu-card design both exploit this 'ace' of a location: two parallel interpretations have been chosen to activate different levels of reference.

First the logo: the objective was to newly interpret the already existing Do & Co signature. Do & Co had already been in existence since 1981, its previous activities included a combined food specialty store/deli as well as an expanded catering service. The objective of the new logo was to express the independence of the new venture as well as the identity of the company, to enact an image-transfer, so to speak. This forbade the design of an entirely new logo. The solution chosen draws on the location as a distinguishing factor: the familiar signature was set inside a stylized cathedral silhouette; a golden, round aureole, broken by fine white lines, holds the elements together and conveys an impression of exquisity.

More modern than the company's original logo, the script-image-composition of the new design represents a definite actualization. Whereas Do & Co's remaining activities, which have grown over a number of years, are represented by a caricature of a man slurping an oyster (done by the Austrian artist Erich Sokol), the more functional look of the new logo represents the USP of the entire Haas-Haus.

The elegant golden aureole may very well be understood as a signal of refinement. Do & Co, generally housed within the upper segment of the market, is also aiming at an exacting clientele in the Haas-Haus. The simplicity of its design keeps the choice of colours free of any baroque-style old-fashioned flavor (or from looking like a post modern take-off).

Whereas the logo is used on the building's facade as well as on business cards, letterheads and on packaging material, a second reference level is used for menu-cards exclusively.

The inspiration here was the striking – in its use of pastel shades amazingly modern – zig-zag and diamond pattern created by the shingles on the roof of St. Stephan's cathedral. This highly decorative motive, only to be seen from above, became the model for the white, green, grey, and yellow pattern now to be seen on Do & Co's menu-cards.

The menu-card's concept is impressing with its ingenious simplicity: glossy, double-layered cardboard with the pattern printed on both sides is cut out diagonally four times front and back. These slits hold the sheets of paper listing the day's menu. A smaller version of this card serves as cheese and dessert menu.

Café and bar employ a cover-version using the same decoration, the sheets are held together by a cord. Here both adaptions of the cathedral motive are brought together: the front of the cover shows the logo set into the ornamental background.

The decoration reappears on the packaging of Do & Co's unique brandname-product, the Dom-Spitz, sold at the company's Stephansplatz location. This sweet specialty is an experiment as far as brand-name-transfer goes; the triangular box decoratively varies the graphical motive.

The fact that the visual representation is so entirely focused on the cathedral is more than just an obvious marketing calculation. The truth is: only the sensational view qualifies the location as one of the best in town. Take it away, and its value is reduced by half. To open up a restaurant on the 7th floor of any building – no matter how good the food – takes considerable courage, especially if (as in the case in Haas-Haus) there is absolutely no supporting customer frequency during the evening hours.

Seen from this angle, the Do & Co concept at Haas-Haus could only be realized thanks to the venerable vis-à-vis and the connected viewing-experience. This explains the integral role of the cathedral element in the enterprise's profile.

At the same time, the connection of reputable location and gastronomical commitment – strongly emphasized by corporate design – creates quite a raise in prestige for the entire Do & Co group. No doubt, a pleasant and desirable side-effect!

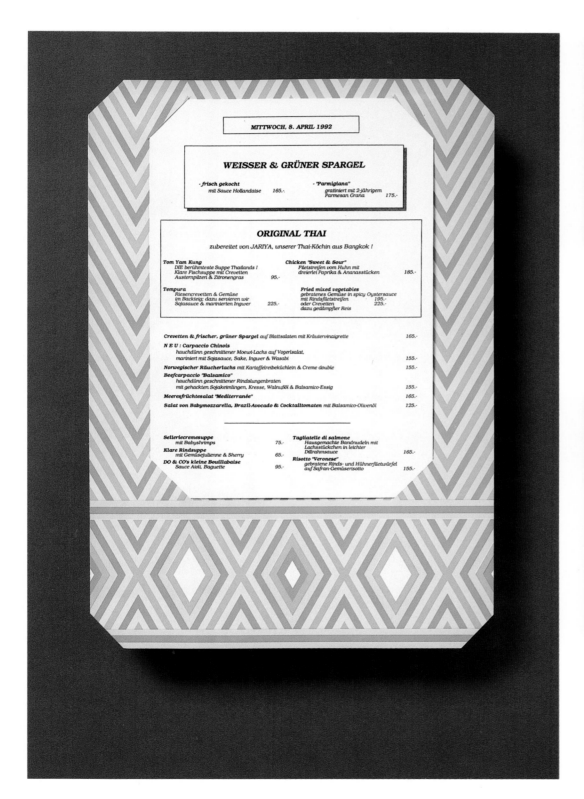

MITTWOCH, 8. APRIL 1992

WEISSER & GRÜNER SPARGEL

- *frisch gekocht*
  mit Sauce Hollandaise   165.-

- *"Parmigiana"*
  gratiniert mit 2-jährigem
  Parmesan Grana   175.-

ORIGINAL THAI

zubereitet von JARIYA, unserer Thai-Köchin aus Bangkok !

Tom Yam Kung
DIE berühmteste Suppe Thailands !
Klare Fischsuppe mit Crevetten
Austernpilzen & Zitronengras   95.-

Chicken "Sweet & Sour"
Filetstreifen vom Huhn mit
dreierlei Paprika & Ananasstücken   185.-

Tempura
Riesencrevetten & Gemüse
im Backteig; dazu servieren wir
Sojasauce & marinierten Ingwer   225.-

Fried mixed vegetables
gebratenes Gemüse in spicy Oystersauce
mit Rindsfiletstreifen   195.-
oder Crevetten   225.-
dazu gedämpfter Reis

Crevetten & frischer, grüner Spargel auf Blattsalaten mit Kräutervinaigrette   165.-

N E U : Carpaccio Chinois
hauchdünn geschnittener Moewi-Lachs auf Vogerlsalat,
marimiert mit Sojasauce, Sake, Ingwer & Wasabi   155.-

Norwegischer Räucherlachs mit Kartoffelreibeküchlein & Creme double   155.-

Beefcarpaccio "Balsamico"
hauchdünn geschnittener Rindslungenbraten
mit gehackten Sojakeimlingen, Kresse, Walnußöl & Balsamico-Essig   155.-

Meeresfrüchtesalat "Mediterranée"   165.-

Salat von Babymozzarella, Brazil-Avocado & Cocktailtomaten mit Balsamico-Olivenöl   125.-

---

Selleriecremesuppe
mit Babyshrimps   75.-

Klare Rindsuppe
mit Gemüsejulienne & Sherry   65.-

DO & CO's kleine Bouillabaise
Sauce Aioli, Baguette   95.-

Tagliatelle di salmone
Hausgemachte Bandnudeln mit
Lachsstückchen in leichter
Dillrahmsauce   165.-

Risotto "Veronese"
gebratene Rinds- und Hühnerfiletwürfel
auf Safran-Gemüserisotto   155.-

Proprietor:

Attila Dogudan, Do & Co group, Vienna.

Interior design:

Hans Hollein, Vienna, Do & Co.

Logo:

Erich Sokol, Vienna.

Menu-card:

Mang & Partner, Vienna.

A case of successful cultural transplantation

The Sakura at the Basel train station disproves two widely held convictions. The first is: elevated Japanese cuisine simply can't be done for Europeans. The second is: – especially not if the location is a train station, dominated by hurry, the need to shop for provisions, and a very mixed audience.

The truth is: Japanese restaurants, the fast favourites of a well-to-do, multiculturally oriented clientele, have to be considered the most challenging and difficult to realize of all ethnic concepts. Without a Japanese cook and a Japanese designer, the opening of Sakura (in English: cherry blossom) in 1990 and the soon visible success would not have been possible.

The most important prerequisite for success – at least for this type of concept – is authenticity. But, for heavens's sake, don't take this to mean 'folklore'! The objective is to catch the spirit of Japanese culinary art and culture, in recipes and cooking-techniques used, in presentation and style of service, and – last but not least – in design.

The Sakura's interior shows a very sensitive and modern translation of Japanese aesthetics, more specifically the use of proportions and structures. Conscious reduction, that is: very little, but precious. Simplicity in design, almost ascetic modesty. Following Japanese reason, this serves to direct the diner's attention toward the culinary experience.

Valuable and modern materials, simple shapes, and extreme restraint in decoration create a quiet, almost meditative atmosphere. Generously sized surfaces allow the materials to take effect; soft, harmonious colours, combined with few vibrantly red accents signalize elegance and at the same time unpretentiousness.

The Sakura represents a two-jointed concept. Teppanyaki and Yakitori sector differ in menu, standards – this includes the price range –, 'reasons for coming' and ambiance.

Teppanyaki, that's the exclusive culinary ceremony at the 'Hot Table'; Yakitori – less complicated and time-consuming – concentrates on various little grilled skewers.

In the exclusive Teppanyaki area with its three table formations, the design's focus is on accentuating the 'production' at the table. The exotic backdrop is produced mainly by Japanese Shoji-screens positioned in front of the windows. The ambiance of the Yakitori section is lighter, airier. A skylight and a Buccida tree in front of a scenic window with a view on lush greenery conjure up a garden-like atmosphere.

The Sakura's design exudes so much authenticity because it doesn't rely on simply copying Eastern design examples, but draws its inspiration directly from modern Japanese architecture. On the other hand, decorative elements quoting the traditional style are used very sparingly.

The Sakura's logo with its striking composition shows an empathetic understanding for Japanese culture. Beneath the resounding name, a white circle on a dark grey background - the texture reminds of handmade paper, or maybe the effect of paint on a rough surface. Above the circle a casual blue brushstroke, a fleeting impression of Japanese calligraphy.

The logo is governed by the same design principles as the interior – no naturalistic touch whatsoever! The logo's imagery is inspired by the banners which in Japan mark a restaurant open for business. The symbol of the circle – strictly stylized – represents the filled plate, the ultimate embodiment of gastronomical service, on, if it so pleases, a cherry-blossom.

From the very first step, when going up the passage to the restaurant entrance – made to look like a Japanese draw-bridge – the logo accompanies the customer: it graces the paper wrapping of the non-reusable chopsticks, appears on the matchbooks, and serves as label for the Sakura's own rosé wine (a Piemontese vintage poured from very attractive, slender bottles) – though in this case with the addition of the

Japanese pictograph for 'Sakura', which is also to be seen as a generously-sized painting in the lounge. And of course, it is also used on the menu-card's covers.

The enterprise's card concept is exemplary. The threefold card-ensemble – drinks, as well as one card each for both of the restaurant's sections – impresses by visual impact and format. 40 respectable centimeters high, its slender shape saves it from appearing too weighty. The covers – made of laminated cardboard – vary the colours of the logo – blue background for the Yakitori-card, black for Teppanyaki and drinks.

The entire card can be unfolded from left to right just like an accordion, additionally, both menu-cards use the concept of exchangeable slide-in cards in their center. This facilitates easy variation of special Teppanyaki-menus and Yakitori-skewers.

Differing from the Teppanyaki-card, which is completely devoid of any illustration, the Yakitori-card illustrates its mainstay of items with small coloured pictures. These little images, whose water-coloured style is reminiscent of coloured Japanese ink-drawings, make it unnecessary to explain a dish with any words – and also give the customer an idea of the size to be expected of his chosen skewer.

In general, though, visual means are used with great discretion. The menu-card's most important design elements are the Japanese pictographs – meant as a special accommodation for Japanese visitors. The generous lay-out makes the most of the pictographs' visual impact: together with the phonetic transcription and the German explanation – each in a different typographical design – they make up a very expressive face. A perfect harmony of information and design!

31

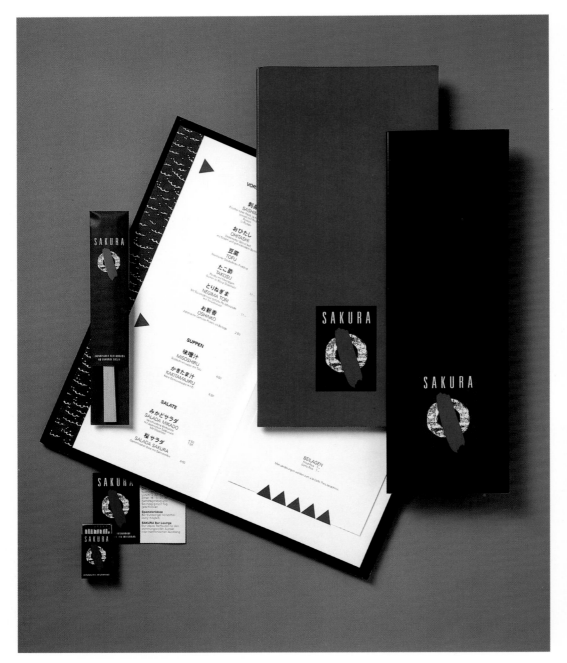

Proprietor:

Hans Berchtold, Basel.

Architect:

Nicolas Goetz, Basel.

Interior design:

Susanne Biedermann, Joshiharo Ishii, Basel/Paris.

Logo/menu-card:

Luis Rempert, Werbebüro Dr. René Sidler, Basel.

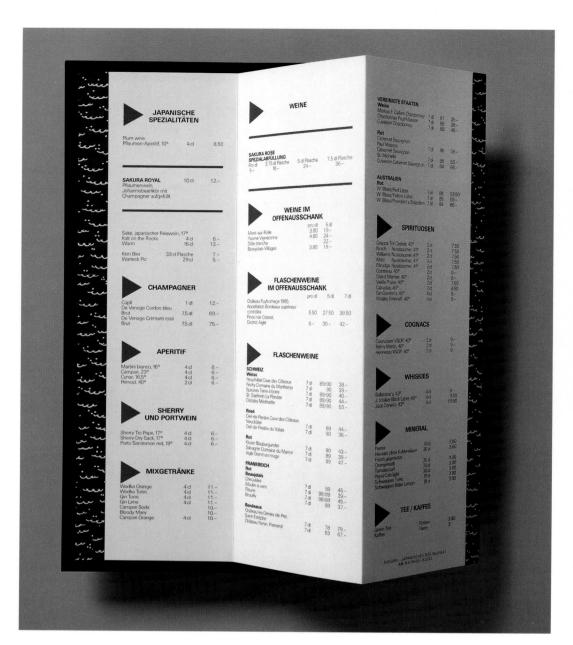

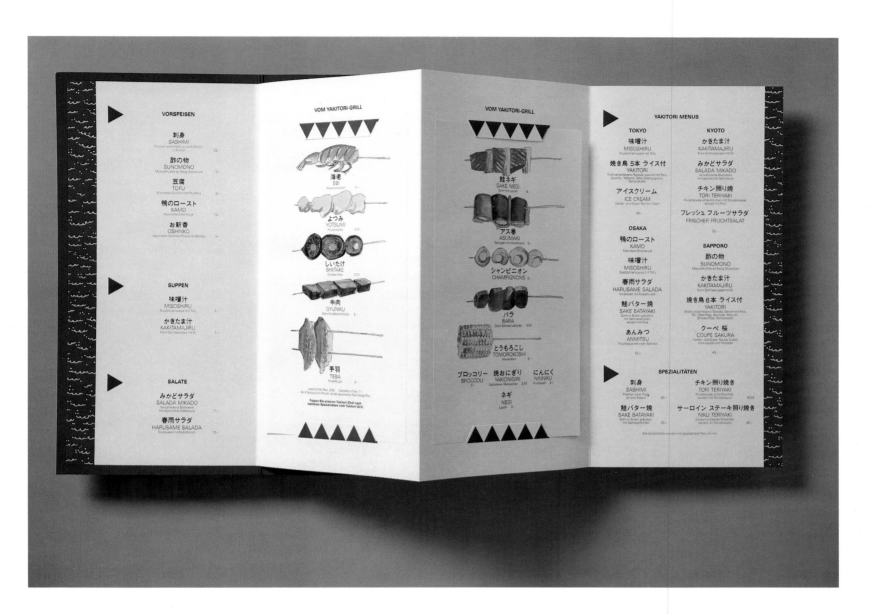

The charm of alienation

Quite a historical site: as early as the 15th century we find mention of an inn called the 'Blaue Ente' (Blue Duck) at this address. This institution was followed by a brewery, which in turn made place for a mill. Much later again the site was used as a cold storage depot. So opening a restaurant there in 1986 in a way meant going back to the roots – but coming up with an entirely new result.

The new owner took the liberty to put the old name into a totally different context. At the end, all that remains is a quotation: reduction to a purely allusive design led to a yellow letter 'e' on a symbolized wave, in front of a circular blue background.

To actually depict the duck was no longer discussed anymore. A new interpretation was needed since proprietor and conceptionists had taken the entire building out of its habitual context. This of course also had to govern the choice of logo – no more little animals, please – let's get away from traditional imagery and emotions.

The charm and the excitement lie in the alienation. After 400 years, the 'Blaue Ente' now finds itself in a new habitat, under totally new social conditions.

The Zurich restaurant is part of a model example of putting former commercially-used premises to new use. Here architecture has the definite desire to communicate with the cosmopolitan multicultural clientele in a timely way.

So during the mid-eighties, the old depot was turned into a light-flooded steel construction. Architecture and ambiance fully draw on the contrast between historical and non-historical elements.

The inimitable centerpiece of the restaurant is a cooling-compressor manufactured in 1918 – without this 'piece de résistance' of industrial culture, the object most probably wouldn't be quite as unique and rich in contrast.

An unplastered grey wall of unplastered roughly hewn sandstone – the rear wall of the restaurant – together with a big wheel and the connected compressor are the only antique elements represented. Everything else is moderately post-modern.

The entire look is one of openness and light, but without glare. A giant glass-front, bulky white ventilation ducts, together with graceful halogen lights fixed on cobweb-thin wires dominate the impression. There are supposedly almost 100 of these little lights, giving each customer the feeling of individual lighting.

The bar has been panelled with a sheet of corrugated chromium-plated steel – this effects a very functional look without at the same time appearing overly sterile. A beautifully-shaped blue vase always contains a lavish arrangement of exquisite flowers; a bright and demonstrative dab of colour in harmony with the season.

In general, blue is used sparingly, setting punctuated accents, – as for example in a blue paravent in the rear of the main dining room.

At night, the glass front and roof set a particularly charming mood.

The restaurant is completed by a piano-bar and a studio, used for special events, parties and banquets.

It is in the piano-bar, on the wall opposite of its dominating bar, that we find the only graphic depiction of the name-giving water fowl; again it has been reduced to a symbol. An oversized, eye-catching stylized duck silhouette of blue acrylic glass, framed by neon lights, sets a playful counterpoint to the otherwise strictly conceptionalized ambiance and the more abstract use of the restaurant's historical name.

The enterprise draws on the upper market segment, consequently the menu-cards employ the system of cover plus daily/monthly changing insert sheets. Typically the offerings are handwritten by the chef de cuisine; the same is true for a giant slate-board listing the seasonal specialties.

A play of colours on the covers of both food and drink menu-cards mirror the different items offered. Both formats used – small for banquet, children's and digestive, resp. bar card, large for the restaurant card – employ the same cover layout, enlivened by logo-space-word compositions dynamized by varying use of colour combination.

The colours used are all within the realm of blue and its complemetary shades; colours that tie in with the logo's content and at the same time represent a high standard. Only the 'e', with dashing yellow impertinence dares to cross the harmony of muted shades.

Another outstanding feature: the 'Blue Duck's' logo fulfils a main requirement on logos in exemplary fashion: its effect remains strong even without the use of colours. It also lends itself to variation: the 'e' may be used in exchange with the full name, colouring can be vivid or very subdued. The effect achieved is livelyness – in contrast to the rigid design-politics as for instance for classical brands of consumer articles.

The 'Blaue Ente' is yet another example of how form needs to be filled by gastronomical reality. Only then do symbols and enterprise categories contain and express meaning.

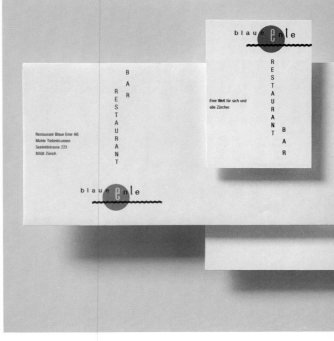

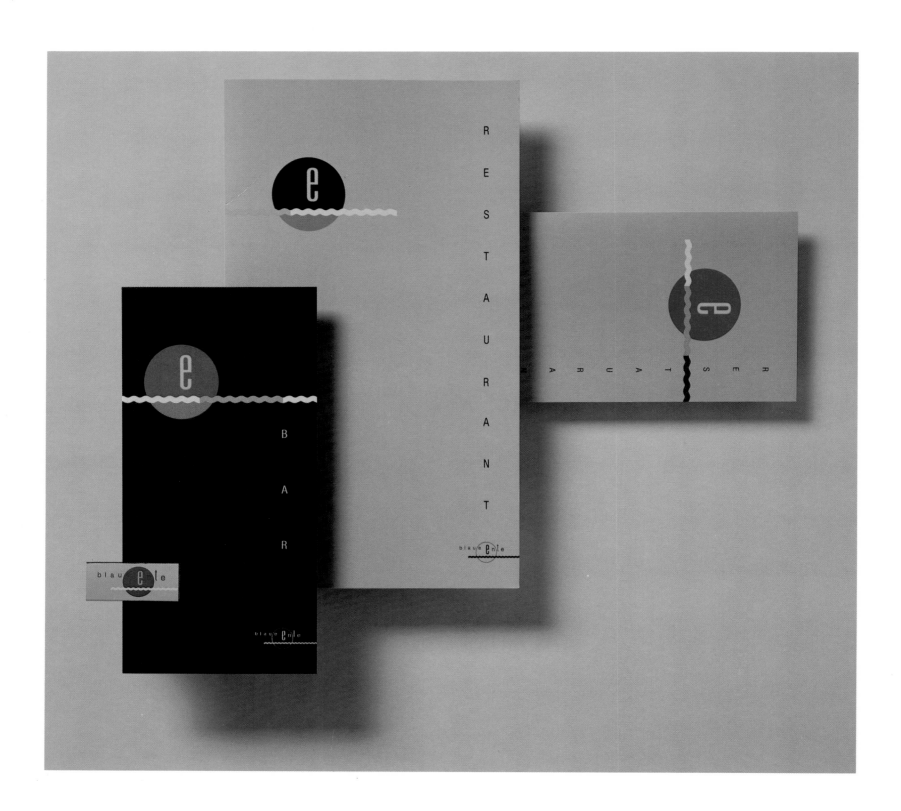

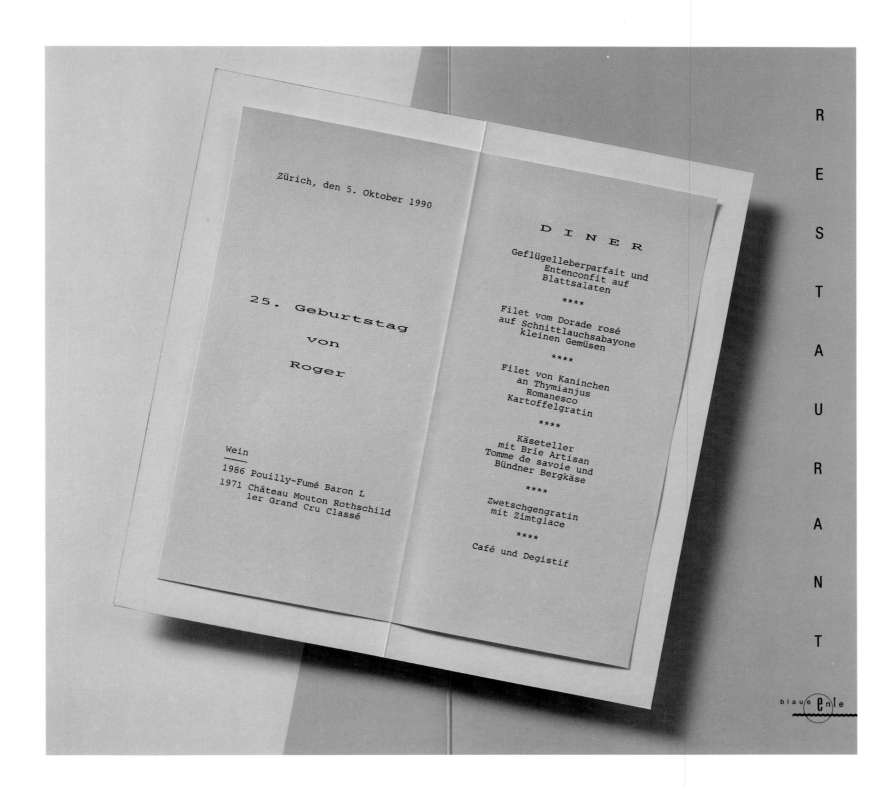

Proprietors:

Monica and Rolf Weber, Zurich.

Interior design:

Gerd Burla, Zurich.

Logo/menu-card:

Rolf Weiersmüller, AG für visuelle Kommunikation,
Zurich.

Unleashed geometry

The fascination of this project lies in the creative consequence which had been used in interior architecture and design. The fact that the Croixement opened in 1989 had to fold after only three years in business was not due to, but rather in spite of the intense aesthetic vibration of the object. It slithered into the economical offside because the location did not fulfil seemingly justified expectations.

From the point of view of design this was doubly a loss: Croixement is almost a showpiece of contemporary interior design, and by now a historical model of exemplary corporate design, which deserves to be recalled to life for the purpose of demonstration:

Croixement was inspired by the avantgarde atmosphere permeating Parc de la Villette. Definitely purist in form, the restaurant aims to achieve perfect harmony between interior and surroundings. And these surroundings are determined by the excitement created by integrating futuristic high-tech architecture into the natural landscape of the Parc de la Villette. The yet unfinished ambitious park-project in the eastern part of Paris defines itself as a combination of culture and leisure.

The Croixement building at the Canal d'Ourcq on the park terrain also reflects this tendency towards the extreme: its acute-angled ground plan resembles a piece of pie. Significant outside features of the building are grey-black lines, decorating the entire length of each exterior wall. This design-feature reappears as basic feature in the interior furnishment and corporate design, which is pointedly futuristic: Croixement is concepted as a 'Brasserie of the year 2000'.

What emerges, is a work of art ruled by modernity, each little detail an essential part of the overall composition. Perfect – almost obsessively so.

Unleashed geometry: the interior is dominated by an artful use of straight lines. Not to be overlooked: the contrast of white and pale-yellow horizontal stripes lining the walls, echoing the 'beam'-motive of the exterior. The open space is vertically structured by high columns. Most of the more than seven-meters-high front wall has been given over to a gigantic glassfront; vertical and horizontal crossbeams cut it into many small rectangles.

The sheer monumental impression of the interior to a large extent is a consequence of the building's unusual dimensions. The height of the ceiling effects the almost sacral character of the Croixement architecture – this feature is further emphasized by a lofty gallery.

A spiral staircase connects the main restaurant space with the gallery, which also harbours an additional bar. The parallel symmetry of the bannister again quotes the motive of simple lines.

This strict coherence in design becomes obvious when looking at details. One of the logo's elements – three rectangles on top of each other – keeps popping up as a decorative motive: three lighted glass squares are set into each step of the marble stairs. The trio keeps recurring as a formal continuum on the columns as well as on the back of each chair. The effect achieved is one of structured space, with visual landmarks 'breaking' it and giving it contour.

The logo itself substitutes the 's' in the French 'croisement' (crossroads, crossing) with a graphically accentuated 'x'. This letter expresses the idea of a crossing – at the same time it can also be understood as a symbol of geometric principle.

The furniture – designed exclusively for Croixement – adheres to the severe design-language of the premises; albeit softer, curved shapes were used to create appealing counterpoints. But then again: the grey obtusely-angled block of granite which serves as a bar, its contours traced by ceiling spot-lights; the colossal rectangular glass-sculpture in the entrance area – a creation by the artist Guillaume Saalburg;

the symmetrically spaced rows of small window-panes. They all reproduce the shape-enamoured structural principle of the Croixement design.

Architectural severity also governs the choice of materials used. Most of them are put to use unadultered, without much 'softening'. Hard materials, such as glass, granite, marble and metal, underline the abstract functionality of the ambiance. Black and white, the favourite colours of the nineties, represent precisely the same emotional (non)-valence. And black and white are the dominant moodsetters in the restaurant.

Black-and-white stripes even decorate the staff's socks; following the corporate design's inherent logic, it is to be expected to also find black-and-white menu-cards. The entire ensemble of standard and additional cards, including all other carriers of information, such as business cards or matchbooks, employ the same familiar pattern of stripes. Here the use of contrast has been reduced to pure graphic art; with a minimum of formal variables, the typographical representation of the services offered – black on white, white on black – turns into a major design element.

It is especially this reduction in design which makes the multitude of variations in card-design so fascinating. The recurring rectangular shape – solo, as a trio or as entire series – allows for an experience of visual recognition. The menu-cards shape itself quotes this geometrical archetype.

Within the highly stylized design context of Croixement, the use of figurative imagery is of course out of the question. The menucard, too, is a proclamation of the abstract principle.

As extravagant the design, as simple and relaxed the gastronomical concept. Croixement wanted to be open to anyone; a challenge, but to a large extent independent of design. The location turned out to be the critical factor.

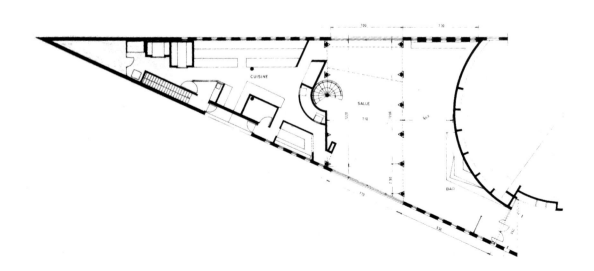

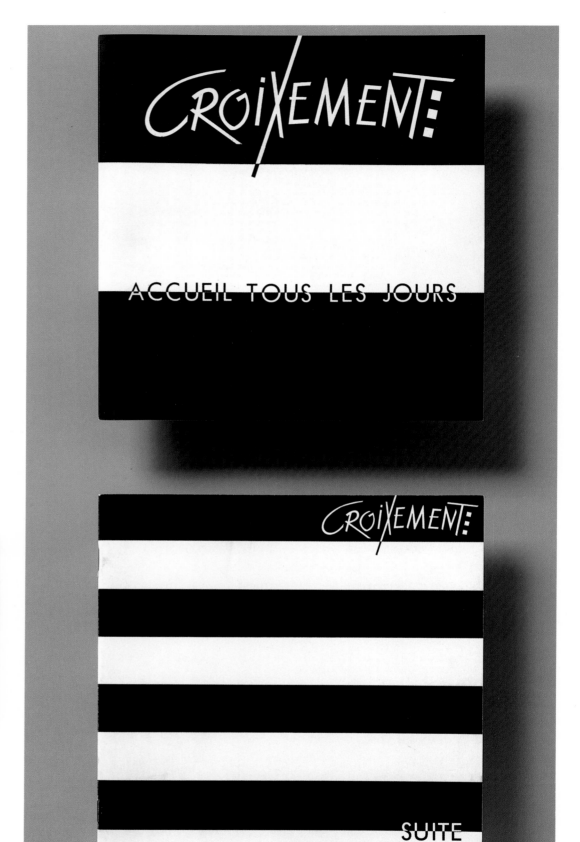

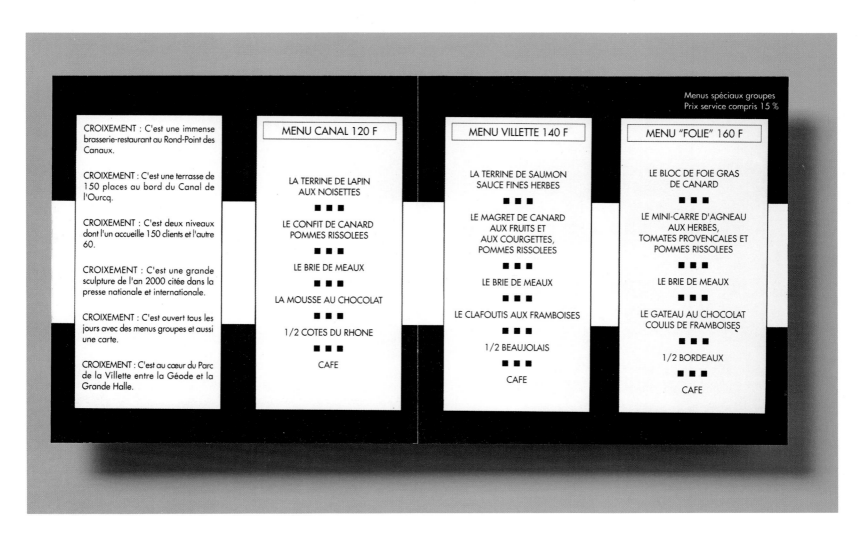

CROIXEMENT : C'est une immense brasserie-restaurant au Rond-Point des Canaux.

CROIXEMENT : C'est une terrasse de 150 places au bord du Canal de l'Ourcq.

CROIXEMENT : C'est deux niveaux dont l'un accueille 150 clients et l'autre 60.

CROIXEMENT : C'est une grande sculpture de l'an 2000 citée dans la presse nationale et internationale.

CROIXEMENT : C'est ouvert tous les jours avec des menus groupes et aussi une carte.

CROIXEMENT : C'est au cœur du Parc de la Villette entre la Géode et la Grande Halle.

Menus spéciaux groupes
Prix service compris 15 %

MENU CANAL 120 F

LA TERRINE DE LAPIN
AUX NOISETTES

■ ■ ■

LE CONFIT DE CANARD
POMMES RISSOLEES

■ ■ ■

LE BRIE DE MEAUX

■ ■ ■

LA MOUSSE AU CHOCOLAT

■ ■ ■

1/2 COTES DU RHONE

■ ■ ■

CAFE

MENU VILLETTE 140 F

LA TERRINE DE SAUMON
SAUCE FINES HERBES

■ ■ ■

LE MAGRET DE CANARD
AUX FRUITS ET
AUX COURGETTES,
POMMES RISSOLEES

■ ■ ■

LE BRIE DE MEAUX

■ ■ ■

LE CLAFOUTIS AUX FRAMBOISES

■ ■ ■

1/2 BEAUJOLAIS

■ ■ ■

CAFE

MENU "FOLIE" 160 F

LE BLOC DE FOIE GRAS
DE CANARD

■ ■ ■

LE MINI-CARRE D'AGNEAU
AUX HERBES,
TOMATES PROVENCALES ET
POMMES RISSOLEES

■ ■ ■

LE BRIE DE MEAUX

■ ■ ■

LE GATEAU AU CHOCOLAT
COULIS DE FRAMBOISES

■ ■ ■

1/2 BORDEAUX

■ ■ ■

CAFE

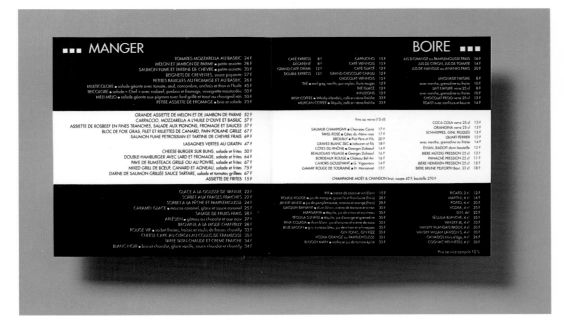

Some Heavy Marketing

Menu-card examples from the world of German and Central European gastronomy

The art of visualizing gourmet sophistication

A mere three percent of the population – this at least is an estimate by those who should really know: the celebrated chefs themselves – make up the small but distinguished clientele of gourmet restaurants. This probably just as much is true in Switzerland, France, or any other place as it is in Germany.

As no other segment of the gastronomical business, these first-class restaurants depend on their customers' conscious decision to visit this place and no other; spontaneous drop-ins or 'accidental' guests are rarely to be seen.

When thinking about this category of restaurants, it would be wrong to consider only the ones that have been honoured with stars or little chef's hats. These places comprise only maybe one fourth – if not less – of all restaurants in this deluxe class, which is defined by a high level of refinement both in regard to the delicacies offered and the standard of prices charged.

Guests come here with rather high and well-defined expectations. Exquisite ambiance, excellent service and of course an inspired and creative cuisine are taken for granted. After all, this kind of entertainment has its price.

Also: different than in any other type of gastronomical enterprise, from a customer's standpoint of view these top-notch establishments are represented by one single person: the cook – the chef de cuisine – who in many cases also is the owner.

His expertise makes or breaks the reputation of the house. Nowhere else is the image of a restaurant so closely tied to the name of its chef.

As a consequence, high-class restaurants are strongly influenced by a certain chef's personality. His style of cooking, his culinary signature, define the character of the house. He is the creative source, who draws the admiring guests. And much like

devoted pilgrims, they have to put up with quite a few inconveniences: getting to such a noble restaurant often involves traveling 30 minutes to one hour by car. First-class restaurants definitely draw their customers from a much wider surrounding area.

Creativity, personality and price level – this trio defines the marketing margin of top-notch restaurants. And where there is so much emphasis on personality, the menu-card's design may definitely express a very individual character. Very often the design chosen not only represents the chef's personal taste, but also reflects his preferences, some biographical elements, toys with his name or maybe makes some kind of reference to the location.

It is understood that the menu-card should reveal the set of values and aesthetic refinement which defines this genre of restaurants as a whole. But discreet understatement in white and gold is for the most part a thing of the past. Nowadays, menu-card design is a means of displaying and illustrating a highly-elevated level of creativity. It is not by chance that this is where we most often find artist-designed menu-cards. They express the philosophy of a first-class restaurant – no mass production or mediocrity. These artists' designs – very often done expressly for this particular house – underline the uniqueness of the services offered. In the first place, they document the gourmet-cooks affinity with the world of art.

Very rarely does one see photographies; just as atypical are designs using common symbols of culinary opulence – these are exchangeable and have no ties to a particular establishment.

The reasons why today so many first-class proprietors go for a significant, visually refined statement in their menu-card design, are twofold. Not only do they aim to fulfill the customer's expectation of creativity in a more complete and all-embracing manner – just as the visual presentation of food has moved into focus to a much higher degree. Consequently, top-chefs have more of a tendency to develop their own corporate design.

Apart from this, a visually impressive menu-card is also designed to help a customer effortlessly define the identity of a particular restaurant. Aesthetically pleasing visual effects create a lasting impression of uniqueness.

And last not least: any kind of effort to create visual impact also has its emotional quality. No matter whether using 'only' a logo or 'telling a story' – both are much more likely to create a positive emotional response than starkly naked lettering.

The ideal is met when the card's design harmoniously corresponds with the 'spirit' of the establishment. This may or may not include the style of furnishing. In any case the card should reflect the concept's overall style, be it formal or relaxed, more modern or traditional.

By the way, more and more gourmet temples are abandoning the age-old tradition of oversized, heavy and unwieldy menu-cards. Today, the rule is a much smaller format; tables are smaller, space is more precious – a little understatement in size allows for much better handling.

In general the artistic efforts are limited to the card's cover, this is explained by the typical marketing-strategy employed by first-class restaurants. To strive for culinary excellence and creativity usually effects a constant rhythmic change in items offered. Many establishments use the concept of a daily changing menu, even though within this class of restaurants the proprietor rarely expects a particular customer to dine there twice within one week.

But at least a weekly rotation is expected in a top-notch restaurant; the appropriate design-solution is a cover with easy-to-change pages on the inside. A more elaborate alternative is a completely styled folder with exchangeable stickers. In any case, a flexible solution is absolutely necessary in a restaurant enjoying a first-class reputation.

Name:
Schwarzer Hahn, Deidesheim

Business type/character:
Star-awarded restaurant in the Romantik Hotel Deidesheimer Hof, kitchen headed by Manfred Schwarz.

Card:
Menu card with artistically designed logo

Card system:
Simply folded cover, printed on the outside, card entirely high-gloss laminated, size when closed: 21×40 cm. Double-glued cardboard, interior pages with diagonal insertion slits. Menu and à-la-carte selection on colored insertion sheets; printed by typewriter or PC printer and reproduced. Wine list designed analogously, however thread-stitched.

Special features:
Corporate design conception, rooster motif also on special cards and calling cards. Logo is considered an allusion to the chef de cuisine's name (Schwarz = black) as well as the location, the seat of the winegrowing family Hahn (Hahn = rooster)

Draft/Design:
The artist Hans Engelram, Hasloch (logo)/Artur Hahn

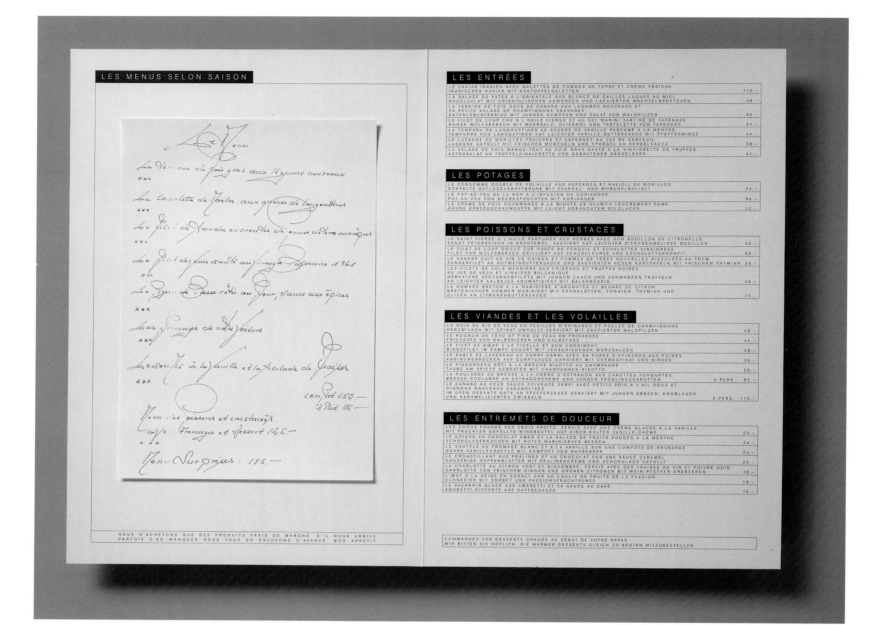

Name:
Petermann's Kunststuben, Küsnacht

Business type/character:
2-star restaurant operated by the renowned Swiss chef Horst Petermann

Card:
Menu card with artistically designed cover sheet.

Card system:
Simply folded cardboard cover, printed on both sides, size when closed: 29.5 × 43 cm; inside front cover blank, hand-written seasonal card is reproduced and glued in.

Special features:
Artistic character of menu card (incl. inside; note the printed sheet in the style of the '50s!) as equivalent to the restaurant's profile: annexed art gallery; alternating exhibitions in the restaurant! The menu card was the first to be awarded the gold medal by the Swiss Art Directors Club in 1983.

Draft/Design:
The artist Willi Rieser, Lufingen-Augwil

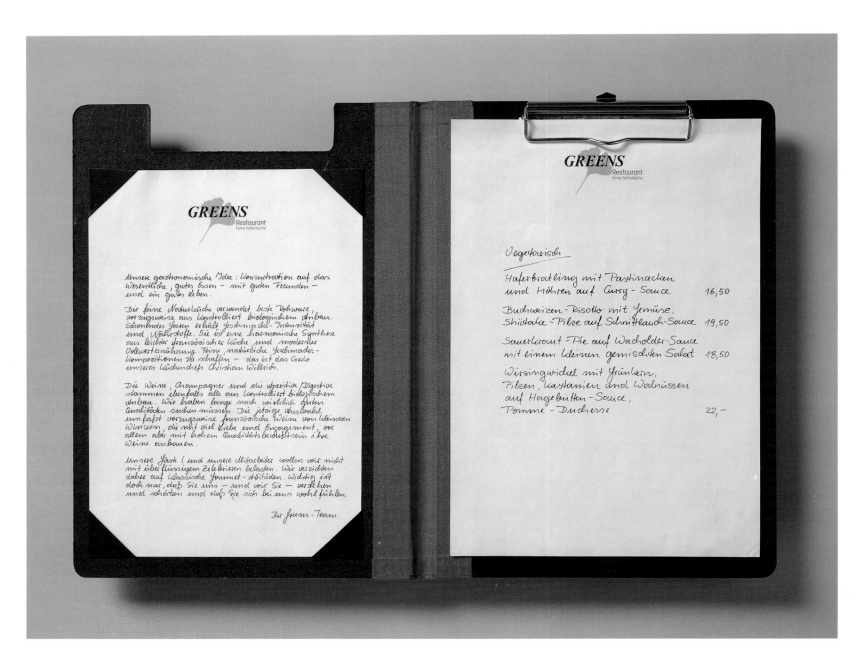

Name:
Greens, Düsseldorf

Business type/character:
Gourmet restaurant; kitchen headed by Christian Willrich, emphasis on light French and exquisite natural cuisine.

Card:
Menu card with unique presentation solution.

Card system:
Black unadorned cardboard spring folder with lid as cover; selection groups on separate sheets, hand-written, copied on Greens paper and fastened en bloc by clip. Reticent logo solution black on gray: Greens logo and a Gingko leaf, wine list designed analogously.

Special features:
Unpretentious card approach—analogous to the interior's design. New version: selection group titles marked with color chalk. Information on the restaurant's philosophy on the lid's inside.

Draft/Design:
Dreesen Design, Düsseldorf

Name:
Orion Le Gourmet, Zurich
(until spring 1990: Kramer Restaurationsbetriebe, Uitikon-Waldegg)

Business type/character:
Upper-class market segment

Card:
Menu card 1989

Card system:
Meticulously designed card, 8 pages including cover, size when closed: 26.5 × 36 cm, stapled, with high-gloss laminated cover, cover sheet printed on outside. Basic printing on inside with food motifs, the actual selection can be added by print later on. Wine list analogous, but with different pictures.

Special features:
Photographic style illustrates the conceptual statement; light cuisine.

Draft/Design:
Agency Marty, Köniz (Bern)

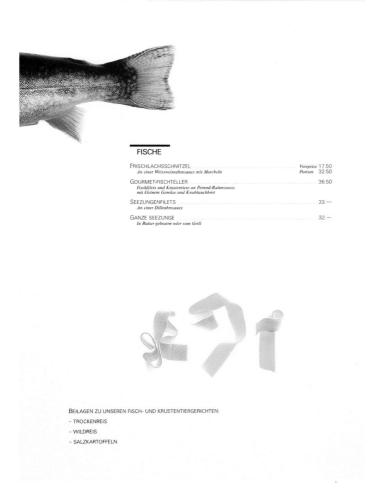

FISCHE

FRISCHLACHSSCHNITZEL	*Vorspeise* 17.50
An einer Weissweinrahmsauce mit Morcheln	*Portion* 32.50
GOURMET-FISCHTELLER	36.50
Fischfilets und Krustentiere an Pernod-Rahmsauce,	
mit kleinem Gemüse und Knoblauchbrot	
SEEZUNGENFILETS	33.—
An einer Dillrahmsauce	
GANZE SEEZUNGE	32.—
In Butter gebraten oder vom Grill	

BEILAGEN ZU UNSEREN FISCH- UND KRUSTENTIERGERICHTEN:
- TROCKENREIS
- WILDREIS
- SALZKARTOFFELN

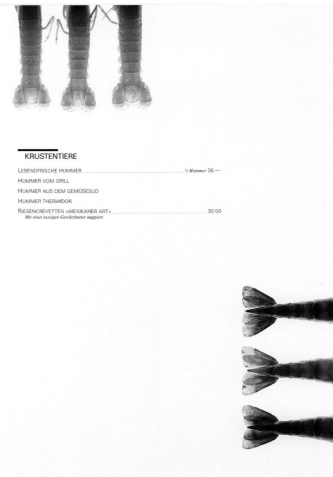

KRUSTENTIERE

LEBENDFRISCHE HUMMER	*¼ Hummer* 36.—
HUMMER VOM GRILL	
HUMMER AUS DEM GEMÜSESUD	
HUMMER THERMIDOR	
RIESENCREVETTEN «MEXIKANER ART»	30.50
Mit einer rassigen Gewürzbutter nappiert	

	MILANESE DI VITELLO *paniertes Kalbschnitzel*	DM 24,00	
	SCALOPPINE AL VINO BIANCO *Kalbschnitzel in Weißwein*	DM 25,00	
	SCALOPPINE ALLA PROVINCIALE *in Kräuter-Tomaten-Sahnesauce*	DM 25,00	
	SCALOPPINE AI FUNGHI *mit Champignons*	DM 26,00	
CARNE **CON CONTORNO**	SALTINBOCCA ALLA ROMANA *Kalbfleisch mit Parmaschinken in Weißwein*	DM 26,00	
	PAILLARD DI VITELLO *gegrilltes Kalbschnitzel*	DM 24,00	
	FEGATO DI VITELLO BURRO E SALVIA *Leber in Butter und Salbei*	DM 24,00	
	FEGATO DI VITELLO VENEZIANA *Leber mit Zwiebeln und Weißwein*	DM 24,00	
	PIZZAIOLA *mit Oliven, Kapern, Knoblauch, Tomatensauce*	DM 27,00	

	BISTECCA AI FERRI *gegrilltes Steak*	DM 25,00
	FILETTO ALLA GRIGLIA *gegrilltes Filet*	DM 30,00
CARNE **CON CONTORNO**	FILETTO AL PEPE VERDE *Filet mit grünem Pfeffer*	DM 31,00
	FILETTO BELLINI *Spezialität des Hauses*	DM 32,00
	COTOLETTE D'AGNELLO *Lammkotelett*	DM 24,00

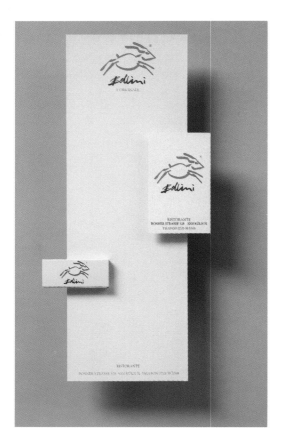

Name:
Ristorante Bellini, Cologne
(Spitz-Gruppe, Cologne)

Business type/character:
Exquisite Italian restaurant.

Card:
Standard menu card for foods and beverages.

Card system:
All-in-one solution, 12 pages plus cover, stapled. Size: 21 × 21 cm. Material: high-quality salmon-pink structured cardboard. Unorthodox arrangement of selection group titles. Comprehensive additional selection complementing the basic menu card changing daily, mounted on flip-chart. Separate wine list for bottled wines.

Special features:
Corporate-design-conception; Bellini logo and colors on card cover as well as on calling cards, matchboxes as well as on billheads. Colors harmonizing with interior design. The fantasy creature hopping over a logo is the restaurant's very own fairy-tale heraldic animal.

Draft/Design:
Advertising agency Axiz, Cologne (logo and card)

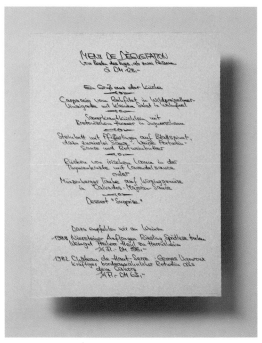

Name:
Restaurant Hessler, Maintal-Dörnigheim

Business type/character:
Star-awarded restaurant with natural-cuisine philosophy, kitchen headed by Doris Katharina Hessler.

Card:
Spring season menu card with artistically designed cover sheet, the motif: a portrait of the chef de cuisine.

Card system:
Simply folded cover, cover printed, gloss-laminated. Inner pages and cover backside bordeaux-red. Size when closed: 40 × 40 cm. Loose sheets with selection superscribed by hand (menus) or by PC printer and fixed with adhesive points.

Special features:
A total of four seasonal portrait motifs matching the restaurant's seasonal cooking. These motifs are solely used for the menu cards. Elucidations on the paintings and the artist on the outside back cover.

Draft/Design:
The artist Wilfried Abels, Frankfurt

Name:

Landhaus Scherrer, Hamburg

Business type/character:

Two-star restaurant, regionally-oriented cuisine, kitchen headed by Heinz Wehmann.

Cards:

Menu card and wine list as painting folder; limited graphic edition. Corresponding design: sensual-erotically colored motifs; a mixture of Art Nouveau and fantastic realism.

Card system:

Both cards are meticulously designed; size when closed: 34 × 42 cm. Silver-colored cover with sketch of country house on cover sheet. Inside material: genuine drawing paper, each side completely printed with graphic drawings. Menu card: ten folded pages including inside front cover. The left side features a colored drawing, the same motif is found on the right side screened in a mosaic-like pattern. All sections are printed on transparent parchment paper by laser printer and fixed to the screened pages with adhesive strips. Wine list: 18 pages including inside front cover. Bound with sewing thread. A colored drawing on the left pages, macrophotographs centered around wine on the right side. Selection presentation like in menu card.

Special features:

Comprehensive approach: charger plates designed in same style. Original pictures by Fratzscher also exhibited in the restaurant. In 1989, first prize awarded by the Sommelier-Union: Germany's best wine list. Information on the card's creator to be found on the outside back cover.

Draft/Design:

The artist Wolfgang K.H. Fratzscher, Hamburg/the publisher Luciano Tezzele, Hamburg (realization)

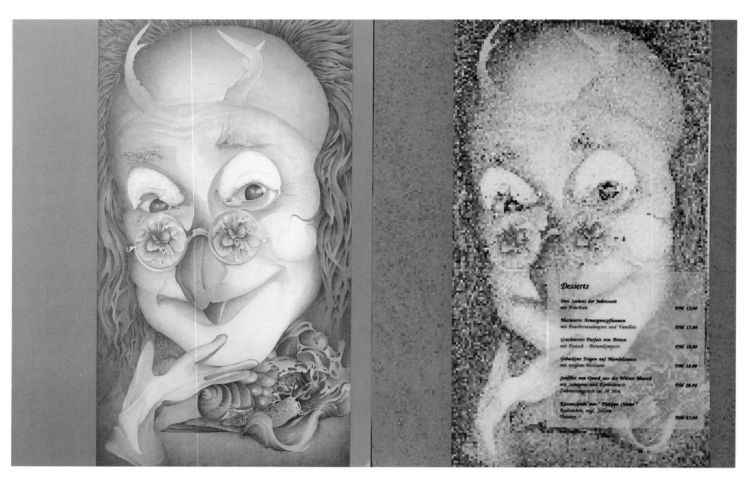

Desserts

Drei Sorbets der Jahreszeit
mit Früchten   DM 15,00

Marinierte Armagnacpflaumen
mit Feuchtreesabayone und Vanilleis   DM 17,00

Gratiniertes Parfait von Birnen
mit Punsch - Birnenkompott   DM 18,00

Gebackene Feigen auf Mandelsauce
mit weißem Mocineis   DM 18,00

Soufflee von Quark aus der Wilster Marsch
mit Sabayone und Kirschenis
Zubereitungszeit ca. 30 Min.   DM 20,00

Käsenauswahl von " Philippe Olivier "
Radieschen, engl. Sellerie
Trauben   DM 27,00

Zwischengerichte

Kräuterpfannküchlein
mit Kalbsbries und Pfifferlingen   DM 34,00

Geschnorster Kalbskopf
mit winterlichen Gemüsen
Balsamicojus   DM 37,00

Hausgemachte Nudeln mit weißem Trüffel
aromatisiert   DM 58,00

Gratinierte Sylter Royal Austern
auf Rosenkohlblätter, Rieslingsauce   DM 36,00

1/2 Hummer à la nage
mit Gemüsewürfel und Dill   DM 64,00

Norddeutsche Gerichte

Steinbutt im Stück gekocht
mit Sahnemeerrettich, Butter
Kartoffeln   DM 65,00

Rehrückenfilet mit Rosenkohlblätter
Pfifferlingen, Semmelknödel, Kronsbeeren
Wacholdersauce   DM 62,00

Krosse Vierländer Ente im Ganzen gebraten
Brust mit Gemüsen und Pfeffersauce
- Zubereitungszeit 65 Min.
Keulen mit Salaten serviert
für 2 Personen -preis Person-   DM 67,00

Name:
Grill-Restaurant Vier Jahreszeiten, Düsseldorf
(Stockheim-Gastronomie, Düsseldorf)

Business type/character:
Sophisticated airport restaurant with elevated selection and price level. International à-la-minute cuisine with seasonal character.

Card:
Menu card for foods and beverages with art reproductions on the cover sheet.

Card system:
All-in-one card, cover plus eight selection pages, entirely cellophane-coated. Stapled, size when closed: 23×39 cm. Center spread empty for Offer of the Season/Offer of the Day. Additional cards for specialty products, wine list. Menu selection in three languages—location!

Special features:
The cover sheet scene shows a quartet of paintings by the Dutch painter Adriaen van de Venne titled "The Four Seasons." Information about the artist on the inside front cover. The respective seasonal motif is repeated on the menu card's loose leaves in yellow, green, orange, or blue. A visual support of the conceptual statement: seasonal cooking. Painting reproductions to be found in the restaurant.

Draft/Design:
Ingo Bergmann, Design Division, Krefeld

GRILL-RESTAURANT VIER-JAHRESZEITEN

LES VAÇANCES
Chez Max

VORSPEISEN / PREMIERS PLATS

THE **NICE** SALADE "RICH AND BEAUTIFUL" 17.--

INSALATA MISTA 11.--

INSALATA DI RUCOLA CON PESCE A L'OLIO D'OLIVA 22.--

CRUDITES AVEC TROIS SAUCES 18.--

SCOTCH WILDE SALMON MARINATED WITH DILL 25.--/48.--

TRANCHE DE MELON AVEC JAMBON DE PARME 24.--

LOBSTERSALAD WITH ARTICHOKE AND NUTOIL 35.--/65.--

RAUCHLACHS COUPE "CHEZ MAX" MIT TOAST UND BUTTER 28.--/42.--

SUPPEN / SOUPES

SOUPE DE POISSON DES ROCHES, PAIN GRILLE ET ROUILLE 14.--

GRANDE PORTION EN CAQUELON 27.--

SOUPE DE RATATOUILLE FROIDE OU CHAUDE 12.--

MINESTRONE ALLA TICINESE 10.--

WARME VORSPEISEN
PREMIERS PLATS CHAUDS

CANNELLONI DI CAPRIOLO AL FORNO 19.--

RAVIOLI ALLA RICOTTA E FUNGI AL BURRO E SALVIA 16.--/29.--

SPAGHETTIS OU NOUILLES MAISON A LA CREME AVEC CAVIAR 52.--

SPAGHETTIS OR NUDELS WITH CREAM AND SMOKED SALMON 28.--/42.--

SPAGHETTI O TAGLIATELLE CON PEPERONCINI, AGLIO E OLIO D'OLIVA 15.--/25.--

COUVERT LE SOIR 3.--

**************************** H E U T E ****************************

KALBSKOPFSALAT MIT
SENFSAUCE
16.--

LES VAÇANCES
Chez Max

HAUPTGERICHTE / PLATS PRINCIPAUX
MAIN COURSES

JAPON / FRANCE

EINE MARSEILLER BOUILLABAISSE IM TOPF SERVIERT, DAZU ROHER FISCH,
MUSCHELN, KRUSTENTIERE UND GEMUESE, UM IM TOPF KURZ ZU GAREN
46.--

MIT HUMMER + 24.--

******

COUS - GNUSS

EIN FEINES COUSCOUS NACH IHRER WAHL

PORTUGIESISCH

MIT PIRI-PIRI HUEHNCHEN UND GEMUESE 38.--

MAROKKANISCH

MIT LAMMFLEISCH, BOHNEN, LAUCH, ZWIEBELN UND KAROTTEN 36.--

******

SAUCISSON SUR PAPETTE VAUDOISE 29.--

POLLO AL VINO DI MONTEPULCIANO CON TARTELETTE DE MAIS 36.--

CHICKEN-CURRY WITH FRUITS - BASMATI RICE 38.--

NOIX D'AGNEAU AVEC RATATOUILLE ET POMMES ECRASEES AU ROMARIN 39.--

RAGOUT DE CHEVREUIL AUX MURES ET SPAETZLI AU BEURRE 36.--

FILET DE BOEUF AUX CHANTERELLES, LEGUMES ET POMMES RISSOLEES 56.--

**************************** H E U T E ****************************

AILE DE RAIE
AU BEURRE NOISETTE
POMMES PERSILEES 34.50

Name:
Les Vacances Chez Max, Zollikon

Business type/character:
Exquisite bistro operated by top-notch chef de cuisine Max Kehl. Internationale Ferienküche für Gourmets (international vacation cuisine for gourmets).

Card:
Menu card with artistically designed cover.

Card system:
Simply folded cover, outside high-gloss laminated cardboard, size when closed: 22 × 31 cm. Cover sheet with picture motif and logo. Same cover solution for menu and à-la-carte selection as well as beverages; selection leaves with pre-printed colored logo are glued in. Lettering by PC printer.

Special features:
Picture motif/logo are ubiquitous: on standard and special cards, calling cards and post cards. Unique product approach (Ferienküche [vacation cooking]) as peg for visual appearance.

Draft/Design:
Cartoonist René Fehr, Zurich (card and logo)

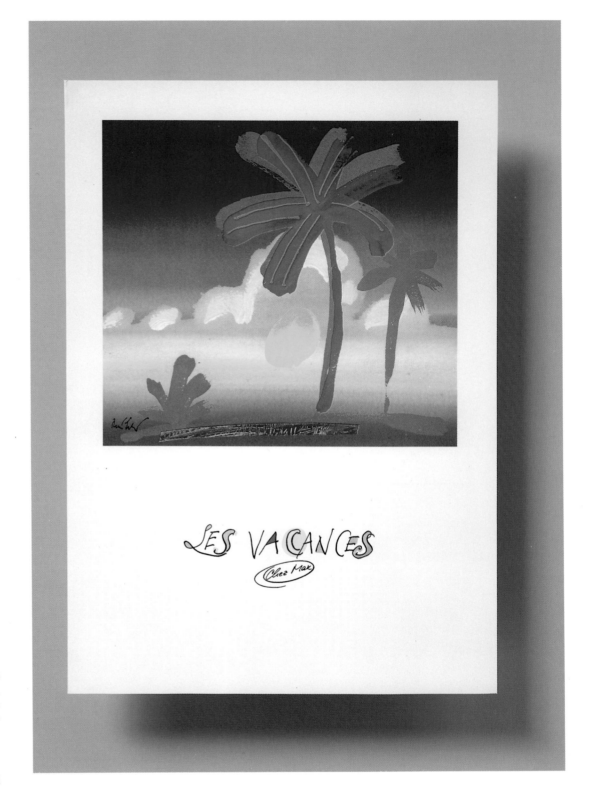

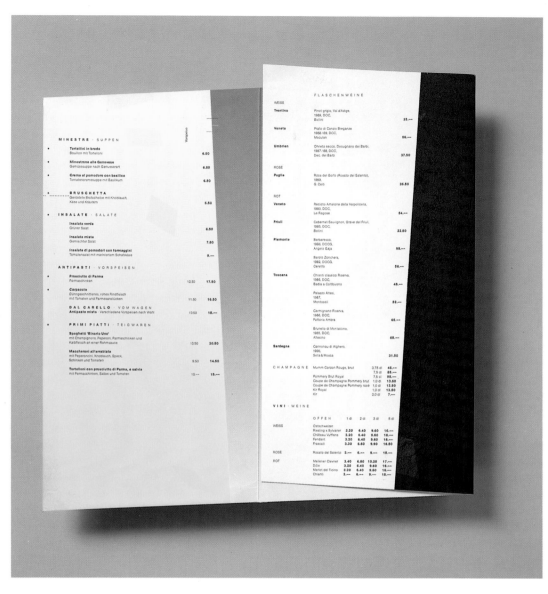

Name:
Binario Uno, Zurich-Kloten
(airport restaurants Zurich)

Business type/character:
Exquisite Italian restaurant in Zurich airport's railway station. Predominantly selected audience, flight passengers of minor importance. Modern approach in respective ambiance, menu card design, and philosophy: menu not mandatory.

Card:
Modernly styled selection card with elaborate design analogue to the restaurant interior.

Card system:
All-in-one solution, high-quality absorbent offset paper. Modified miscellaneous folding: resembles a napkin in folded condition. Asymmetrical effect is achieved through trapezoidal shape. Size when closed: 19.5 × 40 cm (maximum). Card printed on both sides; color, design, and typography match the restaurant's overall character: modern Italianità. Food selection inside, center spread blank with punched slits (in stairway form!) for half-page-sized insertion cards with week's menu/wine recommendations—lettered by laser printer. Menu card supplemented by blackboard with daily alternating menu offer.

Special features:
The card is element of a comprehensive appearance image for printed matters; corporate identity was created in close cooperation with the architect. Menu card design and logo reflect the black/white chessboard pattern of the restaurant's floor. The chessboard effect on the cover is achieved by transparent water lacquer, which, depending on the influx of light, shows different pictures with a textile appearance. Card and CI are entirely generated by computer.

Draft/Design:
Robert Krügel-Durband, Designagentur Eclat, Erlenbach/Zurich

Design creates individualism

This chapter deals with the 'allrounders' among restaurant operation concepts; their marketing-strategy can only be compared to decathlon competitions. This refers to their wide assortment of products; whereas in other concept dimensions, such as location or sales strategy, they may very well be specialized.

What they have in common, though, is that they offer a wide range of products, covering all types of items. They have chosen a very broad assortment of products, and a wide range of prices, to be able to attract just about any clientele and satisfy the most varied needs.

The advantage of this global strategy is that it spreads the risk. On the other hand, with their all-encompassing range of products, the generalists have a much harder time developing a clearly defined significant profile – compared to the specialists, such as steakhouses or pizza-parlors.

The specific marketing challenge for a generalist is threefold; he has to use his menu-card to communicate the following three concepts:

* to signal diversity and variety

* to allow for the greatest possible flexibility of assortment and at the same time

* to present the establishment in such a memorable way as to give it an edge in competition.

Significance in presentation and total flexibility in range of products – these goals almost exclude each other. It is just this quality of the generalist, his ability to provide 'everything', that brings with it the danger of loosing contour and competence, of being wishy-washy. The typical problem of those who 'can do it all'.

At the same time, while it seems that the generalist theoretically has so many possible directions in which to develop a profile, he practically may not exclude anything, or – even more important – anybody.

The underlying concept-decision usually does not allow exclusion of any segment of possible clientele, by definition the generalists are open to the 'public'. This puts quite a restraint on menu-card design – it has to please everybody. Anything leaving the confines of generally accepted good taste could bring danger and is not appropriate.

There's no doubt: nobody has a harder time than the generalist to visually express the individuality of his services in a significant and memorable way. He has to achieve more than that: because there is a lack of definition in his assortment and profile, his image is so much more endangered by corrosion. In order to 'stay in mind', the generalist has to keep setting 'refreshing' accents much more regularly than his specialized colleague.

This implies that generalists requires flexibility. Flexibility in their assortment of products, which they communicate through their menu-card. And this is where they can use the full potential of marketing-possibilities; exchangeable menu-card pages used in a daily/weekly rotation; supplementary or additional cards for specific times of the day or a particular genre of item; specialty cards. In general: a frequent change of the standard menu-card. The universalist's success depends on his ability to create movement in his assortment of items. He needs to continuously find new ways to meet this challenge. Modern consumers have come to expect this dynamic dimension of constant change from any universalist.

And really, nowhere else do we find such a wide variety of menu-cards, such a colourful mix of basic and supplementary cards as in generalists' establishments.

The volume of products also requires the use of supplementary cards. In order to

adequately present special offers for a specific time of day, for example – in case of doubt the appropriate specialty card communicates competence in a much more convincing manner.

To document widely fanned-out competence: this is the most important marketing achievement of a differentiated use of menu-cards. The main focus is to create landmarks of competence in a wide landscape of products.

First in line are specialty cards: special promotions provide the unique marketing playground for generalists. This is their chance at a partial specialization, or definition of their competence, which in their basic assortment is not open to them. By the way – this is exactly the opposite of how specialists use this marketing instrument.

Generally the inside of a menu-card must be activated as a powerful sales instrument. Dramatization of and emphasis on certain products/groups of products are of primary importance – also in the interest of smooth service-organization.

As far as visual design is concerned, one could say: not too big and not too small, not only in reference to the card's actual size. It has to primarily be balanced, in format and design as well as in items offered. The entire look should be informal and natural, under no circumstances should particular products be used as eye-catchers. More abstract design-concepts are recommended in lieu of concrete visualization: a logo, graphical elements, more general motives. A frequently used alternative is the presentation of overwhelming abundance.

Name:
Restaurant Green House, Rosenberger Hotel Wels
(Rosenberger-Gruppe, St. Pölten)

Business type/character:
Hotel restaurant, medium price range, principal target group: hotel guests.

Card:
Standard menu card.

Card system:
Miscellaneous folding, entirely printed on both sides, high-gloss laminated. Parchment effect for selection groups is achieved by color contrasting. The inside of the center is intended for special offers. Size when closed: 20.5 × 34.5 cm. The restaurant's wine list and the hotel bar's menu card have the same appearance.

Special features:
The menu card's visual mood is reminiscent of the restaurant's garden atmosphere.

Draft/Design:
Volker Uiberreiter, Salzburg

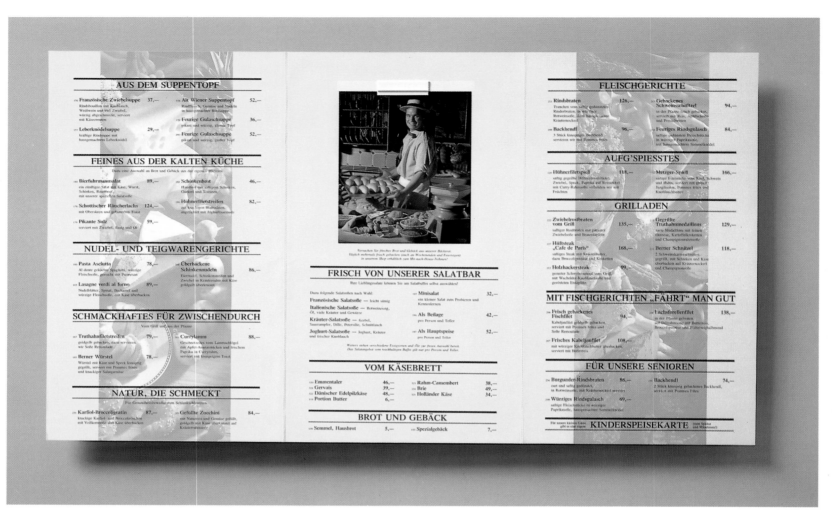

Name:
Rosenberger-Raststätten
(Rosenberger-Gruppe, St. Pölten)

Business type/character:
Road-side gastronomy—expressway restaurant with service, wide-ranged selection and target-group approach.

Card:
Selection card used in all expressway restaurants.

Card system:
All-in-one card; miscellaneous folding, outside front and back covers entirely printed, high-gloss laminated. Size when closed: 20.5×35 cm. Photographs on outside front and back covers are repeated with a blurred effect in the inside. Complementary seasonal offers are communicated by table sets.

Special features:
A photograph in the space for special offers in the card's center assures there is no "visual blank" in case there aren't any special offers.

Draft/Design:
René Juvancic, Vienna

Name:
Bräustuben Spatenhaus, Munich
(Kuffler-Gruppe, Munich)

Business type/character:
Food-oriented with wide-ranged selection, traditional middle-class approach.

Cards:
Menu card and beverage list.

Card system:
Simply folded cover, both sides laminated with matte-finish foil, outsides printed with decoration. Inside covers: information about the establishment and its history. Food selection on folded looseleaf (double office-sized format) typewritten and copied. Card alternating on daily basis. Supplementary special offer sheets. Size when closed: 22.5 × 32.5 cm. Beverage list: inner pages permanently printed, menu card stapled. Format: 18 × 24 cm.

Special features:
Cover design based upon local architectural motifs. Photo composition technique effects reviving of traditional topics.

Draft/Design:
The artist Ricarda Dietz, Munich

SUPPEN

Rindfleischsuppe mit Markklößchen
und frischen Kräutern .... DM 5,50

Deftige Gulaschsuppe .... DM 6,80

WARME SPEISEN

Omelett (3 Eier) mit Champignons,
Salatteller .... DM 12,80

Frankfurter Würstchen (1 Paar), Meerrettichkrem,
Brot oder Brötchen .... DM 6,50

Frankfurter Würstchen (1 Paar), Meerrettichkrem,
Kartoffelsalat .... DM 8,80

„Toast Mozart"-Rumpsteak (120 g) mit Champignons und Kräuterbutter auf Toast ... DM 15,90

Putensteak (150 g) natur, mit Spargelspitzen und
Sauce hollandaise, Butterreis .... DM 18,50

Rib-Eye-Steak (175 g) mit Schmorzwiebeln oder
Kräuterbutter, Bratkartoffeln,
Salatteller .... DM 21,50

FÜR DEN KLEINEN HUNGER

Spaghetti mit pikanter Tomatensauce
und Parmesankäse .... DM 7,80

KALTE SPEISEN & SNACKS

Norwegischer Räucherlachs auf Toast,
garniert mit Meerrettichkrem .... DM 12,80

Bunter Salatteller mit Putenbruststreifen oder
Schafskäse, Eischeiben, garniert mit frischen
Kräutern .... DM 12,80

Sandwich mit:
Knochenschinken (geräuchert) .... DM 5,50
gekochtem Schinken .... DM 5,50
Salami .... DM 4,95
Edamer Käse .... DM 4,95
Emmentaler Käse .... DM 4,95
Frischkäse .... DM 4,95

Camembert (große Portion)
Butter, Brot .... DM 9,80

Käseteller
Butter, Brot .... DM 12,80

DAS AKTUELLE ANGEBOT

WARME SPEISEN / HOT DISHES

505 **Putengeschnetzeltes** in fruchtiger
Apfel-Curry-Soße, Butterreis .... DM 16,50
Chipped leg of turkey in a tangy curry-apple sauce,
butter rice.
öS 118,- / hfl 19,- / FF 59,- / FB 360,-

322 **Tafelspitz** in Schnittlauchrahm,
Salzkartoffeln .... DM 20,50
Prime boiled beef in a cream sauce with chives,
boiled potatoes.
öS 147,- / hfl 23,60 / FF 73,50 / FB 450,-

298 **Rumpsteak** (175 g), mit Kräuterbutter,
Röstkartoffeln, bunter Salatteller ..... DM 26,50
Sirloin steak (175 g), with herb butter, sauté potatoes,
mixed salad.
öS 190,- / hfl 30,50 / FF 95,- / FB 580,-

MENÜ / MENU .... DM 30,50
628 **Klare Hühnersuppe** mit Pfannkuchenstreifen
und frischen Kräutern.
Tafelspitz in Schnittlauchrahm, Salzkartoffeln.
Fruchtdessert "Mango-Aprikose".
Chicken broth with shredded pancake and fresh herbs.
Prime boiled beef in a cream sauce with chives, boiled
potatoes.
Cream dessert "Mango-apricot" (cream cheese and
joghurt with mango and apricots).
öS 219,- / hfl 35,10 / FF 109,- / FB 660,-

DESSERT / DESSERT
611 **Fruchtdessert** "Mango-Aprikose" (Sahnequark,
Joghurt, Mango und Aprikose) .... DM 5,20
Cream dessert "Mango-apricot" (cream cheese and
joghurt with mango and apricots).
öS 37,- / hfl 6,- / FF 19,- / FB 110,-

Die sorgfältige Zubereitung Ihres Gerichtes liegt uns sehr am Herzen,
deshalb rechnen Sie mit ca. 15 Minuten, bis wir Ihre Bestellung servieren. /
All our dishes are freshly prepared. Please accept a delay of approximately 15 minutes before we serve your meal.
5350/M (D-Einl.-ICK) 1.5.91 – 31.5.91

Name:
DSG-Service im Zug
(Deutsche Service-Gesellschaft der Bahn, Frankfurt/Main; German Railroad Service Branch)

Business type/character:
Rail-bound gastronomy; dining car/on-board restaurants, bistro-cafés, seatside service, minibars, sleeper coach service. Wide-ranging performance spectrum for heterogeneous target group. Scope of service and offer dependent upon train system and route. In some cases adaptation of selection and service to time of day.

Cards:
An example from the wide-range menu card selection—altogether about 80 different cards. Cover pages from InterCity-Bord Restaurant (green) and Touristikzug (purple), inside pages from conventional InterCity-Zugrestaurant. Poster with food motifs depicted on cover pages. Example for specialty advertisement: table show-card and matching bottle label.

Card system:
Combination of flexibility and uniformity: half-page sized format is predominant (limited space available on board!), identical design elements: two-colored, bipartite basic layout, small squares for identification of selection elements, food photographs for the card covers. The motifs refer to selection segments: breakfast, beverages, etc. Color differentiation according to train system. Next to that, psychological effect of colors—happy, pleasure-loving atmosphere. Card versions: ranging from insertion sheet for show cards over simply folded covers to multipage stapled cards. In some instances insertion windows for current offers. Cover cellophane-coated on the outside.

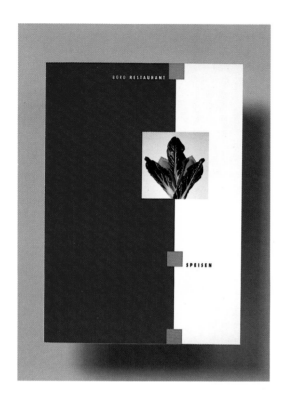

Special features:

Design conception meets complex requirements: versatility, wide-range target group compatibility, high recognition value. Optically improved appearance in context with new service profile. Corporate design approach: all service-in-train-communication and advertising media operate with the card's design elements.

Draft/Design:

Trust Corporate Culture, Frankfurt/Main

71

EIN
KLEINER DENKANSTOSS.

DSG

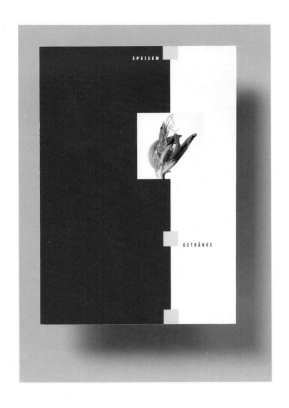

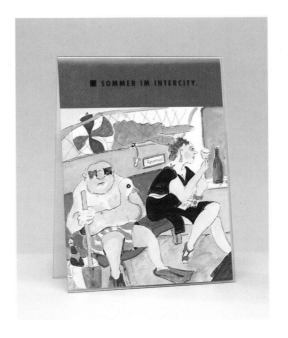

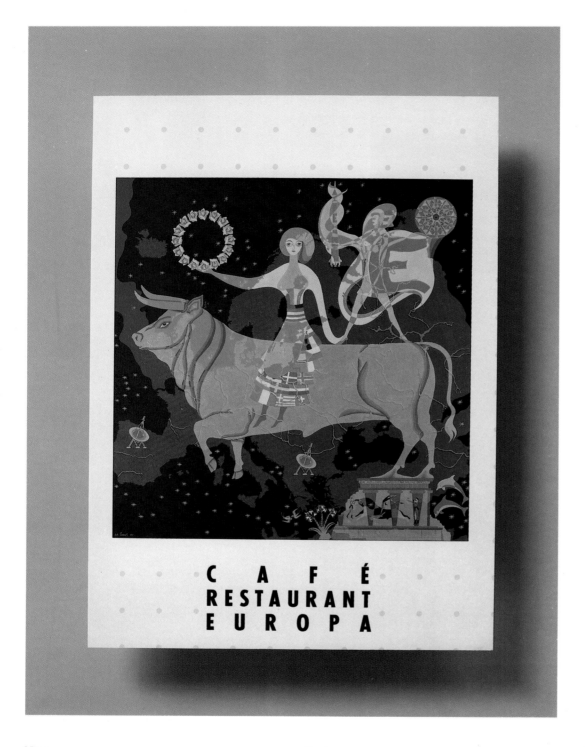

GRILL- UND PFANNENGERICHTE

GRILL- AND PAN SPECIALS – VIANDES EN SAUCE ET GRILLADES

DM

HÄHNCHENBRUST VOM ROST
in Champignonrahm auf badischen Butternudeln 19,80
grilled chicken breast in champignon cream with buttered noodles
poitrine de poulet, sauce aux champignons, nouilles au beurre

GEGRILLTER FLEISCHSPIESS
mit feuriger Paprikarahmsauce, gemischtem Salat
und Curryreis 22,50
beef brochette in hell pepper sauce, mixed salad and curry rice
brochette de viande, sauce pimentée, salade et riz au curry

SCHWEINEFILET AUF APFELSCHEIBEN
mit Pilzen, Sauce Béarnaise und Rösti 23,50
filet de porc grillé avec pommes et champignons, sauce béarnaise et rösti de pommes de terre

WIENER SCHNITZEL
mit Pommes frites und gemischtem Salat 24,00
escalope de veau viennoise, salade et pommes frites

GRILLTELLER
3 Medaillons vom Rost mit Würstchen, Speck,
Kräuterbutter, Speckböhnchen
und Pommes frites 29,50
various mixed grill with herb butter, green beans and french fries

GEGRILLTES RUMPSTEAK
mit gebratenen Champignons, Zwiebeln,
Café de Paris Butter, gebackenen Kartoffel-
stäbchen und gemischtem Salat 33,50
grilled rumpsteak with fried mushrooms, onions, mixed salad and steak fries
entrecôte grillé, champignons, salade et pommes de terre frites

KALBSRÜCKENSTEAK IN MORCHELRAHMSAUCE
Broccoli und Kroketten 36,50
grilled veal steak with morell sauce, broccoli and croquette potatoes
steak de veau grillé, sauce aux morilles et pommes croquettes

FILETSTEAK MIT GRÜNER PFEFFERSAUCE
saisonalen Gemüsen und Kartoffelküchlein 38,00
filet steak with green pepper sauce, market vegetables and potato dumplings
steak de bœuf, sauce au poivre vert, légumes du marché et pommes mousseline

C A F É
R E S T A U R A N T
E U R O P A

Name:
Café Restaurant Europa, Düsseldorf
(Stockheim-Gastronomie, Düsseldorf)

Business type/character:
Airport restaurant, characterized by high traffic volume. Medium to high price level.

Card:
Selection card, entirely printed, with artistically designed cover.

Card system:
All-in-one card, cover plus eight selection pages, entirely cellophane-coated. Stapled. Size when closed: 22 × 30 cm. Overall design motif: dotted screen with color dots. Trilingual selection — location!

Special features:
Cover painting: "Europe and the Bull; Europe and Taurus" — analogous to the restaurant's name. Original picture exhibited in the restaurant. Mental reference to the airport location. Elucidations on the painting and the artist on the inside cover.

Draft/Design:
The artist Curt Stenvert, Cologne (painting)/ Ingo Bergmann, Design Division, Krefeld

Name:
Seerestaurant & Café, Böblingen
(REGA Restaurant und Hotelbetriebe, Sindelfingen)

Business type/character:
Congress-hall restaurant with bistro section and seaside terrace. Guests predominantly business people (congress visitors) and white-collar employees from surrounding locations.

Card:
Bistro's menu card and list of beverages.

Card system:
Simply folded cover, grey-structured cardboard, size when closed: 24 × 38.5 cm. All-in-one solution. Entirely printed, designed cover, illustrations in silhouette for every selection column. Graphics made by computer, text handwritten with exception of column titles. No strict separation of columns of food and beverages; aperitifs and coffee included in the inner section for food. Column titles composed of non-translatable play on words. The basic idea is to get away from conventional order of courses, informal approach. Standard restaurant card in similar design.

Special features:
Matter-of-fact menu card style matching the modern ambiance of the establishment. Logo on cover (stylized waves) form a visual reference to the location. Cost-effective solution allows rapid alternation of card. The word-image-motif of the logo and silhouettes are also used on other communication means of the establishment.

Draft/Design:
Iris Wöhr-Reinheimer, Wöhr Grafik Design, Sindelfingen

Name:
Restaurant Kniese's Gute Stuben, Bad Hersfeld

Business type/character:
Hotel restaurant in the Romantik-Hotel Zum Stern, medium price range, local cuisine. Hotel guests and out-of-house visitors.

Card:
Menu card, artistically designed in naive painting style. Detailed motifs from the inside cover page.

Card system:
Simply folded cover, cardboard with gable-shaped top. Colored cover sheet, inside cover and backside black/white with view of hotel. Size when closed: 23.5 × 43.5 cm (without gables). Selection leaves handwritten, copied and glued in; supplementary menu of the day as looseleaf (PC printer).

Special features:
Original as verre églomisé. Motif also for wine list and calling cards. Information on the establishment's history on the outside back cover.

Draft/Design:
The artist Astrid Störzer, Freyung (Black Forest region)

Name:
Hotel-Restaurant Fröhlicher Rheinfelder Hof, Basel

Business type/character:
Hotel gastronomy; two restaurants: Baiz (plain cooking) and Gryffe Stubb (à-la-carte cuisine, seasonal specialties). Characterized by close association to club activities centered around Basel's Carneval.

Cards:
Menu cards from both restaurants, each with artistically designed cover.

Card system:
Gryffe Stubb: simply folded cover, double-glued structure-laminated cardboard, punched on the inside. Colored selection sheets (yellow, printed by laser printer) are inserted. Size when closed: 24 × 33 cm. Metal corners. Baiz: same principle, however with four selection sheets (pink loose leafs). Colored covers, inside covers and rear page with green brush paintings (logo and clock, emblem of the Basel Sample Fair—location emblem). Separate beverage list in neutral design.

Special features:
Gay exuberant style of illustrations matching the establishment's profile. Corporate design conception: calling cards, banquet sheets, stationery and hotel prospect fanfold with recurring motifs. The originals of the menu card drawings are exhibited in the hotel reception. Very beautifully designed logo. The successful inclusion of the operator's name (Fröhlich = gay, happy) is quite remarkable! Wine and marc labels match the menu card covers.

Draft/Design:
The artist Däge, Däge Design, Basel

Name:
Rasthaus Weiskirchen Süd, Rodgau

Business type/character:
Expressway restaurant, characterized by high volume traffic, wide-range international target group. Combination of service and self-service business. Uncomplicated, "classless."

Card:
Menu card and list of beverages for both establishment sections.

Card system:
All-in-one solution, altar-shape folding, punched, printed on both sides and cellophane coated. Size when closed (without punching) 22 × 27.5 cm. Cover design resembles a radiator grill. Beverage selection on rear side. Food selection with strong visual structure, space for trucker's menu of the day in the card's center.

Special features:
Corporate design conception: colors of card matching service personnel's clothing and entire ambiance. Unusual utilization of menu card in self-service sector, too. Menu not mandatory, but it has a certain service and animation effect. Excerpts from the selection are communicated by chartboard in the self-service-zone. Additional offers are presented directly there.

Draft/Design:
Eugen Stoy, chef de cuisine in the expressway restaurant Weiskirchen

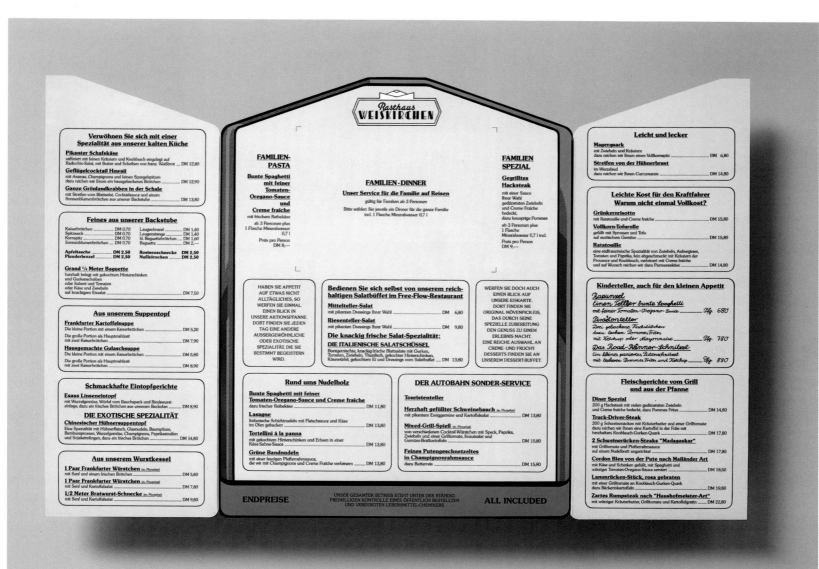

Kinderteller, auch für den kleinen Appetit

Rapunzel
Einen Teller bunte Spaghetti
mit feiner Tomaten-Oregano-Sauce _____ Pfg. 680

Piratenteller
Drei gebackene Fischstäbchen
dazu leckere Pommes Frites
mit Ketchup oder Mayonnaise _____ Pfg. 780

Das Road-Rönner-Schnitzel
Ein kleines paniertes Putenschnitzel
mit leckeren Pommes Frites und Ketchup _____ Pfg. 890

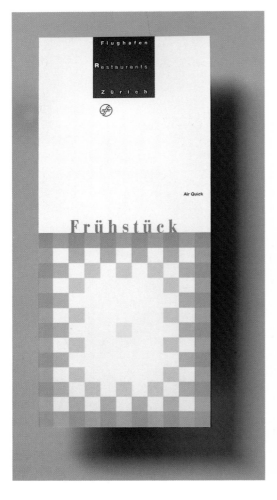

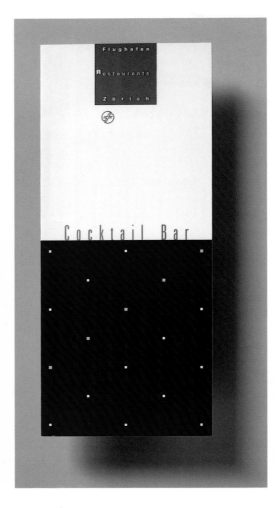

Name:
Flughafengastronomie Zurich-Kloten

Business type/character:
A total of about two dozen gastronomical units; harmonized to meet the requirements of the traffic-intense location. Restaurants, snackbars, bars. Staggered conceptions with differing selection, price, and service design; offer ranging from fast-food to top-notch restaurant.

Cards:
Selection cards of various establishments: Air Quick, Transit, Cocktailbar, Gueti Zyt. Air Quick breakfast menu card and a list of wines used in all businesses.

Card system:
Simply folded or miscellaneous folded cover, entirely printed on both sides and high-gloss laminated. Size when closed 16.5 × 31 cm, breakfast and cocktail cards: 11 × 25.5 cm. Gueti Zyt: 11 × 31 cm. Restaurant and snackbar menu cards as all-in-one solution; supplementary for restaurants: wine lists with bottled wines. Uniform design standards for the cards of all businesses (exceptions: two high-priced restaurants and a nightclub). The outside covers are entirely printed with different graphic decorations; bipartite design, logo at upper edge of card. Each business/type of business with its own decoration; next to that cards used in multiple locations. Uniform appearance on the inside, too: same typography, same basic layout. That assures problem-free handling of alterations. Altogether more than a dozen cards being used.

Special features:
Stylistic relationship between the cards signals variety as well as unity of the businesses run by one operator and allows combination of cards without any problems. There is no culinary reference in the decoration. Photographs from the image prospectus of the airport restaurant; layout is keeping in line with the basic card design.

Draft/Design:
Weiersmüller, Bosshard, Grüninger wgb, Zurich

Flughafen
Restaurants
Zürich

Gueti Zyt

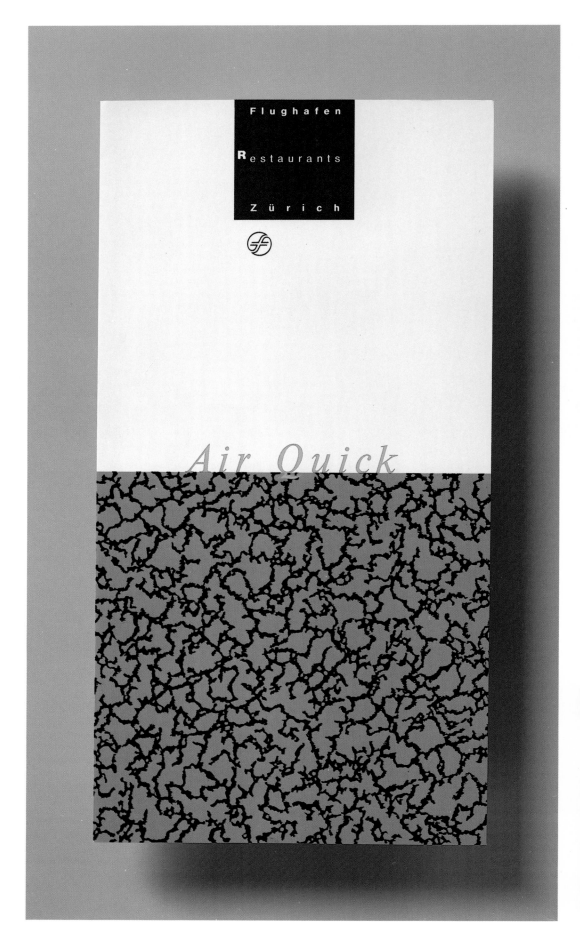

Name:

Henry's Cafe Bar
(Until June 1992: Whitbread-Group, London)

Business type/character:

Emphasis on communication, informal. Refined pub style. Cold and uncomplicated warm dishes. Multiplied—most recently nine units.

Card:

Menu card and list of beverages, cocktail card.

Card system:

Both cards made of matte foil laminated cardboard, analogous appearance with Henry's logo. Menu card: Miscellaneous folding with register look, size when closed: 18 × 27 cm. Printed on both sides. Inside with food and beverage selection on marbled background. Henry's philosophy is introduced on the folded-in back side. Cocktail card: simply folded cover, triangular shape, with register effect. For upright mounting. Maximum size when closed: 16 × 22 cm. Printed on both sides. Inside with selection on marbled background. Cards with different colors: rust-red and green.

Special features:

The logo's picture-element (chameleon) is understood as symbol for the business' changeability during the course of the day—ambiguous slogan: Mood changes at Henry's.

Draft/Design:

Kent & Sendall, Tunbridge Wells, Kent

85

MÖVENPICK
Kantonalbank

Name:
Mövenpick Restaurants Switzerland/Germany
(Mövenpick Unternehmungen, Adliswil)

Business type/character:
Emphasis on enjoyment, casualness. Profile emphasis: quality and diversion. Seasonal cuisine. Uniform basic philosophy; appearance and selection vary.

Cards:
Basic menu cards.

Card system:
Miscellaneous folded cards printed on both sides and high-gloss laminated, folded-in back cover page is narrower with insertion window for promotion card (approximately 10 × 30 cm.) Size when closed: 23 × 37 cm. Basic decoration (food-photography aquarelle paintings), inside and back cover with imprinted selection columns. In addition, there is an individual insert leaf with Menu of the Day and, depending upon special campaigns, photographic cards matching the topic as well as, according to business, a wine list. Aquarelle card with double-glued cardboard, several small windows for alternating selections on the inside left and center. The background resembling handmade paper is technically reproduced. The card's appearance is reminiscent of Japanese painting. Photography of plate is artfully mounted on front cover.

Special features:
Cards belong to the company's central card-pool and can principally be used by all German and Swiss businesses. Cards used approximately for one season each. The business' location is imprinted on cover front page to underline individuality. The card's appearance supports the fresh, modern profile of Mövenpick gastronomy.

Draft/design:
Mövenpick Werbung Restaurants Switzerland, Adliswil

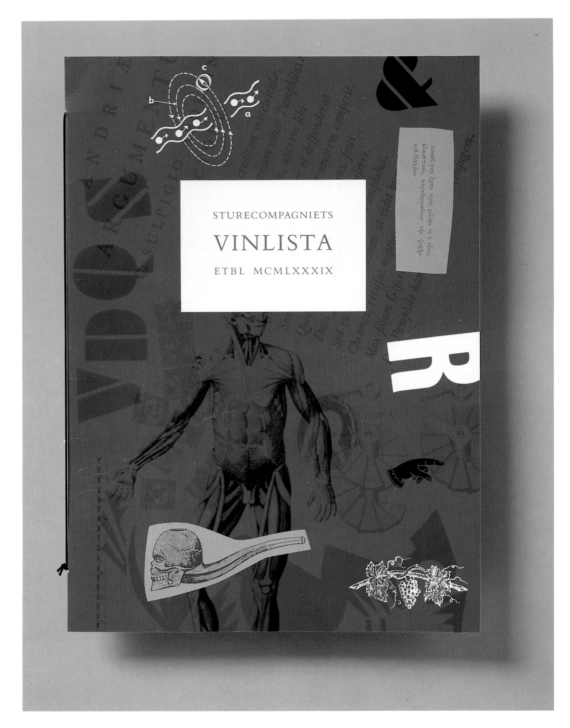

Name:
Sturecompagniet, Stockholm

Business type/character:
"Gastronomical kaleidoscope"; complex with delicatessen, bakery, bar, wine tavern, cafe/ discotheque, and restaurant. The restaurant offers homemade Swedish cooking and classical French cuisine.

Card:
Restaurant's menu card and wine list in different color shades.

Card system:
Designed on both sides, cover simply folded, cardboard laminated with matte foil. Size when closed: 27 × 37 cm. Menu card with one, winelist with two color insertion-sheets, 30 × 42 cm, folded, printed on both sides by PC printer. Fastened with elastic string.

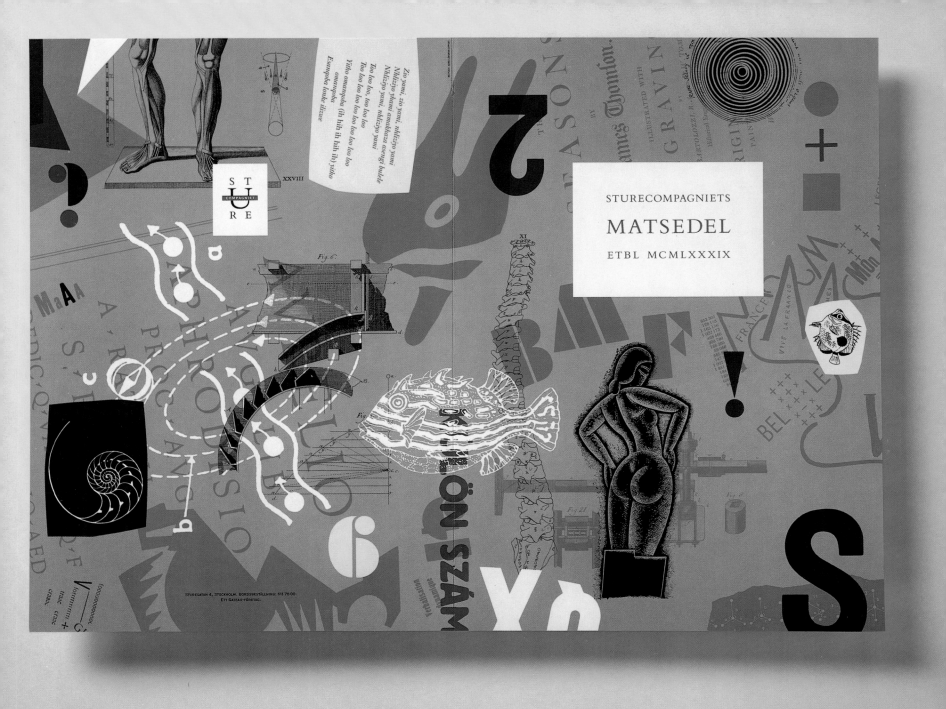

Special Features:
Card designed as allusion to the former owner
of the locality, an inventor, globetrotter, and
constructor; his life's story is narrated in the restaurant's prospectus. Collage technique of card
cover in Dada-fashion, motifs from the world of
technology and research.

Draft/Design:
Kent Nyström, Saatchi & Saatchi, Stockholm

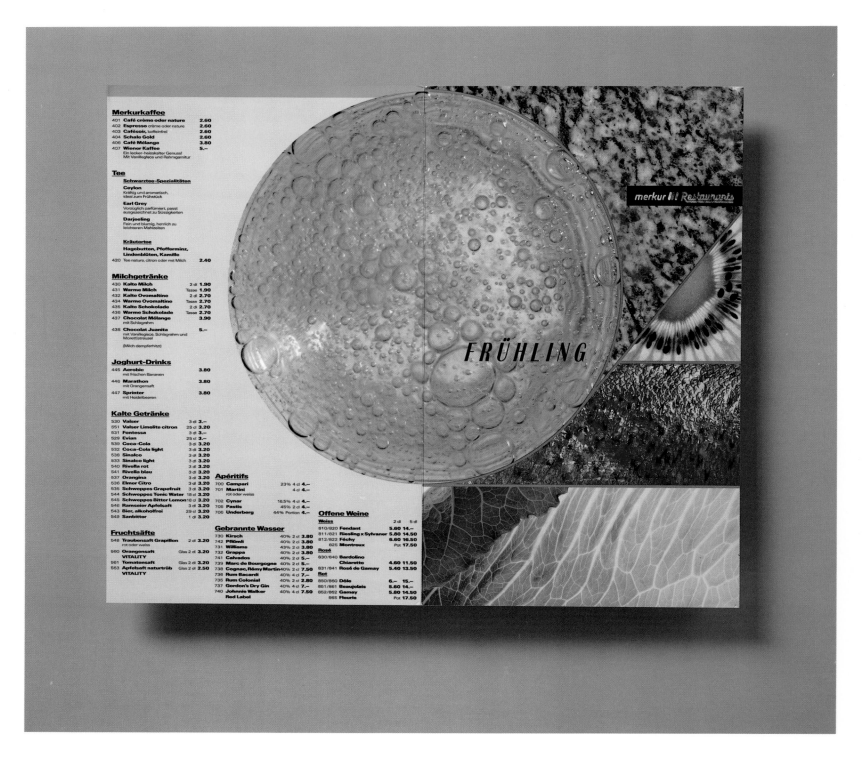

Name:
Merkur-Restaurants Schweiz
(Merkur, Bern)

Business type/character:
Approximately 30 restaurants in shopping centers and highly-frequented urban locations. Oriented toward families.

Card:
Four season-dependent menu cards and beverage lists.

Card system:
Cellophane-coated miscellaneous folding cards printed on both sides, size when closed: 22.5 × 37 cm. All-in-one-cards. Cover sheets with identical photo collage, macro-food-photographs, colors and motifs matching the season. Background color of the selection section also alternating. Uniform structure: food on the inside, clear column structure. Center is blank, individual loose-leaf with selection is attached here. Fold-in cover page with product photographs, rear with beverages. Remarkable detail: Sectional cut of glass on the cover sheet is completed on the rear leaf. In addition there is a list of beverages as simply folded cover in related design as well as special cards.

Special features:
Seasonal character of the selection is to be discernible to the guests through visual hints. Periodical alternation of cards allows flexible adaptation of selection to current events. Servicelife of this card generation: 3 years.

Draft/Design:
Advertising Agency Marty, Köniz (Bern)

Name:
Hotel Gasthof Wöhrmann, Werther

Business type/character:
Hotel, restaurant, and pub. Restaurant with seasonal market—kitchen-conception. Predominantly business guests.

Card:
Restaurant menu card and list of beverages (predominantly used in pub).

Card system:
Both cards on structure-foil laminated cardboard. Uniform design with remarkable details and differing colors. Menu card: cover solution, laminated on both sides, cover design of front and back with logo and triangle as repetitive design-element. Size when closed: 55 × 33 cm. Eight selection sheets, handwritten and reproduced. Special folding technique: Five-page zigzag folding, prepunched. Selection sheets are punched, inserted in the double-fold and fastened with rubberband. Neutrally designed wine lists as supplement. List of beverages: completely laminated and printed on both sides, staggered accordion fold with register effect. Size when closed: 11 × 29.5 cm. Front and back cover identically designed with logo and triangle. Triangle motif as design element in the cards inside.

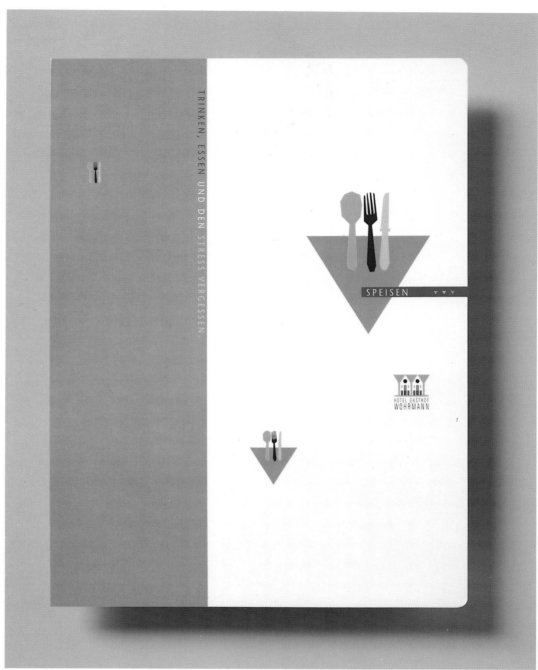

Special features:
Corporate design conceptions as pendant to the restaurant's holistic philosophy. The buildings facade is the origin of the logo. Designed as a picture puzzle, three cocktail glasses frame the double gable. On the inside two stylized figures with suitcases. The logo's colors—dark blue, turquoise—are also the colors of the house and the ambiance. Logo is repeated on all of the business's printing matters. Logo colors are alternately combined.

Draft/Design:
Braun Design, Bartling-Braun, Werther/special folding: Flurer, specialized publisher for menu cards and lists of beverages

Name:
InterCity Restaurants
(Deutsche Service Gesellschaft der Bahn, Frankfurt/Main)

Business type/character:
Restaurant businesses in German railroad stations, travelling atmosphere.

Card:
Breakfast card and wine list with macro-food-photographs on the covers.

Card system:
Gloss-foil laminated cover on both sides, simply folded. Photograph motifs on front and rear cover. Breakfast card (size when closed: 21×30 cm) printed on the inside, selection depiction in breakfast arrangement photograph. Wine list (size when closed: 22×31 cm) blank on the inside, selection sheets are printed locally and fastened in frame/adhesive corners. Menu cards designed analogously with food photography on cover, printed selection sheets (accordion-type folding).

Special features:
Card conception for about twelve InterCity restaurants.

Draft/Design:
Abels & Partner, Frankfurt/Main

Name:
Merkur Snacks und Buffets, Switzerland
(Merkur, Bern)

Business type/character:
About 25 fast-food type conceptions, predominantly located near railroad stations, counter service.

Card:
Selection card.

Card system:
Gloss-foil laminated cardboard, printed on both sides with picture motif, punched. Modified miscellaneous folding: asymmetrical effect achieved through angular format. Maximum size when closed: 15 × 33.5 cm. Front and back cover each show half of a French bread wrapped as express parcel. All-in-one-card; selection sheets are glued to the inside: a trisected office-sheet sized leaf printed with express markers. Inscription (printing or copy) and cutting are handled in central office, the fastening is done locally.

Special features:
Novel variations with the express-marker motif: allusion to speed as conceptual criteria and typical railroad station location. Flexible card solution: same basic card, but varying selection/price constellations of the restaurants can be taken into consideration.

Draft/Design:
Werbeagentur Marty, Köniz (Bern)

Name:
Mövenpick Restaurants, Switzerland/Germany
(Mövenpick Unternehmungen, Adliswil)

Business type/character:
Emphasis on casual, relaxed atmosphere, quality
and diversion. Seasonal cooking. Uniform basic
philosophy; appearance and selection vary.

Card:
Additional card for sweets and beverages.

Card system:
Miscellaneous folded card printed on both sides
and gloss-foil laminated, size when closed:
20 × 31.5 cm. Outside front and back covers
with photographic motif on background decoration resembling hand-made paper, the same
motif to be found reduced in size as diagonal
screen on inside pages and folded-in back cover.
Selection sheets to be glued in feature light-
colored version of the card theme; selection is
copied in.

Special features:
The card features desserts not to be found in the
ice-cream card, as well as hot and non-alcoholic
beverages.

Draft/Design:
Mövenpick Werbung Restaurants Schweiz,
Adliswil

Name:
Restaurant in the Maritim Hotel, Cologne

Business type/character:
Several hotel restaurants, multi-level concepts ranging from gourmet restaurant to more rustic pubs.

Card:
Menu and coffee card of the restaurant Bellevue (high-class level).

Card system:
High-gloss cellophane-coated cover on both sides, size when closed: 28.5×36 cm (menu card), 21×29.5 cm (coffee card). Cover with crayon illustration. Printed inner sheets, fastened with string or stapled. The menu card's first and last inner sheet are made of parchment; the name "Bellevue" written on front. Center pages punched, colored sheets with current menu and special offers (laser printer) are inserted. Basic selection presented successively in three languages. The design principle with slight modifications for other Bellevue cards (drinks, digestifs, desserts, special menus) and all other business types; cover drawing with alternating motifs in same style. Card size and volume varies.

Special features:
Style of drawing is in balance between conservative-dignified and modern style. Required are visual kinship and adaptability to a certain level and target group scope. The Bellevue menu card was awarded a gold medal by the Gastronomische Akademie Deutschland in 1988.

Draft/Design:
Karin Bison, Bremen (illustrations)/Peter Ballach, Advertising Partner, Hanover

Name:
Berns' Bar, Stockholm

Business type/character:
Hotel restaurant in the Hotel Berns' Salonger. Art-Deco ambiance in an old restored hall, at the same time also bar and discotheque, trendy meeting-place for mixed audience, including local clientele.

Card:
Menu card and list of beverages.

Card system:
Cardboard printed on both sides, format: 27 × 40 cm. Entire front side artistically designed with logo and decoration. Chalk drawings, motif: classical café scenes. Rear side longitudinally split in three; the all-in-one offer presentation on the two outer sides.

Special features:
Column heading in bright ornamental type, same typography as logo. Unusual, scattered arrangement of columns.

Draft/Design:
Monica Hellström, Stockholm

99

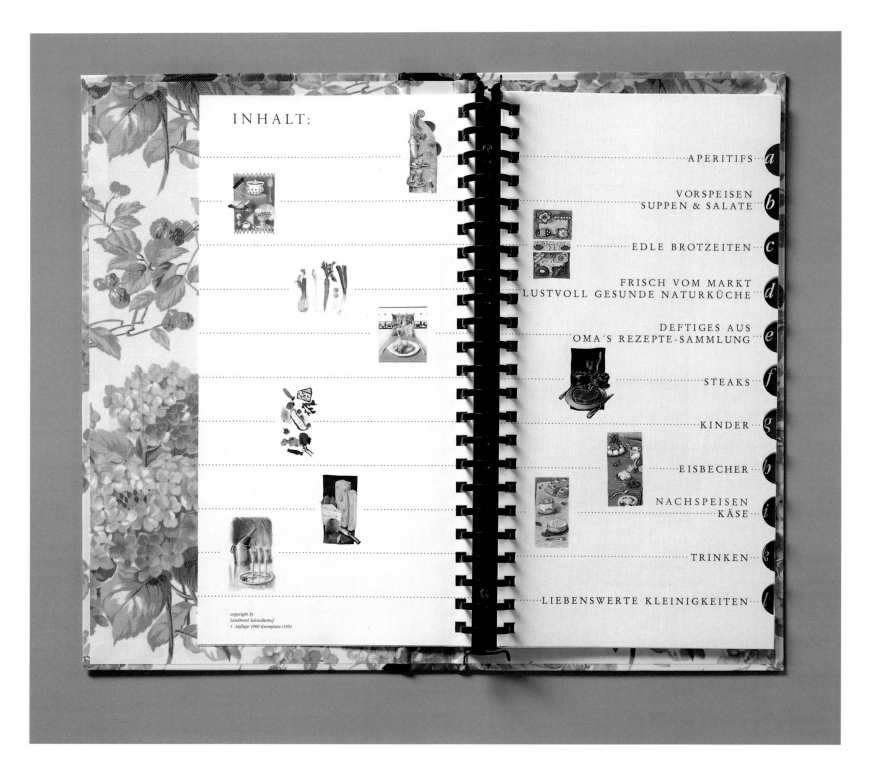

INHALT:

*copyright by
Landhotel Schindlerhof
1. Auflage 1000 Exemplare/1991*

Name:
Landhotel und Kreativzentrum Schindlerhof, Nuremberg-Boxdorf

Business type/character:
Restaurant in the Schindlerhof. Creative, healthy natural cooking, motto: "All Senses are Satisfied."

Card:
The restaurant's selection card.

Card system:
All-in-one card (with the exception of wine), encyclopedia style. Ring-binder with structured foil-laminated rigid binding and 22 insertion sheets made of linen-structured paper and printed on both sides. Size when closed: 18 × 32.5 cm. Extravagant, bibliophile design with introductory text (self-portrait of the company), index and register. The binder's colorful flower decoration in country-house style is repeated as light grey ornament on the selection pages. Another design element of the basic decoration: fancy letters in aquarelle-style. Elegant typographical design in book-printing tradition, two-colored: green/black. Colored drawings (mixed technique) as column openers. Many explanations and excursions. The columns "Directly from the Market" and "Natural Cooking" are only basic decorations; the current offer on colored paper is fastened by staple.

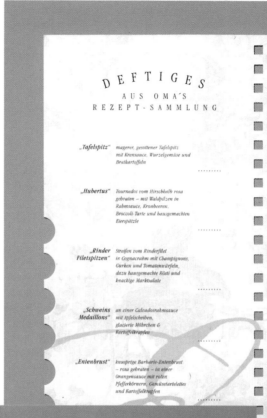

Special features:
Stable, handy ring-mechanisms allow uncompli-cated exchange of individual pages. Corporate design approach: flower motif on the binding is repeated as textile and plate decoration in the restaurant as well as in the restaurant's other printed matter. The originals of the column drawings are exhibited in the restaurant. A menu card with high entertainment values; side effect: time-bridging and communication. The card concept is keeping in line with the holistic philosophy of the Schindler Hof; central motto here: harmony of spirit and emotion.

Draft/Design:
Werner Steiner, Steiner Design, Erlangen

Name:
Café de la Paix, Düsseldorf
(SAS International Hotels, Brussels)

Business type/character:
Hotel-restaurant in the SAS Royal Scandinavian Hotel
Elegant bistro-conception.

Card:
Selection card.

Card system:
All-in-one-card, cover plus eight selection pages, stapled. Entirely high-gloss laminated. Colored drawing on front and back cover, on the inside front cover annotations on the history of the Café de la Paix in Paris. Inside pages blank, selection pages glued on: basic print with logo and monochrome, pastel reproduction of the cover motif, selection printed by laser printer.

Special features:
Card design allows flexible arrangements of selection; individual selection sheets can be changed at any time. Card design and logo are identical with the original in Paris.

Draft/Design:
Adopted from Café de la Paix, Paris

Name:
La Louisiane, Geneva
(Rumba, Basel/UTC-group, Switzerland)

Business type/character:
Refined snackbar conception, small dishes, constantly changing menus.

Card:
List of beverages.

Card system:
Simply folded cover, mat-foil laminated, cover-sheet illustration is a visual translation of the name—Mississippi steamboat, female figure in the style of the 1930s, Dixie atmosphere: elegant gaiety as basic mood. Motif on the inside slightly converted as framing ornament.

Special features:
No menu card; the food selection is presented verbally or on chalk-boards.

Draft/Design:
Freitag&Partner, Zurich

Name:
Mövenpick Restaurants Switzerland/Germany
(Mövenpick Unternehmungen, Adliswil)

Business type/character:
Emphasis on casual, relaxing atmosphere, quality and diversion. Seasonal cooking. Uniform basic philosophy; appearance and selection vary.

Card:
Flexible breakfast menu.

Card system:
Simply folded, gloss-foil laminated outside cover, size when closed: 15×21 cm. Inside blank, selection photocopied on folded insertion sheets. Drawing of chicken on front cover refers to product field.

Special features:
Good-mood atmosphere transported by style of drawing.

Draft/Design:
Mövenpick Werbung Restaurants Schweiz, Adliswil

Name:
Café-Restaurant Mathildenhöhe, Darmstadt

Business type/character:
Café-restaurant in the exhibition halls of the Mathildenhöhe (small hill near the city of Darmstadt). Exhibition visitors, selective groups of guests.

Card:
List of beverages.

Card system:
Gloss-foil laminated cardboard, miscellaneous folding, printed on both sides. Entirely black and white. Art-Nouveau style drawings on cover as ornamental vignette in the interior. Graphic structure and typography in Art-Nouveau style. Supplementary breakfast cards and special offer cards with special dishes and drinks (alternating every 2-3 months) as loose insert sheets also featuring the cover motif. Yet another card with the same motifs for the garden café.

Special features:
Calling cards designed in same style. The Art-Nouveau approach is in context with the location: the first Art-Nouveau exhibitions were staged on the Mathildenhöhe at the beginning of the century. Famous artists of that epoch resided in the nearby artists' colony of the same name still existent today. The illustration is designed after an original drawing in Vienna.

Draft/Design:
Christa Pohl, Dagmar Kniess-Stütz, Café-Restaurant Mathildenhöhe/Manfred Schmidt, Darmstadt

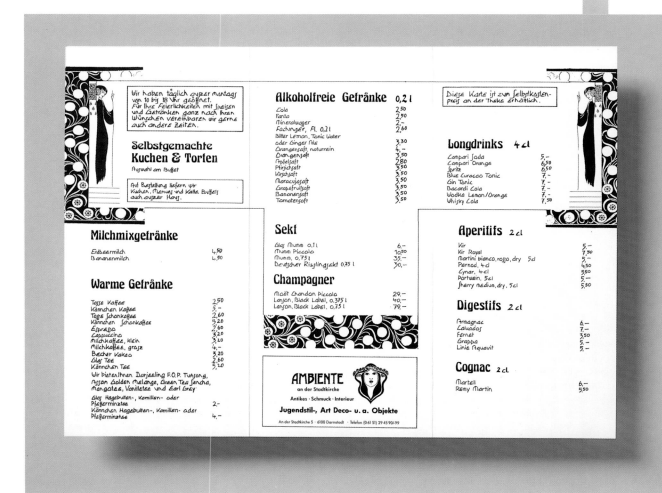

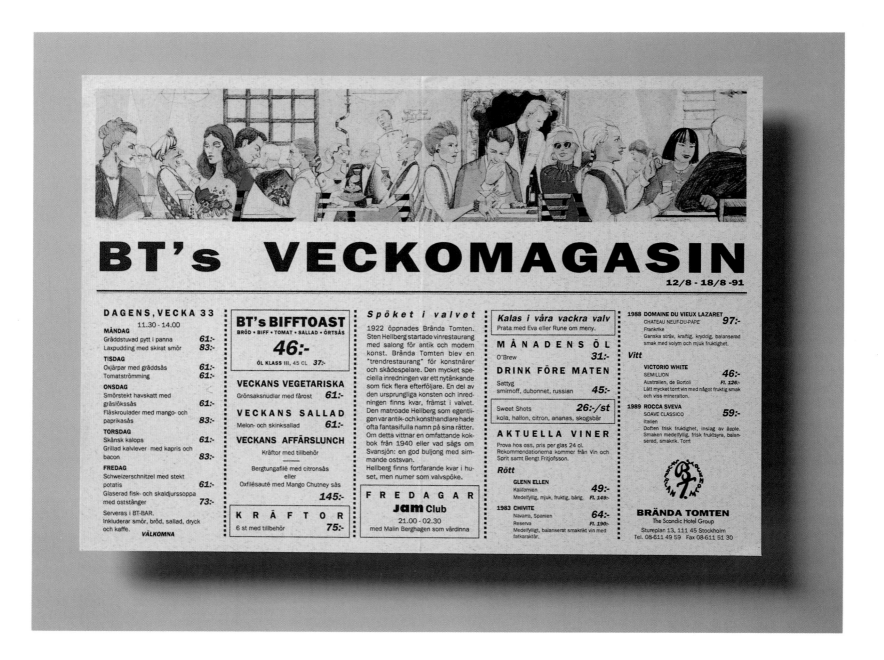

Name:
Brända Tomten, Stockholm
(The Scandic Hotel Group, Stockholm. Converted into an Asian restaurant of the end in 1991)

Business type/character:
Traditional restaurant with artistic flair, casual, with meeting-point character. Annexed bar. Ambiance: combination of the new and the old. Mixed audience, also international.

Card:
Basic menu card and Card of the Week.

Card system:
Both cards consist of colored cardboard printed on one side, menu card in office-sheet-sized format, Card of the Week (Veckomagasin—weekly magazine) with menu card and list of beverages as table set sized 30 × 42 cm. Blank sheets with preprinted illustration, printing by laser printer.

Special features:
Layout in form of a newspaper front page with illustrations and headlines.

Draft/Design:
Ulla Knutsson, Lund (drawing)/Eva Jedin, Stockholm

MATSEDEL

FÖRRÄTTER

Sparris i örtvinegrette med parmaskinka	74:-
Små fyllda nachos	58:-
Sherrymarinerad matjessill med kapris och hackat ägg	62:-
Löjromstoast	87:-

VARMRÄTTER

Fisk- och skaldjursspett med dijonhollandaise	138:-
Halstrad helgeflundra med paprikasås och sockerärtspuré	145:-
Rimmad lax med dillstuvad potatis	98:-
Entrecôte med rödvinssås och oliver	152:-
Biff Rydberg	139:-
Oxfilémedaljonger med calvadospepparsås	158:-
Spare ribs med två såser på majsbädd	94:-
Biff Bearnaise med pommes frites	120:-

SMÅTT & GOTT

BT's Bifftoast	46:-
Fisk- och skaldjurssoppa med aioli	84:-
Ishavsräkor med sauce vert och västerbottenost	68:-

Pasta med parmaskinka, pesto och parmesan	83:-
Krämig gravlaxsallad	65:-
Quiche	66:-
Croque Monsieur	59:-
Pytt i panna	73:-

BT SPECIAL

Kycklingfilé serveras med curry, cocos, mango chutney, banan och ananas	128:-

EFTERRÄTTER

Jordgubbsdessert med vaniljglass	55:-
Dagens sorbet med färsk frukt	44:-
Chokladtårta med frysta hallon och grädde	46:-
Lingonparfait med tjinuskisås	48:-
Petit four	16:-

BRÄNDA TOMTEN
The Scandic Hotel Group

Stureplan 13, Stockholm
Tel 08-611 49 59

Name:
La Fontaine, Grotte-Bar

Cards:
Menu card and list of beverages.

Card system:
Insertion cards in analogous design, double glued, structure-laminated cardboard. Each cover with additional folding page on the inside. Size when closed: 28 × 38 cm. Outside front cover with exquisite photographic design on black background and restaurant logo in gold relief printing. Inside pages punched for selection sheets. Insertion sheets printed with colored decoration design in aquarelle technique.

Special features:
Card cover and insertion sheets with various decorations to be obtained as prefab products; individual logo imprint.

Draft/Design:
Harald Georg Uhl, Purh b. Hallein (Austria)/ imprinting: Hypro, Rothenburg (Switzerland)

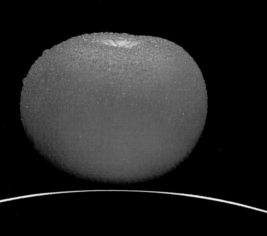

Restaurant

La Fontaine

JOAN CRAWFORD in «Humoresque»

Name:
Mövenpick Restaurant Plaza, Zurich
(Mövenpick Unternehmnungen, Adliswil)

Business type/character:
Emphasis on enjoyment, casualness. Profile emphasis: quality and diversion. Seasonal cuisine. Frequented in the evenings, young audience as typical Mövenpick clientele.

Card:
Basic selection card.

Card system:
Simply folded cover, outside gloss-foil laminated, size when closed: 30 × 42 cm. Stapled, 6 pages including inside front cover. In addition, fold-in window at back cover. Black/white decoration: cover and inside completely printed, illustrated with old film stills. Food listed on the inside, outside back cover features wine.

Special features:
Unusual emphasis on decoration and selection presentation: large-formatted and partially oversized photographs dominate the card, the selection is of minor importance. The card is not part of the central Mövenpick card-pool, but was created specifically for the Restaurant Plaza, the reason being target-group specific design, specific positioning of the business keeping in line with the location.

Draft/Design:
Mövenpick Werbung Restaurant, Switzerland, Adliswil, with photographs taken from the Paramount archives

SUPPEN

MINESTRONE PESTÙ
mit Knoblauch-Brötli   6.80

**TOMATENSUPPE MIT FRISCHEM
BASILIKUM**
und Knoblauch-Brötli   6.80

GERÄUCHERTES UND MARINIERTES

ISLÄNDER SALATTELLER
in Rotwein mariniertes Heringsfilet
mit feuriger Sauce, Blattsalaten,
Tomaten- und Gurkensalat, Cottage
cheese und Knoblauch-Brötli   19.80

GRÖNLÄNDER RAUCHLACHS AUF   60 g   18.50
BUCHWEIZEN-BLINIS
mit saurem Halbrahm, Schnittlauch
und Keta-Caviar

GRÖNLÄNDER RAUCHLACHS   60 g   18.50
MELONE
mit Honigmelone, Cottage cheese und
gerösteten Pinienkernen

RAUCHLACHS-TATAR BELLAVISTA   22.50
mit saurem Halbrahm und Schnittlauch,
Blattsalaten, Tomaten- und Gurkensalat,
Cottage cheese und Knoblauch-Brötli

PICKEREIEN

ATLANTIC-CREVETTEN AUF   16.50
BUCHWEIZEN-BLINIS
mit saurem Halbrahm und Schnittlauch,
Dillrahmgurken-Salat und Keta-Caviar

ARROSTO DI VITELLO   17.80
mit Tomaten-Schnittlauch-Vinaigrette,
Cole Slaw und Knoblauch-Brötli

TATAR

TATAR MÖVENPICK   kleinere Portion 16.50
mild, medium oder feurig.   Portion   22.80
Mit Brioche-Toast und Butter
mit Cognac, Calvados oder Whisky   + 2.50

TATAR MADAGASY (überbacken)   25.80
mit Potato Skins und gebackenen
Zwiebelringen

MARLENE DIETRICH in «Angel»

MÖVENPICKEREIEN

Visual variations of the topic

They are the declared favourites of today's marketing professionals. A typical phenomenon of the 'zeitgeist' which created them and from which they benefit. During the last decades, there has been a tremendous movement towards more and more divison of labour, together with an explosive growth of specialized knowledge in whatever part of life. Specialization has become a necessity. No matter where one looks, this development has touched all branches of industry, economy and science.

More and more companies providing a service or a product are based upon the philosophy of specialization – whether the name is Boss or Benetton, Microsoft or Minolta ... or McDonald's. Outstanding competence is hard to bring across in any other manner, we all have to a large extent equated reduction or concentration with quality.

Consequently we have transferred this equation onto the field of gastronomy. The specialist, or better the product-specialist, enjoys an image-bonus simply because he offers nothing else. He'd be foolish not to exploit it!

Gastronomical specialists aren't an invention of modern days. We all know their precursors, the classical examples of the seafood-restaurant, the ice-cream parlor, and from the 50's and 60's on also the pizza parlor and the Chinese restaurant. Wienerwald belongs in this category, a company which achieved to have its brandname become almost synonymous with an entire genre of products. The dream-come-true for each brandname is to stand for an entire type of product. Just think of Kleenex – who ever uses the word 'tissue paper'?

Nowadays, and this should come as no surprise, we can find a host of gastronomical specialists. Steakhouses, Italian, Japanese, Mexican and natural foods restaurants, potato-concepts ... The majority of specialists seems to stick to ethnic themes, not so much a certain line of products. Although in ethnic restaurants – which of course can only be considered specialists 'away from home' – these criteria may overlap. In any case the most important thing is to dramatize the chosen concept.

Main attraction of such a marketing-specialist is his particular product and its field of association – of course he may and must use all of his resources to charge it emotionally.

An obvious way of doing this would be referring to this particular cuisine's country of origin, by using visual elements in menu-card design as well as atmospheric elements in general decoration and furnishing. An exotic element reminds the customer of vacation; this is a central marketing strongpoint for all restaurants using 'take a holiday from everyday-life' as their main attraction.

Such atmosphere-creating visual effects at the same time cement a restaurant's claim to authenticity, which the customer will unfailingly use to judge an ethnic specialist. In the first place, this authenticity has to be stated by the menu-card. More strongly than anywhere else, culinary competence is synonymous with the 'real' character of the products offered. This means: the menu-card has to document knowledge and expertise, this may also be expressed by the vocabulary chosen. Here the customer has a tendency to translate 'good' with 'authentic'. And vice versa!

This is why it is appropriate to give information on the products and their origins in such a menu-card. Special characteristics of the ethnic cuisine and the ingredients used are well received. After all, the customer likes to experience the unknown delicacies with full awareness and intensity.

Emphasized visualization serves the same goal: it activates the guest's imagination. The objective is to visually vary the chosen theme, or even stronger: to build up a world of emotionally charged images around the particular specialty. To use an extreme expression, one could say: to raise it to a cult.

Because their list of products may be much shorter than average, the specialists may give a lot more attention to visual detail. Instead of length, their menu-card is expected to show depth – just as in any store specializing on a particular item.

Their assortment of items frequently is extremely oriented towards foods – quite logically, as people come here primarily to eat. This includes the fact that a customer beforehand has already made the decision to enjoy a certain kind of food – this is a major difference from the 'generalists'.

Specialization implies a stricter orientation towards a certain clientele, socio-demographically and mentally speaking. The intensity of this orientation may be modified, e.g. by signalling a certain standard; language, materials used, colours, values represented may be used in this context. But a general rule is: specialists are devoted to what they do; and they often appeal to self-proclaimed connoisseurs and hobby experts. These customers like to feel their expertise acknowledged by the presentation – yet another argument for greatest possible authenticity.

This focus on a certain clientele also is the specialist's conceptional weak point. Trends and fashions change, and his dependance on them is considerable. For this reason many entrepreneurs make an effort to widen their field of competence, leaving behind the limitations of their traditional line of products. Specialty promotions offer the opportunity to explore new items, tried-and-true standard dishes can be added to the menu. But in all this, special care needs to be taken: any specialist must be very cautious when making changes. There is too big a danger of loosing profile. Taking small steps is the wisest solution – continuity is as important here as nowhere else.

Name:
El Paso, Wiesbaden

Business type/character:
Mexican restaurant, Tex-Mex cuisine. Second location in Mainz.

Card:
Menu card and list of beverages.

Card system:
All-in-one card, cover plus 8 selection pages, spiral binding. Size when closed: 21.5 × 31 cm. Continuously printed on both sides on white background, gloss-foil laminated. Outside front cover with picture vignette, insides partially with placative illustrations mounted over the text, style and motifs refer to the country of origin. Color stripes in the Mexican national colors lining the pages are another design element. All selection headings are in German and English. Prices hand-written. The El Paso story is narrated on the outside back cover.

Special features:
Product information precedes food columns requiring explanation such as nachos, burritos, enchiladas.

Draft/Design:
Georgios Angelopoulos, El Paso

ALLES
GUTE FÜR
FEIN-
SCHMECKER.

Heinemann®
DÜSSELDORF

Name:

Heinemann Konditoreibetriebe, Mönchengladbach

Business type/character:

Confectionery/Confiserie (sweet shops) with café-restaurants, multiplied.

Card:

Café-restaurant's menu card and list of beverages.

Card system:

All-in-one-selection menu card, altar-shape folding, for upright positioning (small tables!). Punched at top. Printed on both sides and structure-foil laminated. Size when closed: 10.5 × 31.5 cm (without punching). Green/yellow on white background provides for fresh vivid impression. Basic decoration green dots, column headlines with green background and drawings. Cover sheet with advertisement slogan; food selection at one glance in the card center; insertion sheet on right center page with special offers.

Special features:

Corporate design conception. Dominant color green, combined with white, green Heinemann-logo and ribbon as well as dotted motif in alternating arrangements also used for table sets, napkins, and the entire packaging material. A prime example for visual rejuvenation of a traditional company. The CD was honored with the marketing prize by the Chamber of Handicrafts Düsseldorf in 1988.

Draft/Design:

Heinz-Richard und Bernd Heinemann, Heinemann-Konditoreibetriebe.

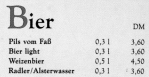

Steaks vom Besten

DM

Hüftsteak 180 g	Das würzige Steak, fein gemasert, kräftig.	14,50
Hüftsteak 250 g		19,40
Rumpsteak 180 g	Der typische Fettrand gibt ihm seinen würzigen	16,90
Rumpsteak 250 g	Geschmack - innen zart und fettarm.	22,80
Filetsteak 180 g	Das zarteste Steak, ohne Fett, fein im Geschmack.	24,90
Filetsteak 250 g		30,30
Entrecôte 200 g	Das Zwischenrippenstück (Rib Eye) mit dem	17,50
Entrecôte 300 g	wichtigen Fettauge, welches ihm Saft und Würze gibt.	24,80
Lammrücken-steaks 200 g	Zwei zarte Steaks vom Lammrücken mit Kräuterbutter, rosa gegrillt.	19,50

Beilagen

DM

Papa Asada, die große gebackene Kartoffel mit Kräuterschaum oder Sauercreme	3,30
Pommes frites	2,90
Maiskolben mit frischer Butter	4,70
Ganze Champignons in Rahmsauce mit Kräutern	5,50

Kombinationen

DM

. . . mit Fleisch

Steak & Salat
saftiges Hüftsteak (150 g) und eine Schale knackiger Salat 13,90

. . . mit Gambas

»Zweimaldrei«
6 Gambas mit Champignons am Spieß gegrillt,
Zitronen-Hollandaise, Knoblauchbrot   29,50

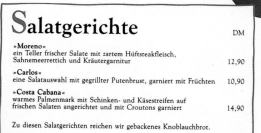

Salatgerichte

DM

»Moreno«
ein Teller frischer Salate mit zartem Hüftsteakfleisch,
Sahnemeerrettich und Kräutergarnitur   12,90

»Carlos«
eine Salatauswahl mit gegrillter Putenbrust, garniert mit Früchten   10,90

»Costa Cabana«
warmes Palmenmark mit Schinken- und Käsestreifen auf
frischen Salaten angerichtet und mit Croutons garniert   14,90

Zu diesen Salatgerichten reichen wir gebackenes Knoblauchbrot.

Bier

DM

Pils vom Faß	0,3 l	3,60
Bier light	0,3 l	3,60
Weizenbier	0,5 l	4,50
Radler/Alsterwasser	0,3 l	3,60

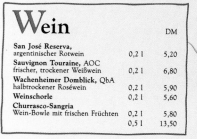

Alkoholfreies

DM

Selters, Mineralwasser	0,25 l	3,20
Coca-Cola light[7]	0,3 l	3,20
Coca-Cola[7]	0,3 l	3,20
Fanta oder **Sprite**[2]	0,3 l	3,20
Apfelschorle	0,2 l	2,80
Apfelsaft, Vaihinger	0,2 l	2,80
Orangensaft, Vaihinger	0,2 l	3,20
Schweppes Bitter Lemon[4]	0,2 l	3,40
Bonaqa, Tafelwasser	0,2 l	2,50

Wein

DM

San José Reserva, argentinischer Rotwein	0,2 l	5,20
Sauvignon Touraine, AOC frischer, trockener Weißwein	0,2 l	6,80
Wachenheimer Domblick, QbA halbtrockener Roséwein	0,2 l	5,90
Weinschorle	0,2 l	5,60
Churrasco-Sangria Wein-Bowle mit frischen Früchten	0,2 l	5,80
	0,5 l	13,50

Kaffee

DM

Kännchen Kaffee	6,20
Cappuccino-Churrasco	3,30

Eis

DM

Drei Kugeln Eis nach Wahl mit Sahne	5,50

Copa Amigos – das Eisvergnügen für zwei
Eine bunte Mischung aus Walnuß-, Pistazien-,
Schokoladen-, Erdbeer-, Waldbeere-Joghurt-,
Rumtopf- und Vanilleeis auf Baiser, mit
Schokoladen- und Waldbeersauce, Schlagsahne,
Walnüssen und frischen Früchten garniert.   18,50

Name:
Churrasco Steakrestaurants Germany
(Whitbread Restaurants Holding Germany,
Düsseldorf/Whitbread Group, Great Britain)

Business type/character:
Steakhouse conception, multiplied.

Cards:
Menu card and list of beverages, terrace card.

Card system:
Both cards all-in-one, printed on both sides and
gloss-foil laminated. Size when closed: 17.5 ×
30 cm. Basic card: miscellaneous folding, cover
sheet: photomontage with ingredients floating
in the air. Interior basic decoration: depiction of
selection chosen at will freely floating in the air
before reddish background, rectangular selection columns on white background. Product information on the rear side. Terrace card: simply
folded cover. Cover sheet design and interior
layout analogous to the basic card, but less
bulkiness through white background. Additional dessert card.

Special features:
Basic card's colors: black/red—matching logo.
Typical symbolic color constellation, related to
profile product.

Draft/Design:
Churrasco Steakrestaurants, Germany

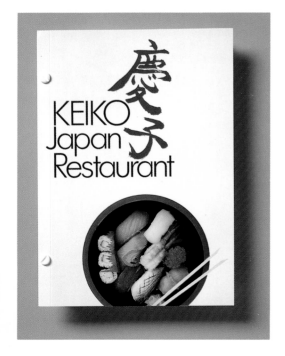

Name:
Mangostin Asia, Munich
(Kaub-Gruppe, Munich)

Business type/character:
Several business types/company divisions under one roof: Lemon Grass (Thai specialties, wok), Keiko Japan Restaurant (sushi, tempura, sukiyaki), Papa Joe's Colonial Bar & Restaurant, Mangostin Garden. Second location in Karlsruhe.

Cards:
Card ensemble with uniform layout. Restaurant card and cocktail card.

Card system:
Varying cover solutions: simply folded cover for cocktail card, size when closed: 23.5 × 34.5 cm. Folded cover of same size with kinking groove and punched holes for Lemon Grass and Papa Joe selection cards, office-sheet sized insertion sheets are punched and fastened with plastic screw buttons. Same principle, but office-sheet sized cover for Keiko card. Covers gloss-foil laminated on both sides, white background, photo motif and logo on outside front cover. Lemon Grass/Papa Joe: identical cover, product information on cover inside, illustrated with photos. All-in-one cards, selection sheets light grey/green paper with parchment structure, printed on one side with laser printer. Volume: 15 to 17 pages (variable). Keiko cover with own logo and picture motif, inside cover pages blank, 14 inside pages, yellow paper with parchment structure. Cocktail card with product-related picture motif, selection presentation with product photographs on cover inside.

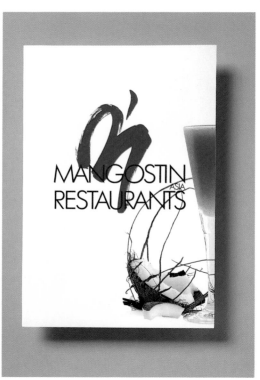

Special features:
Flexible economical system, selection modification always possible by exchanging individual sheets. Exception: cocktail card (fixed selection). Self-contained design appearance.

Draft/Design:
Studio Rastorfer, Munich

Name:
Wienerwald Restaurants Austria
(Wigast, Vienna)

Business type/character:
Poultry specialties, also in Wigast Tourast businesses (expressway restaurants). Multiplied, altogether 53 locations.

Card:
Menu card and list of beverages.

Card system:
All-in-one card, cover solution plus four inside pages, punched. Stapled, size when closed: 18 × 35 cm (without punching). Entirely printed on both sides and gloss-foil laminated, cover outside artfully designed motif: naive depiction shows model of the most recent tourist restaurant opened in May 1992. Inside with white background, illustrated with product photographs.

Special features:
Cover aquarelle by Gottfried Kumpf—artful character of the card as profilation moment.

Draft/Design:
The artist Gottfried Kumpf (cover illustration)/
Wienerwald Austria

Name:
Ristorante Golfo di Napoli, Frankfurt

Business type/character:
Classical Italian restaurant (no pizzas).

Card:
Menu card and list of beverages.

Card system:
All-in-one card, cover with fold-in flaps and 16 selection pages, stapled. Size when closed (without flaps) 23.5 × 34 cm. Outside covers including flaps illustrated, gloss-foil laminated. Cover inside blank. Selection sheets classically designed, tri-lingual—Italian, German, English.

Special features:
Cover illustration by Wilhelm Schlote in typical line-drawing style; abstract interpretation of the topics "gastronomy" and "Naples."

Draft/Design:
The artist Wilhelm Schlote (cover drawing)/ Golfo di Napoli

123

Name:

La Part du Lion, Paris
(CRC Compagnie de Restaurants et Caféterias,
Bagneux)

Business type/character:

"Theme restaurant"; logo, ambiance and card in
afro-colonial style. Selection emphasis upon
grill dishes, exotic accents. One franchise business in Bordeaux.

Cards:

Menu card and list of beverages, dessert card.

Card system:

Both cards have the same basic decoration; the
cover features a stylized silhouetted jungle scene
with the logo's word/picture motif. Both sides
of the two cards printed and gloss-foil laminated. Basic card: simply folded cover in unconventional broad-side size. Size when closed:
33.5 × 24 cm. Basic colors in green, somewhat
lighter on the interior, two-color surfaces plus
framing palm leaf ornaments. Selection columns
(foods and wine) box-shaped on white background. Miscellaneous beverages on rear cover.
Dessert card: simply folded cover, size when
closed: 16.5 × 24 cm. Analogous layout, but basic colors yellow/brown, inside yellow/orange.

Special features:

Corporate design conception with imaginative
variations. Billheads with graphic interpretation
of the jungle motif in pastel green tones. Table
sets made of brown paper, logo designed as
stamp imprint in black and brown. Tablecloth
decoration matching the card's design.

Draft/Design:

La Part du Lion

Name:
Hippodrom, Cologne-Weidenpesch
(KGSG Kaufhof Gastronomie Service Gesell-
schaft, Cologne)

Business type/character:
Carvery conception, principle: buffet service,
entrées and roast buffet, dessert buffet. Table
service for drinks. Fixed prices for food and
the restaurant's own wines. Second location in
Neuss.

Card:
List of beverages and ice creams with racecourse
motif on cover.

Card system:
Simply folded cover plus four inside pages (stapled). Size when closed: 21 × 29.5 cm. Photo
motif spread out over front and rear cover, the
original is a b/w photograph reproduced in
duo-tone technique (b/w with additional color
bordeaux). Gloss-foil laminated. Cover inside
blank, selection sheets with bordeaux-colored
writing on white background.

Special features:
Cover photograph makes reference to location
at the racecourse. Bordeaux repeated as predominant color in restaurant interior. Extensive
concept explanation and buffet prices on two inside pages.

Draft/Design:
Werbehaus, Cologne

Name:
Ristorante Fiorello, Hamburg
(Bleichenhof-Restaurantbetriebe, Hamburg)

Business type/character:
Italian restaurant in the Bleichenhof-Passage
(shopping passage).

Card:
Menu card and list of beverages.

Card system:
All-in-one card, miscellaneous folding with punching, resembles napkin when folded. Size when closed: 11 × 34 cm (without punching). Entirely mat-coated cardboard printed on both sides in four colors, basic color white, colored drawings on cover and inside, colored column titles. Inside logo visible when folded. Additional ice cream card/terrace card, designed analogously.

Special features:
Compact but clearly structured design; space-economic card format (small tables!).

Draft/Design:
Fiorello/Agentur Horstmann & Werbung, Hamburg (illustrations)

Name:
Bella Vista, Schluchsee

Business type/character:
Italian restaurant/pizza parlor in the Hetzel Hotel Hochschwarzwald. Uncomplicated, casual.

Card:
Menu card and list of beverages.

Card system:
All-in-one card, printed on both sides and gloss-foil laminated. Altar-shaped punching, size when closed: 21 × 30 cm. Photo motifs on the cover sides complement each other to form a sectional view of a filled plate; motif is taken up again on the inside of the card. List of beverages on the backside on neutral grey background.

Special features:
Original variation of motif with filled and empty plate.

Draft/Design:
Lothar Scheding Graphic-Design, Staufen i.Br.

Name:
Chili's, Innsbruck
(System-Gastronomie, Innsbruck)

Business type/character:
Tex-Mex restaurant, product emphasis: Mexican specialties, steaks, burgers. Strong atmosphere.

Card:
Menu card and list of beverages.

Card system:
All-in-one card, printed on both sides, gloss-foil laminated. Miscellaneous folding, size when closed: 21 × 35 cm. Photo motif covering both cover sheet and rear sheet, Chili's logo printed on cover. Selection on ochre-colored background on the inside and folded-in rear side.

Special features:
The card's photo motif shows a poster by the Mexican artist Sergio Bustamante. The topic and color tone underline the conceptual statement and correspond with the interior colors. Original plastics and more posters by the artist exhibited in the restaurant. Cover motif is repeated on the restaurant's calling card.

Draft/Design:
The artist Sergio Bustamante (cover photo)/ System-Gastronomie, Innsbruck

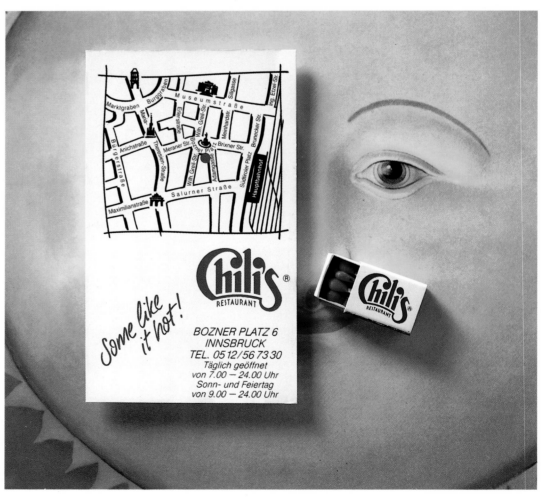

SPECIAL THANKS TO:

Mark Anderson, Chicago Meat Market Representative
Anderson Food Concepts; Chicago, Illinois

Rocio Martinez, Director General
VIP-Tours; Chapultepec, Mexico

Andreas Rupprechter, General Manager
Buenaventura Hotels****; Puerto Vallarta, Mexico

Sergio Bustamante, Artist
Galería de Arte en Joyas Y Artesanías;
Tlaquepaque, Mexico

Ruth's Chris Steak House — Home of Serious Steaks
Ft. Lauderdale — San Francisco — Dallas

Old San Francisco Steak House
Dallas, Texas

Baby Doe's Matchless Mine
Dallas, Texas

Butcher Shop Steak House
Dallas — Knoxville — Memphis — Little Rock — Orlando

Senior Frog's
Cancun, Mexico

Captains Cove Seafood Restaurant & Bar
Cancun, Mexico

La Mansion Restaurantes
Mexico City, Mexico

Carlos O'Brian's — Bar & Grill & Clothesline
Puerto Vallarta, Mexico

Carlos'n Charlie's — Bar & Grill & Pawnshop
Cancun, Mexico

Pirámide Charlie's — Members & Non/Members Only
Pirámides de Teotihuacan, Mexico

J.P. & Catalina 1
Marina Puerto Vallarta, Mexico

and...

...LULU & other great friends!

Name:
Spaghetti Factory, Switzerland
(Bindella Unternehmungen, Zurich)

Business type/character:
Young restaurant conception with product emphasis on spaghetti; profile basis: the Italian-American spaghetti culture. Multiplied.

Cards:
Special cards "Super Specials" and "Desserts."
Show cards with beverage list.

Card system:
Both special cards with uniform layout; simply folded cover, printed on both sides, mat-foil laminated. Size when closed: 19 × 29.5 cm. Basic color white, outside with logo screen as basic design, cover front with picture motif. Selection in colored rectangles on white background on the inside. Both cards vary the colors pink/turquoise. In analogous cover design: foreign language cards. Show cards for beverages: two punched cardboards printed on both sides and inserted into each other. Basic format (without punching) 21 × 21 cm. Regular selection communicated via table sets.

Special features:
Super Specials card promotes special offers also printed on table sets. Photograph taken from current image brochure.

Draft/Design:
Werbeatelier Gerhard Brauchle, Thal/Lesch + Frei Werbeagentur, Zurich (logo); Spaghetti Factory Corso/Werbeatelier Gerhard Brauchle (show cards for beverages); Spaghetti Factory Corso/Atelier am See, Zurich (cards); Helmut J. Koch, Spaghetti Factory Corso/Farner Publics FCB, Zurich (image brochure)

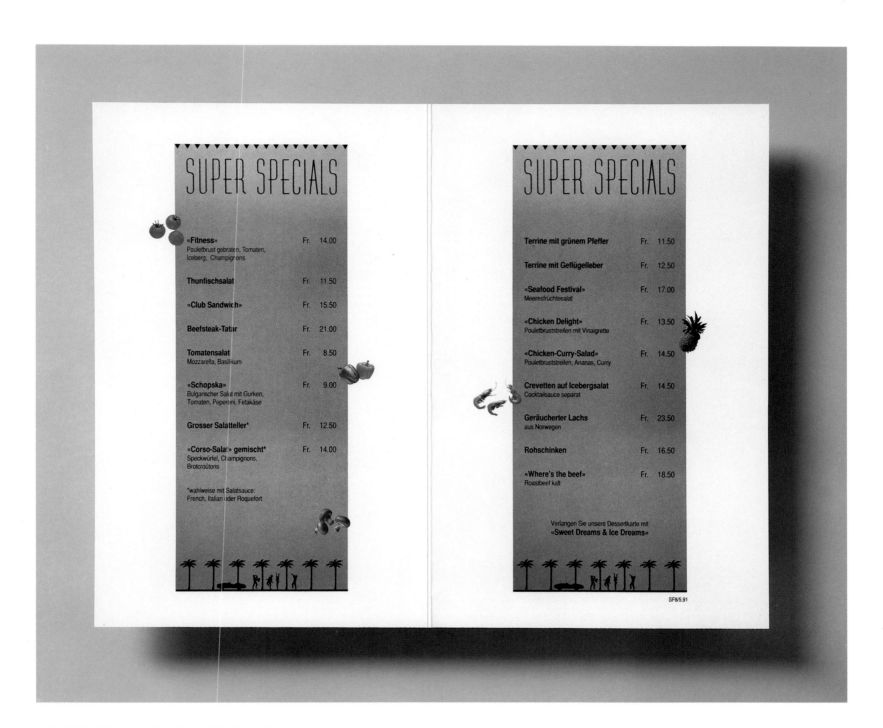

SUPER SPECIALS

«Fitness» Pouletbrust gebraten, Tomaten, Iceberg, Champignons	Fr.	14.00
Thunfischsalat	Fr.	11.50
«Club Sandwich»	Fr.	15.50
Beefsteak-Tatar	Fr.	21.00
Tomatensalat Mozzarella, Basilikum	Fr.	8.50
«Schopska» Bulgarischer Salat mit Gurken, Tomaten, Peperoni, Fetakäse	Fr.	9.00
Grosser Salatteller*	Fr.	12.50
«Corso-Salat» gemischt* Speckwürfel, Champignons, Brotcroûtons	Fr.	14.00

*wahlweise mit Salatsauce:
French, Italian oder Roquefort

SUPER SPECIALS

Terrine mit grünem Pfeffer	Fr.	11.50
Terrine mit Geflügelleber	Fr.	12.50
«Seafood Festival» Meeresfrüchtesalat	Fr.	17.00
«Chicken Delight» Pouletbruststreifen mit Vinaigrette	Fr.	13.50
«Chicken-Curry-Salad» Pouletbruststreifen, Ananas, Curry	Fr.	14.50
Crevetten auf Icebergsalat Cocktailsauce separat	Fr.	14.50
Geräucherter Lachs aus Norwegen	Fr.	23.50
Rohschinken	Fr.	16.50
«Where's the beef» Roastbeef kalt	Fr.	18.50

Verlangen Sie unsere Dessertkarte mit
«Sweet Dreams & Ice Dreams»

SF8/5.91

Name:
Lokales, Darmstadt

Business type/character:
Pizza parlor, mixed audience, many students, casual. Emphasis on communication.

Card:
Menu card and list of beverages.

Card system:
All-in-one card, simply folded cover, asymmetrical format, punched. Maximum size when closed: 35 × 50 cm. Printed on both sides, coated with printing varnish. All cover sides with different ground color, basic decoration in chalking technique plus cartoon-like drawings. The selection is printed-in separately. Column lines in alternating typography.

Special features:
Card is presented in magazine folders. Format with wave-like punching, decoration and typography underline the unconventional appeal (motto: the entirely different pizza parlor). Only the selection text must be renewed for alteration of selection.

Draft/Design:
Müller, Stoiber & Reuss, Darmstadt

S ALA T

Lokales Salat (Sahnesoße)	10,90
kleiner Salat Lokales	7,50
Chef Salat (Knofi - Sahnesoße)	10,90
kleiner Chefsalat	7,50
Red Lokales Salat (Cocktailsoße)	10,90
kleiner Red Lokales	7,50
Keimlingsalat (verschiedene Sprossen)	10,90
kleiner Keimlingsalat	7,50
Chickensalat	12,40
kleiner Chickensalat	9,00
Französischer Salat	11,90
kleiner Französischer Salat	8,50
Italienischer Salat (Vinaigrette Soße)	9,50
Italo Spezial (mit Thunfisch)	10,50
Beilagensalat (Vinaigrette Soße)	5,50
Schafkäse Teller	8,00
Mozzarella Teller	8,00

PIZZA fantasy

FANTASY die neue Lokales-Pizzaidee

	groß	klein
Fantasy Mozzarella	11,30	10,80
Fantasy Thunfisch	11,30	10,80
Fantasy Hot (Vorsicht scharf!)	11,30	10,80
Fantasy Vegetarisch	11,30	10,80
Fantasy Knofi	11,30	10,80
Fantasy Ei (mit gekochtem Ei)	11,30	10,80
Fantasy Gouda	11,30	10,80
Vollkorn Fantasy		
Fantasy Mozzarella	11,80	11,30
Fantasy Thunfisch	11,80	11,30
Fantasy Hot (Vorsicht scharf)	11,80	11,30
Fantasy Vegetarisch	11,80	11,30
Fantasy Knofi	11,80	11,30
Fantasy Ei (mit gekochtem Ei)	11,80	11,30
Fantasy Gouda	11,80	11,30

PIZZA

VOLLWERT	groß	klein
Broccoli (Peperoniwurst, Broccoli, Gouda überbacken)	11,50	11,00
Rohkost (Karotten, frische Tomaten, frische Gurken, Gouda überbacken)	10,50	10,00
Gucci (Zucchini, Gouda)	10,00	9,50
Feta (Zucchini, Schafskäse)	10,00	9,50
CHICKEN		
Chicken Curry (Chicken, frischer Paprika, Mais, Curry, Knoblauchsoße)	12,90	12,40
Bangkok (Chicken, Mais, frischer Paprika, Chinagewürz, Sojasoße, frischer Knoblauch)	13,40	12,90
Chicken Fresh (Chicken, Zwiebel, frische Tomaten, Curry)	11,50	11,00
Chicken süß-sauer (Chicken, Ananas, Banane, Curry)	12,40	11,90
Oriental (Chicken, Banane Mandeln, Curry)	12,90	12,40
SPINAT		
Poppi (Spinat, Ei)	9,90	9,40
Popparella (Spinat, Mozzarella, Ei)	11,40	10,90
Popschi (Spinat, Schinken, frz. Knoblauch)	10,60	10,10
Poppep (Spinat, Peperwurst, fr. Knoblauch)	10,40	9,90
MOZZARELLA		
Sizilia (Mozzarella, frische Tomaten, Oliven, Basilikum)	12,40	11,90
Mozzarella Spezial (Peperwurst, frischer Lauch, Mozzarella)	12,40	11,90
Pepino (Peperoniwurst, Erbsen, Mais, Zwiebel, Curry)	10,30	9,80
Sam (Karotten, frische Champignons, Curry, Knoblauchsoße, Käse überbacken)	9,80	9,30
Teufelsch (Tomatenpaprika, grüne Peperoni, Zwiebel, Pilze, Knoblauch, Zembiesoße)	12,40	11,90
Tresen (Peperoniwurst, Curry, frische Champignons, Knoblauchsoße)	10,00	9,50
Topic (Peperoniwurst, Thunfisch, frische Tomaten, Zwiebel, frischer Pfeffer)	11,30	10,80
Sirtaki (frischer Paprika, Schafskäse, frische Tomaten, frische Champignons)	11,90	11,40

Unsere Preise sind Endpreise.

Küche durchgehend bis 0.30 Uhr.
An Freitagen, Samstagen und vor Feiertagen bis 0.45 Uhr

Name:

La Cantinetta, Solothurn
(Bindella Unternehmungen, Zurich)

Business type/character:

Classic Italian restaurant (no pizzas)/Enoteca
(integrated wine tavern with degustation).

Cards:

Menu card, list of beverages, and wine card.

Card system:

All cards with the same layout. Cover plus four
pages (menu card, list of beverages) respectively
eight inside pages (wine card). Stapled. Differing formats: menu card when closed: 21 × 30
cm, wine card: 16 × 30 cm, list of beverages:
10.5 × 30 cm. Outside cover with vine runner
ornaments in different colors, matte-laminated.

Selection pages on white structured paper, first
page logo only. Menu card's inside front cover
with explanations of Cantinetta philosophy; the
restaurant's own wine-growing estate in Italy is
introduced in the wine card.

Special features:

Unobtrusive card appearance. The cover's vine
runner motif shows the decoration of a typical
florentine school-book wrapper—a reference to
the Tuscan cuisine prepared in the restaurant.

Draft/Design:

Atelier Jacquet, Bern

Vorweg oder zwischendurch

Omelette "Valencia"	12,80
ein flaches Omelette mit Gemüsen, Kartoffeln, Champignons und Garnelen*[2], in der Pfanne serviert	
Gravad Lachs	kleinere Portion 14,50
kräutergebeizter, norwegischer Lachs	Portion 24,50
mit Senf-Dill-Sauce, Toast und Butter	
Grönländer Garnelen*[2] und grüner Spargel	13,50
auf Eisbergsalat, mit pikantem Dressing, im Cocktail-Glas serviert, mit Toast und Butter	
Gourmet-Teller "von Eicken"	20,80
Gravad Lachs, rosa gebratenes Roastbeef, Garnelen*[2] und gebratene Poulardenbrust, mit Salaten garniert, dazu zwei leckere Saucen und Baguette	
Carpaccio vom Rind	16,90
hauchdünn geschnitten und bestens abgeschmeckt, serviert mit Stangenweißbrot	
Roastbeef kalt – rosa gebraten	kleinere Portion 14,90
mit Bratkartoffeln und Sauce Remoulade	Portion 19,80

Aus dem Suppentopf
immer frisch und hausgemacht

Westfälische Kartoffelsuppe	6,20
mit frischem Sauerrahm und Schnittlauch	
Hausgemachte Gulaschsuppe	6,70
kräftig und deftig	
Tomatencreme-Suppe	5,90
mit Crème fraiche und Buttercroutons	

Frühstück–Kuchen–Party-Service

Frühstück und Kaffeezeit
Frühstück wird bei uns "Groß" geschrieben!
Lassen Sie sich von unserem vielfältigen Angebot überraschen.

Den ganzen Tag ist bei uns Kuchenzeit.
Alle Kuchen auch zum Mit-nach-Hause-nehmen.

Von Eicken-Party-Service
Wir organisieren für Sie ganz nach Ihren Wünschen
Ihre Feier bei Ihnen zu Hause oder auch außerhalb
- selbstverständlich alles auch im Full-Service!
Nähere Informationen erhalten Sie gerne von
unserer Restaurant-Leitung.

Vom Salat-Buffet

Zu jeder Jahreszeit erwartet Sie eine Vielfalt verschiedener Salate.
Wählen Sie nach Herzenslust am Buffet und stellen Sie sich Ihren
Salat selbst zusammen.

Salat	7,90
großer Salat	10,90

Dazu unsere hausgemachten Salatsaucen:
- **"von Eicken-Dressing"**
  eine phantasievolle Salatsauce, würzig-pikant, mit vielen Kräutern, und, und ...
- **"French-Dressing"**
  die originale, französische Salatsauce
- **"Swiss-Dressing"**
  sahnig, mit Eigelb, mildem Sherryessig, bestem Salatöl und ausgesuchten Gewürzen

Salat-Hits wie in Kalifornien…

"Sunset Boulevard"	16,20
Gravadlachs, sautierte Babycalamares und Champignons auf Blattsalaten, Tomaten und Gurken mit würziger Vinaigrette angemacht. Dazu geröstetes Kräuterbaguette.	
"American"	18,50
eine knackig-frische Salat-Komposition mit saftig gebratener Poulardenbrust, rosa Grönland-Garnelen*[2], krossen Speckscheiben und "von Eicken-Dressing". Dazu geröstetes Kräuter-Baguette	

Nudeln & Toasts

"Grüne Nudeln -du Chef-"	15,80
mit Schinkenstreifen, Tomaten, Sahne, ausgewählten Kräutern und Parmesan	
Spaghettini "Frutti di Mare"	18,50
Lachswürfel, Crevetten, Zucchini und Baby-Calamares in Kräuterbutter frisch gebraten, auf geschmolzenen Tomaten und Basilikum	
"Von Eicken - Toast"	16,70
zwei zarte Schweinemedaillons mit frischen Champignons, Sauce Hollandaise gratiniert	
Poularden - Spargel - Toast	15,80
eine saftige Poulardenbrust mit grünem Spargel und Sauce Hollandaise	

Mal etwas anderes…

Broccoli mit Käsesahnesauce gratiniert und warmem Knoblauchbrot serviert	13,80
Baked Potatoes mit Kräuterquark, marinierten Lachsstreifen und Garnelen belegt	12,50

von Eicken-Steaks

Pfeffer-Steak	120 g	17,50
in einer rassig pikanten Sauce aus Schalotten, Cognac und grünem Madagaskarpfeffer, Kartoffelkroketten	180 g	22,40
Rumpsteak "Strindberg"	180 g	23,50
mit einer Zwiebelsenfkruste, Bratkartoffeln		
Filetsteak "Gärtnerin Art"	120 g	22,50
mit frischen Gemüsen umlegt, Sauce Bearnaise, Kartoffelkroketten	180 g	32,50
Grill-Teller		21,80
3 Medaillons mit frischen Champignons, Sauce Bearnaise, Grilltomate, Pommes frites		
Schweinerücken-Steak	180 g	18,80
mit frischen Champignons in Rahm, Pommes frites		
Schweinerücken-Steak "Teppan Yaki"	180 g	18,80
mit Zwiebeln, Chinakohl, Soyasprossen und anderen Gemüsen, kurzgebraten, fernöstlich mit Soya und Sesam gewürzt, dazu Reis		
"Entrecôte Double" (für 2 - 3 Personen)	360 g	54,00
ein doppelt großes Rumpsteak mit 3 Marktgemüsen, frischen Champignons, Bratkartoffeln mit Speck, Pfeffer- und Kräutergarten-Sauce in der Riesenpfanne serviert		

Steaks natur
mit geröstetem Baguette, Steaksauce oder Kräuterbutter serviert

Hüftsteak	180 g	18,50
aus dem Herzstück der Rinderhüfte, kernig und kräftig	250 g	23,90
Rumpsteak	180 g	21,30
herzhaft im Geschmack mit dem typischen Fettrand	250 g	28,90
Filetsteak	180 g	27,20
aus der Rinderlende besonders zart und saftig	250 g	34,00

Dazu empfehlen wir:

Pommes frites, Kartoffelkroketten,Butterreis, Bratkartoffeln	3,50
Tagesfrisches Gemüse, kleiner Salatteller	4,50
Rahm-Champignons, grüner Spargel mit Sauce Hollandaise	5,50
Sauce Hollandaise, Sauce Bearnaise	3,50
Baked Potato mit Kräuterquark	4,20

von Eicken-Pfannen
originell und heiß in der Pfanne serviert

"die von Eicken-Grill-Pfanne"	25,90
ein Huft-, Poularden- und Schweine-Medaillon mit frischen Champignons in Rahm, drei Marktgemüsen, Bratkartoffeln mit Speck und dreierlei Saucen	
"die asiatische Gemüse-Pfanne"	17,80
vielerlei von frischem Gemüse in der Pfanne kurz gebraten, mit Glasnudeln, interessant fernöstlich gewürzt, dazu Reis	
"die mediterrane Seafood-Pfanne"	23,50
Lachs, Tiefseecrevetten, Babycalamares und Champignons in der Pfanne mit Knoblauchbutter gebraten, mit Zitrone und frischen Kräutern gewürzt, serviert mit Reis	
"die herrliche Nudel-Pfanne"	20,80
ein saftig-gebratenes, mit Schinken gefülltes Poulardenbrustfilet mit Mascarpone, geschmolzenen Tomaten, an frischer Sahne und grünen Nudeln	

Aus Meer & See…

Norwegischer Frischlachs vom Grill	kleinere Portion	15,90
mit grünem Spargel und Kräutergarten-Sauce, wahlweise Butterkartoffeln oder Butterreis	Portion	23,90
Heilbuttsteak vom Grill mit Kräuterbutter		18,50
dazu Salzkartoffeln und bunter Salat		
Heilbuttsteak "Schöne Müllerin"		19,80
in Butter gebraten, mit Tomatenwürfeln und Kräutern, mit Zitrone gewürzt, dazu reichen wir Salzkartoffeln und Tagesgemüse		

Ihre Lieblings-Gerichte…

Geschnetzeltes vom Schweinefilet "Züricher Art"	20,80
mit frischen Champignons, Weißwein und viel Rahm zubereitet, dazu grüne Nudeln	
Poulardenbrust "gratiniert"	18,80
saftig gebraten, mit einem halben Pfirsich, Schinken und Käse überbacken, dazu Pommes frites	
Schnitzel "Wiener Art"	19,50
vom Schweinerücken - paniert und in Butter gebraten, dazu Pommes frites und ein bunter Salatteller	
Streifen von der Poulardenbrust	17,90
in Curryrahm und in Kokos gebacken, servierter Ananas, serviert mit Butterreis	
Filetspitzen "Mexicana"	21,80
ein feuriges Gericht mit Geschnetzeltem vom Rinderfilet, mit mexikanischem Gemüse, im Reisring serviert	

Name:
von Eicken essen & trinken.
(Casserole Feine Fleischkost, Herten/West)

Business type/character:
Restaurant with product emphasis on steaks and meat dishes. Multiplied.

Card:
Menu card and list of beverages.

Card system:
All-in-one card, altar-shape folding, size when closed: 18 × 30 cm. Printed on both sides, gloss-foil laminated. Cover side with product-related naive illustration and logo, design in form of a crest on grey background. Selection pages white background with green column headings and green frame. Food on the inside, beverages on the fold-in outer sides.

Special features:
Fresh, "natural" appearance through accentuation of color green. Cover illustration refers to restaurant's product emphasis.

Draft/Design:
The artist Marlis Lunau, Essen (cover illustration)/Agentur Strauff & Weiss, Essen.

Name:
Ristorante da Paolino, Hamburg

Business type/character:
Classic Italian restaurant (no pizza); trendy.

Card:
Menu card and list of beverages.

Card system:
All-in-one card, cover plus eight pages, stapled. Size when closed: 24 × 43 cm. Printing lacquer. Front cover b/w photograph of Paolino and logo on white background, inside double-paged b/w photograph: landscape and people in Paolino's home of Sardinia. Selection columns in white squares. Column headlines underlined in the Italian national colors—a reference to the logo and stimulating color accent. In addition there are numerous Specials of the Day; oral recommendation.

Special features:
Total dominance of photo motifs, the selection is entirely pushed to the background. The large-format photographs have a high degree of conceptual aura: visual experience as sales promoter. Marketing by imagination.

Draft/Design:
Paolino Cherchi, da Paolino

PESCE / FISCH

Calamari Fritti *Gebackener Tintenfisch*	DM
Calamari alla Livornese *Tintenfisch in Tomatensauce*	DM
Scampi e Calamari alla Griglia *Scampi und Tintenfisch auf dem Rost gegrillt*	DM
Scampi alla Griglia *Gegrillte Scampi*	DM
Fritto Misto *Gemischte Meeresfrüchte gebacken*	DM
Scampi alla Livornese *Scampi in Tomatensauce*	DM
Scampi del Pirata *Scampi in Knoblauch-Petersiliensauce*	DM
Scampi al Pernod *Scampi mit Pernod-Sahnesauce*	DM
Scampi della Casa *Scampi nach Art des Hauses*	DM

CARNE / FLEISCH*

Bistecca di Manzo alla Griglia *Rumpsteak auf dem Rost gegrillt*	DM
Bistecca alla Pizzaiola *Rumpsteak in Tomatensauce*	DM
Filetto alla Griglia *Rinderfilet auf dem Rost gegrillt*	DM
Filetto al Gorgonzola *Rinderfilet in Gorgonzolasauce*	DM
Filetto alla Nerone *Rinderfilet in pikanter Cognacsauce*	DM
Saltimbocca alla Romana *Kalbsmedaillons mit Schinken und Salbei*	DM
Scaloppine al Vino Bianco *Kalbsmedaillons in Weißweinsauce*	DM
Scaloppine al Limone *Kalbsmedaillons in Zitronensauce*	DM
Piccata alla Paolino *Geschmortes Kalbsmedaillon mit Artischocken und Pilzen in Weißweinsauce*	DM
Costeletta di Agnello all'Aglio e Rosmarino *Lammkoteletts mit Knoblauch und Rosmarin*	DM
Fegato di Vitello con Burro e Salvia *Kalbsleber mit Butter und Salbei*	DM
Grigliata Mista *Verschiedene Sorten Fleisch auf dem Rost gegrillt*	DM

*Tutti i piatti verranno serviti con verdura di stagione
Alle Gerichte werden mit Gemüse der Saison serviert

ANTIPASTI / VORSPEISEN

Antipasto all'Italiana	DM
Italienische Salami, Parmaschinken und Oliven	
Antipasto della Casa	DM
Gemischte Vorspeisen vom Buffet	
Prosciutto e Melone	DM
Parmaschinken und Melone	
Mozzarella, Pomodoro e Basilico	DM
Mozzarella, Tomaten mit frischem Basilikum	
Insalata di Frutti di Mare	DM
Salat aus Meeresfrüchten	
Carpaccio	DM
Robes Rinderfilet fein geschnitten mit Olivenöl und Parmesan	

INSALATE / SALATE

Insalata Verde	DM
Grüner Salat	
Insalata Mista	DM
Gemischter Salat	
Insalata di Pomodoro	DM
Tomatensalat	
Insalata-Capricciosa	DM
Salat nach Art des Hauses	

MINESTRE / SUPPEN

Minestrone	DM
Italienische Gemüsesuppe	
Tortellini in Brodo	DM
Tortellini in frischer Fleischbrühe	
Stracciatella alla Romana	DM
Frische Fleischbrühe mit Eiereinlauf	

BIBITE / GETRÄNKE

APERITIF

Campari Bitter mit Soda	DM
Martini Bianco	DM
Martini Rosso	DM
Ramazotti	DM
Cynar	DM
Sherry	DM
Rossantico	DM

WHISKY

Jim Beam/Cola	DM
Scotch Whisky/Cola	DM
Bourbon/Cola	DM

COGNAC

Martell	DM
Vecchia Romagna	DM
Stock 84	DM
Courvoisier	DM

SPIRITUOSEN

Wodka	DM
Rum	DM
Gin	DM
Fernet Branca	DM
Grappa Libarna	DM
Sambuca	DM
Amaretto Gambarotta	DM
Cointreau	DM
Amaro Averna	DM

BIER

1 Flasche Holsten	DM
1 Flasche Moravia	DM
1 Glas Moravia 0,3	DM

ALKOHOLFREI

Coca Cola	DM
Fanta	DM
Orangensaft	DM
Apfelsaft	DM
San Pellegrino Mineralwasser	DM

WARM

1 Tasse Kaffee	DM
1 Tasse Espresso	DM
1 Tasse Cappuccino	DM
1 Glas Tee	DM

VINO / WEIN

OFFENE WEINE weiß, rot, rosé

¼l DM 6,–   ½l DM 10,–   1l DM

VINO BIANCO / WEISSWEIN

Verdicchio Fazi Battaglia	DM
Soave Bolla	DM
Aragosta	DM
Pino Grigio Marco Felluga	DM
Vernaccia Giannina	DM
Gavi La Scola	DM
Chardonnay	DM
Terre Bianche	DM

VINO ROSSO / ROTWEIN

Chianti Classico	DM
Barbera	DM
Brunello di Montalcino	DM
Tignanello	DM
Barolo	DM
Barbaresco Gaja	DM
Cabernet	DM

ROSÉ

Five Roses	DM
Rosé Bolla	DM

CHAMPAGNER / SPUMANTE

Moët Chandon	DM
Dom Perignon	DM
Ferrari	DM
Fürst von Metternich	DM

Name:
al dente, Innsbruck
(System-Gastronomie, Innsbruck)

Business type/character:
Café-restaurant conception with emphasis on pasta dishes; Italian ambiance.

Card:
Menu card and list of beverages.

Card system:
All-in-one card, simply folded cover with fold-in flap at inside back cover, size when closed (without fold-in flap) 21 × 29.5 cm. Printed on both sides, gloss-foil laminated. Outside front cover full-formatted photo motif, with al dente logo. Selection on inside pages on yellow background, insertion sheet with special offers on inside front cover. Desserts on one side of flap, beverages on the other.

Special features:
Unconventional and witty photo design of cover motif, artistic alienation of the profile product: food art. Corporate design approach: repetition of the motif on the restaurant's calling cards. The photo motif of the promotion card "La Spaghettata" is related: office-sheet sized leaflet printed on one side, text integrated into the picture.

Draft/Design:
Otto Kasper Studios, Rielasingen (cover photo)/
System-Gastronomie, Innsbruck

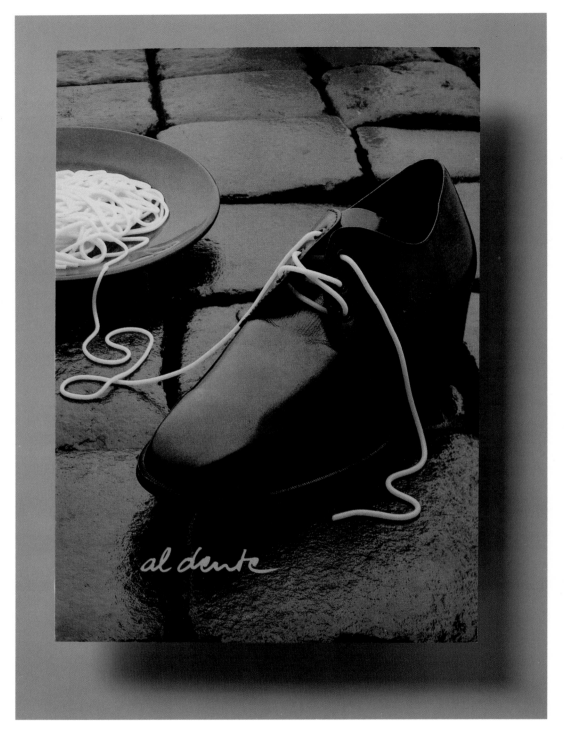

Name:
Papa Joe's Grill-Cantina-Bar, Innsbruck
(System-Gastronomie, Innsbruck)

Business type/character:
Tex-Mex concept with distinct US accent. Casual, emphasis on communication and drinks (large bar counter). Remarkable ambiance.

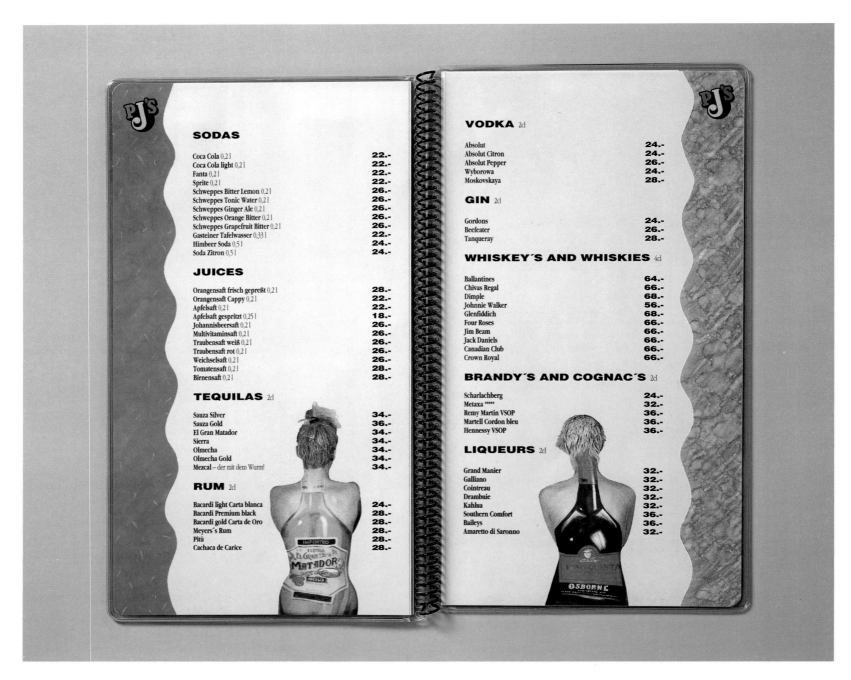

SODAS

Coca Cola 0,2 l	22.-
Coca Cola light 0,2 l	22.-
Fanta 0,2 l	22.-
Sprite 0,2 l	22.-
Schweppes Bitter Lemon 0,2 l	26.-
Schweppes Tonic Water 0,2 l	26.-
Schweppes Ginger Ale 0,2 l	26.-
Schweppes Orange Bitter 0,2 l	26.-
Schweppes Grapefruit Bitter 0,2 l	26.-
Gasteiner Tafelwasser 0,33 l	22.-
Himbeer Soda 0,5 l	24.-
Soda Zitron 0,5 l	24.-

JUICES

Orangensaft frisch gepreßt 0,2 l	28.-
Orangensaft Cappy 0,2 l	22.-
Apfelsaft 0,2 l	22.-
Apfelsaft gespritzt 0,25 l	18.-
Johannisbeersaft 0,2 l	26.-
Multivitaminsaft 0,2 l	26.-
Traubensaft weiß 0,2 l	26.-
Traubensaft rot 0,2 l	26.-
Weichselsaft 0,2 l	26.-
Tomatensaft 0,2 l	28.-
Birnensaft 0,2 l	28.-

TEQUILAS 2cl

Sauza Silver	34.-
Sauza Gold	36.-
El Gran Matador	34.-
Sierra	34.-
Olmecha	34.-
Olmecha Gold	34.-
Mezcal – der mit dem Wurm!	34.-

RUM 2cl

Bacardi light Carta blanca	24.-
Bacardi Premium black	28.-
Bacardi gold Carta de Oro	28.-
Meyers´s Rum	28.-
Pitú	28.-
Cachaca de Carice	28.-

VODKA 2cl

Absolut	24.-
Absolut Citron	24.-
Absolut Pepper	26.-
Wyborowa	24.-
Moskovskaya	28.-

GIN 2cl

Gordons	24.-
Beefeater	26.-
Tanqueray	28.-

WHISKEY´S AND WHISKIES 4cl

Ballantines	64.-
Chivas Regal	66.-
Dimple	68.-
Johnnie Walker	56.-
Glenfiddich	68.-
Four Roses	66.-
Jim Beam	66.-
Jack Daniels	66.-
Canadian Club	66.-
Crown Royal	66.-

BRANDY´S AND COGNAC´S 2cl

Scharlachberg	24.-
Metaxa *****	32.-
Remy Martin VSOP	36.-
Martell Cordon bleu	36.-
Hennessy VSOP	36.-

LIQUEURS 2cl

Grand Manier	32.-
Galliano	32.-
Cointreau	32.-
Drambuie	32.-
Kahlua	32.-
Southern Comfort	36.-
Baileys	36.-
Amaretto di Saronno	32.-

Cards:
Menu card, list of beverages.

Card system:
Both cards with analogous layout, cover and one inside sheet inserted in transparent folders. Spiral binding. Cover design resembles that of a newspaper. Cover motif: still life with vegetables respectively bottles realized as body painting. Menu card: size when closed: 22 × 32.5 cm. Cover plus six inside pages. Inside pages in two colors, the design resembles Indian folklore with alternating contemporary color contrasts. Cover-photo details on inside pages. First inside page: Papa Joe's message. List of beverages: size when closed: 17 × 29 cm. Cover plus six inside pages. Decoration analogous to the menu card, illustrations in the inner part vary accordingly.

Last inside pages feature film strips from the body-painting photo productions.

Special features:
Extremely original fundamental idea, combination of art and life. Visual appeal of cards—colorful, graphic and forceful, resembling the Santa Fe style—underlines the business' positioning. Cover text, column headings, product names in English, partially also product descriptions and inside remarks. Keeping in line with conception, authentic fiction. Cover motifs also used for calling cards. Transparent folder solution allows partial alteration of the selection.

Draft/Design:
Werbeagentur Mallner & Fuchs, Innsbruck/ Henrik Müller-Künast, Samerberg (body painting)/Gerold Tomas, Munich (photography)

PJ's

CANTINA

Seafood Quesada
gebratene Weizentortilla, gefüllt mit Tiefseekrabben, Tintenfisch, Miesmuscheln, Seezungenfilet, frischen Champignons und Lauchstreifen, dazu Chili-Salsa und Kräuterrahm **98.-**

Beef Burrito
gerollte Weizentortilla, gefüllt mit frisch gebratenen Rindfleischstreifen, roten Bohnen, Mais und Tomaten, dazu Chili-Salsa und Kräuterrahm **98.-**

Chicken Burrito
gerollte Weizentortilla, gefüllt mit gebratenem Hühnerfleisch, Paprikastreifen, Tomaten und Zwiebeln, dazu Chili-Salsa und Kräuterrahm **98.-**

Fajitas

Fajita, ein ursprünglich texanisches Nationalgericht, entstammt dem spanischen „Falditas" (kleine Stücke) und ist ein Rezept der Chicano-Cowboys des 19. Jahrhunderts. Mundgerecht geschnittenes Fleisch, serviert in der heißen Guß-eisenpfanne, wird mit Kidney-Beans, Guacamole, Shredded Cheese, Eisbergsalat und Kräuterrahm in warme Weizentortillas gerollt und von Hand gegessen.

Pork Fajitas Ab 2 Personen!
gebratene Schweinsfilets mit sautierten Zwiebeln und Paprikastreifen pro Person **124.-**

Beef & Chicken Fajitas
gebratene Rind-und Hühnerfleischstreifen mit Mais, Tomaten und roten Bohnen pro Person **124.-**

Seafood Fajitas
Tiefseekrabben, Miesmuscheln und Seezungenfilet in leichter Weißweinsauce pro Person **138.-**

Texas Style Chili
feuriger Chilitopf mit ausgesuchten Rindfleischstücken, roten Bohnen, Knoblauch, Tomaten und Paprika, dazu wilder Reis **108.-**

Mexican Style Chili
rassiges Ragout aus faschiertem Rindfleisch, mit roten Bohnen, Knoblauch, Tomaten und Paprika, dazu wilder Reis **108.-**

Corn on the Cob

am Grill goldbraun gebratener Maiskolben mit Kräuterbutter **30.-**

PJ´s GRILL

Steaks

Anderson´s Gourmet Steak
180g Rindersteak aus der Hüfte mit **Mark Anderson´s Spice Mix**™, einer speziellen Kräutergewürzmischung, dazu Baked Potato und Grilltomate **160.-**

Beef & Pork
gegrillte Rindfleisch- und Schweinsfiletstreifen mit Tomaten, grünen Bohnen und Paprika, in der heißen Gußeisenpfanne serviert **148.-**

Steak & Salad
180g Rindersteak aus der Hüfte, dazu eine Auswahl knackfrischer Salate und warmes Knoblauchbrot **160.-**

Mini Steak
kleines Rindersteak aus der Hüfte, dazu Pfefferrahmsauce und Baked Potato mit Kräuterrahm **132.-**

Filet Spieß
Stücke vom Rinderfilet, dazu grüne Bohnen, Kräuterbutter und Baked Potato mit Kräuterrahm **190.-**

IT'S PRIME TIME

Im ganzen medium gebratener Rinderrücken, zart marmoriert mit dem typischen Fettrand, dazu Baked Potato mit Kräuterrahm

Regular Cut	King Cut	Papa Joe´s C...
180g **170.-**	280g **270.-**	460g **44...**

US-Steaks

Fleisch allerhöchster Qualität – richtig gelagert – wunschgerecht zub... ein herzhafter Genuß!

Sirloin	Filet	Si...
190g **164.-**	210g **190.-**	2... **20...**

——————————— dazu wahlweise: ———————————

Chili´s Maiskolben	**30.-**	Knoblauchbrot	
Baked Potato	**20.-**	Champignons	
Pommes frites	**24.-**	Grüne Bohne...	
Wildreis	**22.-**	Zwiebeln – ...	

Falls Sie keinen anderen Wunsch äußern, grillen wir Ihr...

SORRY, we are not responsible for steaks ord...

Atmosphere as sales vehicle

Fun, entertainment, having a good time – naturally this dimension of experience is more or less part of every visit of a gastronomical establishment. Yet there is a species of enterprises which has made it its objective to provide primarily this aspect – maybe we could call it the 'emotional surplus value of provided services'.

Fun or communication-oriented gastronomy: here the customer's expectation or his reason for coming is not that of being supplied with food and drink; his main interest here will be in a more immaterial dimension, which is to have fun, to be entertained – communication, emotional experiences setting a counterpoint to everyday life.

Modern interpretations of this theme usually address themselves to a younger clientele – to a large degree singles or small groups.

In this case food and beverages function as a material vehicle for the actually anticipated experience. Hold it – the sequence is just the other way around: it's drink and food! In a typical fun-concept-establishment, sales of beverages figure way ahead of the edibles.

Analogically, beverages make up the major part of such a restaurant's menu card. The assortment of drinks is usually much more varied. As limited as the choice of foods is here anyway, some fun-oriented concepts don't have any on their menu at all.

But there is no rule without its exception: a small segment of the entertainment-gastronomy attaches more importance to food – examples of this are a number of the so-called Tex-Mex-concepts, which are sprouting up everywhere. Here the idea is to offer ethnic specialties. Food specialists with emphasis on cuisine; on the menu as well as in the entire range of products sold. These restaurants are part of a certain trend in lifestyle, which seeks the exotic to

be 'in'. The customer is attracted primarily by emotional and communicative experiences, culinary enjoyment is secondary.

Consequently, within the entertainment-gastronomy you will find 'mixed' as well as 'just drinks' menues. Both are expected to achieve much more than simple communication of items offered:

* They reflect the self-image of a particular business and help to define its identity – as is the case in all other branches of this line of industry. A profiling element.

* Their function – with the aid of visual and linguistic means – is to attract a certain clientele by creating connection to specific lifestyle categories: without much thought a customer decides whether he'd like to be a part of the symbolized value system. Design and language used in a menu card, together with other design concepts, strongly influence this decision.

* They are an extremely important means of addressing the customer, an instrument of communication par excellence. A well-made card will aim directly at the customer's inherent desire for entertainment, it will set the mood, so to speak. The more exciting, the better; it is the first delivery on the conceptual promise: You'll have a good time here!

A classy appearance is very rarely the style to choose. To the contrary: such a card can, or should be, funny, smart and crazy. The emotional message is: "Isn't it fun to be alive?!" and this message should be carefully aimed to reach the desired clientele.

Differing from traditional pubs or neighbourhood watering holes – which actually do belong within this category of establishment – modern fun-concepts aim at a very well-defined clientele and employ precise marketing-concepts. The first question to answer is always: "Who do I want to attract?" Trendy yuppies, academically trained cosmopolitans, arty Bohemians … or a less discriminating teenage crowd?

Even if a relaxed, informal design has become more common, styles differ greatly depending on the envisioned clientele.

Free and easy – or 'letting it all hang out', flippant asiders or funny comments on the offerings; far out, more conservative, shrill: humor knows many variations.

The same goes for the visual means used. Not all fun-concepts rely on a certain lingo, but rather use neutral language and employ visual means to define their place on the map of lifestyles. If using both means, it is very important that they be well-matched. A general rule is: the more extreme the choosen language or imagery, the more closely-defined the desired clientele. A more discreet design tends to attract a wider public.

An outstanding example in this discipline has been presented by T.G.I.Friday's, a chain of restaurants originating in the US, but now also operating in Great Britain. T.G.I. Friday's is a model representative of mixing 'fun & food', and during the 80's definitely offered one of the most innovative menu-card designs in the United States. Friday's inspiration and influence in North America could be compared to that of Mövenpick restaurants on the European market.

It is remarkable, though, that at least in Germany the beverage-oriented segment of the gastronomical industry frequently is not exploiting full marketing potential of menu cards. Of all gastronomical branches, this one puts the least emphasis on presenting itself by this means.

Such neglect has its reason: in the past, marketing had been completely left to the breweries. Only now, with the rise of professional systems on this market (such as restaurant chains), the situation is changing. The menu card is now very consciously being activated as an extremely powerful instrument of animation.

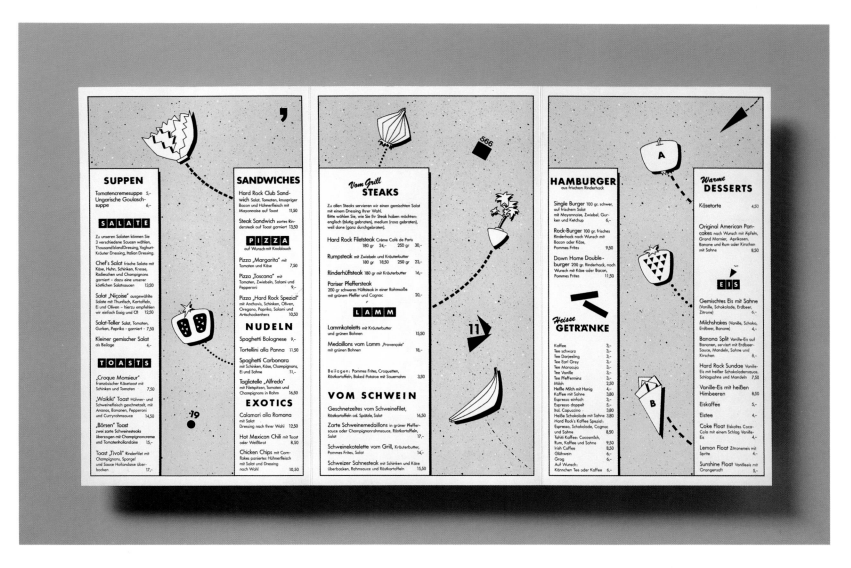

Name:
Hard Rock Café, Frankfurt/Main

Business type/character:
Music pub, emphasis on drinks, with meeting-point character. Not with classical hard rock appeal, designed in lofthouse style.

Card:
Menu card and list of beverages.

Card system:
All-in-one card, miscellaneous folding, entirely printed on both sides and gloss-foil laminated. Size when closed: 21 × 36.5 cm. Outside front cover shows stylized New York skyline, mint green as background color on all outside covers. Pink background on the inside. Highly individualistic background decoration, selection listed in white squares. Foods and hot drinks on the insides, other beverages on the rear side and folded-in outside. Varying typographical design of the column headings. Supplementary insertion sheet with Menus of the Day.

Special features:
Highly individualistic matter-of-fact zeitgeist design, modernized Hard Rock logo. Skyline motif on cover corresponds with neon wall sculpture in the restaurant.

Draft/Design:
Frank Martin Petschull, Wiesbaden

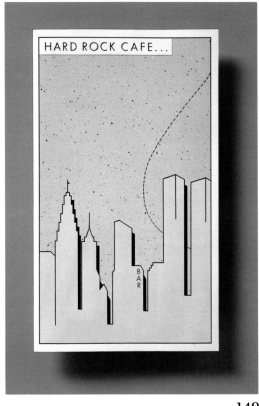

Noodles

aperitivi

cynar soda		5 cl	5.00
punt e mes		5 cl	4.00
campari* soda		5 cl	7.00
campari* orange		0.2 l	8.00
martini	weiß, rot, dry	5 cl	5.00

degistivi

fernet branca		2 cl	4.00
fernet menta		2 cl	4.00
linie aquavit		2 cl	5.00
grappa sigillo		2 cl	4.50
grappa piave		2 cl	5.50
grappa sigillo nero		2 cl	5.00
streitberger hausbrand	waldhimbeer, schlehe, kirsch, birne	2 cl	4.00
ramazzotti		2 cl	4.00
averna		2 cl	4.00
wodka		2 cl	4.00
tequilla weiß		2 cl	3.50
tequilla braun		2 cl	4.50

weißweine offen

frascati secco d.o.c. trocken	0.2 l / 0.5 l / 1.0 l	5.00 / 12.00 / 24.00
verdicchio castelli d.o.c. trocken frischfruchtig	0.2 l / 0.5 l / 1.0 l	5.00 / 12.00 / 24.00
orvieto classico d.o.c. umbrien trocken, feinherb	0.2 l / 0.5 l / 1.0 l	5.50 / 13.00 / 26.00
pinot grigio trocken, feines bukett	0.2 l / 0.5 l / 1.0 l	6.50 / 16.00 / 32.00

rosé offen

bardolino classico	0.2 l / 0.5 l / 1.0 l	5.50 / 13.00 / 26.00

rotweine offen

chianti classico d.o.c.g. trocken	0.2 l / 0.5 l / 1.0 l	5.50 / 13.00 / 26.00
montepulciano d'abruzzo d.o.c. trocken, zarte herbe	0.2 l / 0.5 l / 1.0 l	5.00 / 12.00 / 24.00
valpolicella classico superiore a.o.c. würzig, kräftig	0.2 l / 0.5 l / 1.0 l	5.50 / 13.00 / 26.00

Name:
Noodles, Munich
(Kaub-Gruppe, Munich)

Business type/character:
Restaurant and bar with emphasis upon pasta specialties, slogan: 1. münchner spaghetti oper (1st Munich Spaghetti Opera). Modern ambiance, emphasis on communication, meeting-place character. zeitgeist, trendy.

Card:
Menu card and list of beverages 1990.

Card system:
Cover plus 8 selection pages, stapled. Size when closed: 21 × 29.5 cm. Cover gloss-foil laminated on both sides. Outside front cover b/w photograph, with Noodles logo. Selection in script typography on white background on the inside. Noodles logo as headline on every page.

Special features:
The card only lists drinks, antipasti, and desserts. Noodle dishes were only advertised on chalkboards (different conception today). Cover motif with ironical and erotic touch—underlines positioning of the restaurant: unconventional, saucy, pleasure-oriented.

Draft/Design:
Kruse & Specht, Munich

Name:

Zoozie'z, Munich
(Kruse & Specht Unternehmensgruppe, Munich)

Business type/character:

Café-bar restaurant. Predominantly young mixed audience. Multi-conceptual, dependent on time of day. Bistro character in the evening.

Card:

The card is not depicted here. Advertisement means: a multi-purpose leaflet in office-sheet sized format, two invitation cards for the annual summer festival. Sheet with complete word-image logo; in black on white it also serves as cover illustration of the menu card.

Special features:

Creative variation is to transport a certain atmosphere and at the same time is to prevent any sign of fatigue—this concept has been running strong for 12 years.

Draft/Design:

Kruse & Specht, Munich

152

Name:
Spitz, Cologne/Bonn
(Spitz-Gruppe, Cologne)

Business type/character:
Mixed conception: pub, café, bistro. Trendy meeting point, emphasis on communication and drinks. Multiplied.

Cards:
Three versions of the menu card and beverage list.

Card system:
Simply folded cover, recycled paper. Size when closed 15.5 × 25.5 cm. Outside front cover with b/w photo motif and logo in blue. Selection pages with blue column titles. All-in-one card with basic menu offer, additional Menu of the Day offers.

Special features:
Deliberately simple card structure, uncomplicated manufacturing, designed as consumer good for daily alteration (high customer frequency!). The establishment's prime color blue is the only additional color. The card is made available to franchisees by the central office free of cost. Individual cover sheet motif for each establishment: historic photographs of the respective Spitz location approximately 40 years ago.

Draft/Design:
Spitz-Gruppe, Cologne

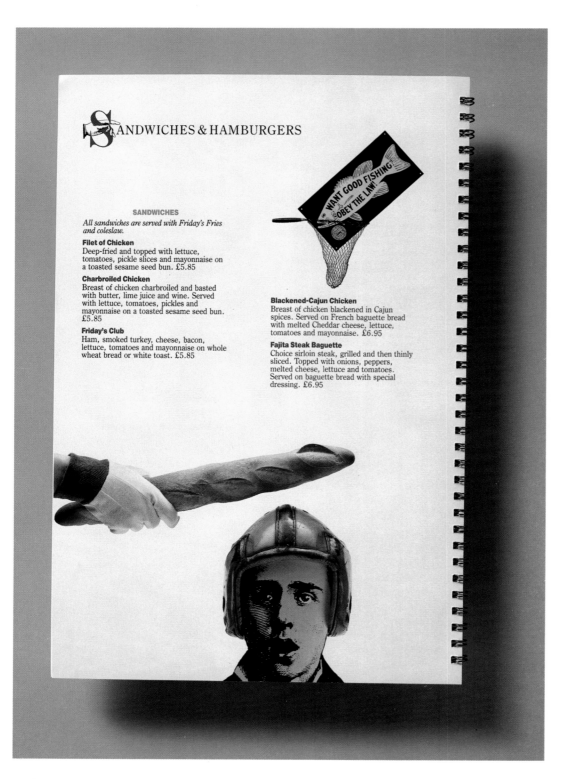

Name:
T.G.I. Friday's Great Britain
(Whitbread-Gruppe, London)

Business type/character:
American bistro—prominent in atmosphere and decoration, animating, vivid; fun and entertainment are central conception moments. Comprehensive offer of foods and beverages. Large centrally located bar counter. Multiplied.

Card:
Menu card and list of beverages.

Card system:
All-in-one card (only a small selection of cocktails, approximately 500 cocktails available), spiral binding, altogether 18 pages plus two cover sheets inserted in transparent plastic folders, entirely mat-foil laminated. Size when closed: 23 × 33 cm (folder), selection pages: 21 × 31 cm. Selection pages are entirely colorful designed on yellow background, a double page per column. A large number of curiosities is depicted, collector's items of all kinds. Typography in several colors. The same card stapled, in b/w and reduced in size to 14.5 × 21 cm can be had as take-along. New: Cocktail and beer card, also formatted 14.5 × 21 cm with 48 pages, with colorful unique decoration.

Special features:

Highly individual unmistakable card profile with high entertainment value. Visuals as atmospheric vehicle. The basic decoration is pre-printed; alterations of selection therefore are relatively easy to be effected. Card depictions refer to distinct decoration elements of the establishment itself: related original objects ("elegant clutter") create a distinct atmosphere. The logo is very sparsely used—only as gold relief printing on the card folder (original in black writing on red/white background).

Draft/Design:

Adopted from T.G.I. Friday's USA

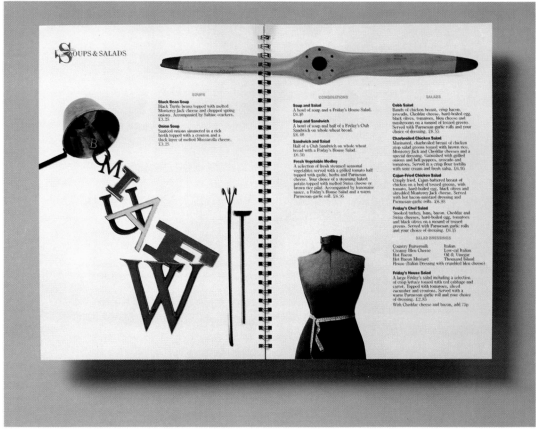

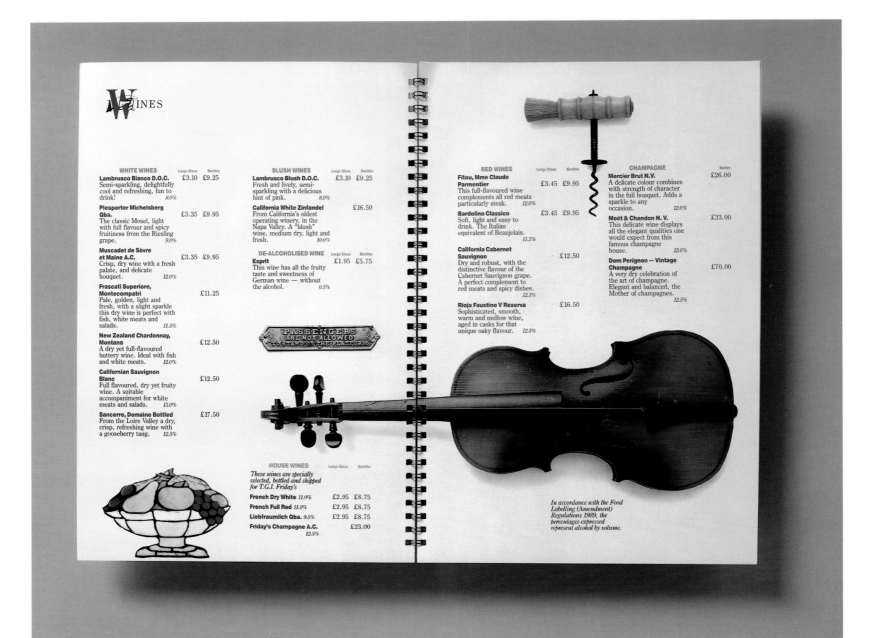

W INES

WHITE WINES

	Large Glass	Bottle
Lambrusco Bianco D.O.C. Semi-sparkling, delightfully cool and refreshing, fun to drink! *8.0%*	£3.10	£9.25
Piesporter Michelsberg Qba. The classic Mosel, light with full flavour and spicy fruitiness from the Riesling grape. *9.0%*	£3.35	£9.95
Muscadet de Sèvre et Maine A.C. Crisp, dry wine with a fresh palate, and delicate bouquet. *12.0%*	£3.35	£9.95
Frascati Superiore, Montecompatri Pale, golden, light and fresh, with a slight sparkle this dry wine is perfect with fish, white meats and salads. *11.5%*		£11.25
New Zealand Chardonnay, Montana A dry yet full-flavoured buttery wine. Ideal with fish and white meats. *12.0%*		£12.50
Californian Sauvignon Blanc Full flavoured, dry yet fruity wine. A suitable accompaniment for white meats and salads. *13.0%*		£12.50
Sancerre, Domaine Bottled From the Loire Valley a dry, crisp, refreshing wine with a gooseberry tang. *12.5%*		£17.50

BLUSH WINES

	Large Glass	Bottle
Lambrusco Blush D.O.C. Fresh and lively, semi-sparkling with a delicious hint of pink. *8.0%*	£3.10	£9.25
California White Zinfandel From California's oldest operating winery, in the Napa Valley. A "blush" wine, medium dry, light and fresh. *10.0%*		£16.50

DE-ALCOHOLISED WINE

	Large Glass	Bottle
Esprit This wine has all the fruity taste and sweetness of German wine — without the alcohol. *0.5%*	£1.95	£5.75

HOUSE WINES

These wines are specially selected, bottled and shipped for T.G.I. Friday's

	Large Glass	Bottle
French Dry White *11.0%*	£2.95	£8.75
French Full Red *11.0%*	£2.95	£8.75
Liebfraumilch Qba. *9.5%*	£2.95	£8.75
Friday's Champagne A.C. *12.5%*		£23.00

RED WINES

	Large Glass	Bottle
Fitou, Mme Claude Parmentier This full-flavoured wine complements all red meats particularly steak. *12.0%*	£3.45	£9.95
Bardolino Classico Soft, light and easy to drink. The Italian equivalent of Beaujolais. *11.5%*	£3.45	£9.95
California Cabernet Sauvignon Dry and robust, with the distinctive flavour of the Cabernet Sauvignon grape. A perfect complement to red meats and spicy dishes. *12.5%*		£12.50
Rioja Faustino V Reserva Sophisticated, smooth, warm and mellow wine, aged in casks for that unique oaky flavour. *12.5%*		£16.50

CHAMPAGNE

	Bottle
Mercier Brut N.V. A delicate colour combines with strength of character in the full bouquet. Adds a sparkle to any occasion. *12.0%*	£26.00
Moët & Chandon N. V. This delicate wine displays all the elegant qualities one would expect from this famous champagne house. *12.0%*	£33.00
Dom Perignon — Vintage Champagne A very dry celebration of the art of champagne. Elegant and balanced, the Mother of champagnes. *12.5%*	£70.00

PASSENGERS ARE NOT ALLOWED TO STAND ON THE PLATFORM

In accordance with the Food Labelling (Amendment) Regulations 1989, the percentages expressed represent alcohol by volume.

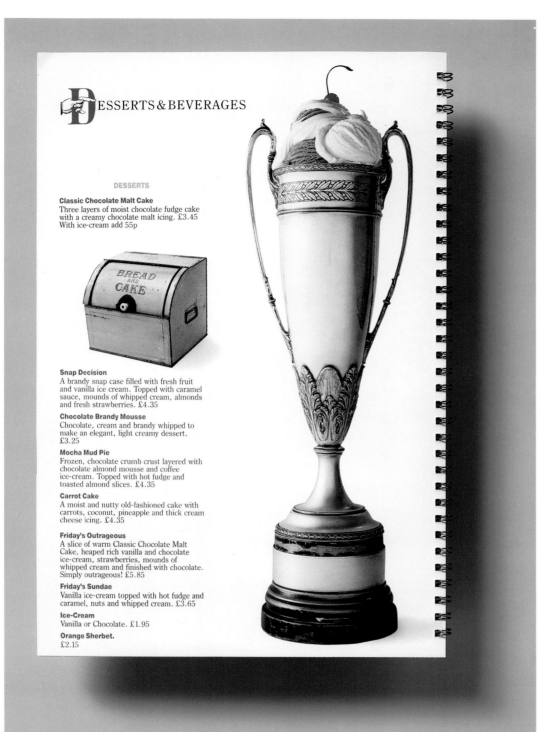

DESSERTS & BEVERAGES

DESSERTS

Classic Chocolate Malt Cake
Three layers of moist chocolate fudge cake with a creamy chocolate malt icing. £3.45
With ice-cream add 55p

Snap Decision
A brandy snap case filled with fresh fruit and vanilla ice cream. Topped with caramel sauce, mounds of whipped cream, almonds and fresh strawberries. £4.35

Chocolate Brandy Mousse
Chocolate, cream and brandy whipped to make an elegant, light creamy dessert.
£3.25

Mocha Mud Pie
Frozen, chocolate crumb crust layered with chocolate almond mousse and coffee ice-cream. Topped with hot fudge and toasted almond slices. £4.35

Carrot Cake
A moist and nutty old-fashioned cake with carrots, coconut, pineapple and thick cream cheese icing. £4.35

Friday's Outrageous
A slice of warm Classic Chocolate Malt Cake, heaped rich vanilla and chocolate ice-cream, strawberries, mounds of whipped cream and finished with chocolate. Simply outrageous! £5.85

Friday's Sundae
Vanilla ice-cream topped with hot fudge and caramel, nuts and whipped cream. £3.65

Ice-Cream
Vanilla or Chocolate. £1.95

Orange Sherbet.
£2.15

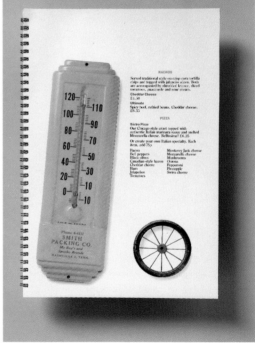

Name:
Pupasch
(Pupasch-Gruppe, Hannover)

Business type/character:
Beer-joint appeal with emphasis on having a good time and communication. Motto: the totally crazy bar. Rustic appeal, the limited space makes setting-up contact easy, controlled animation. Young audience. Multiplied.

Card:
Menu card and list of beverages.

Card system:
Simply folded cover, punched. Size when closed 15 × 30 cm (without punching). Outside front cover designed as clown's mask with openings for eyes, nose, and mouth. Two mask versions: female and male. Basic color yellow as in Pupasch logo. Selection on interior pages on yellow background framed by earthy aphorisms. The presentation of the selection itself with deliberately risqué undertone.

Special features:
The card's design underlines the positioning: loud, hearty and fun-loving gastronomy.

Draft/Design:
B + B Gastronomie Marketing, Ostrittum/Berlin

Name:
Jimmy's Diner, Berlin

Business type/character:
Emphasis on atmosphere, action, and communication. Slogan: "Not just a restaurant but a way of life." The selection and ambiance resembles the typical US diners of the 1950s: fastfood kitchen ranging from burgers to chili con carne, furnished in chrome and pink.

Card:
Menu card and list of beverages.

Card system:
All-in-one card, simply folded cover plus four inside pages, punched, both sides gloss-foil laminated. Stapled, size when closed (without punching) 19 × 32 cm, inside pages 19 × 13 cm. Entirely printed in color, the cover illustration resembles a jukebox. Record motif on inside cover. Column titles/list of dishes predominantly in English.

Special features:
Colorful approach and illustration topics refer to the diner conception origin, at the same time to music as important conception element. The English language is meant to underline the selection's authenticity.

Draft/Design:
Jimmy's Diner

Name:
Alex
(Alex-Gruppe, Oldenburg)

Business type/character:
Mixed conception: pub, café, bistro. Young, strong on communication and drinking. Emphasis upon good atmosphere, slogan: "Breakfast. Lunch. Dinner. Always." Multiplied.

Cards:
Two ice cream card generations, the elder version (Heiss auf Eis [hot on ice]) and the current version (I love Eis).

Card system:
Both cards simply folded cover, printed on both sides. Heiß auf Eis: outside gloss-foil laminated, inside mat-foil laminated. Size when closed: 14 × 31 cm. Outside covers with colorful decoration, inside pages à la Alex: trendy visuals, hip wording, cartoon-bubble communication. I love Eis: both sides gloss-foil laminated, size

when closed: 16.5 × 33 cm. Designed as picture story in three parts, outside front cover, both inside covers, and outside back cover each with full formatted photo motif with typical Alex scene. Selection presented in squares. Ice cream card supplements the basic offer card.

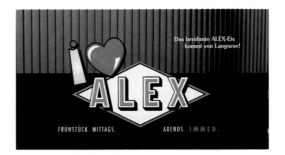

Special features:
Text is used to develop a specific Alex feeling. Intensive work with the logo—brand formation! The second version—more colorful, more snappy, more with it—as advanced development of animation via card: narrative approach, the card narrates a (love) story. The picture's message is more important than the presentation of the selection. Effect: emotional charging of product.

Draft/Design:
B + B Gastronomie Marketing, Ostrittum/Berlin

160

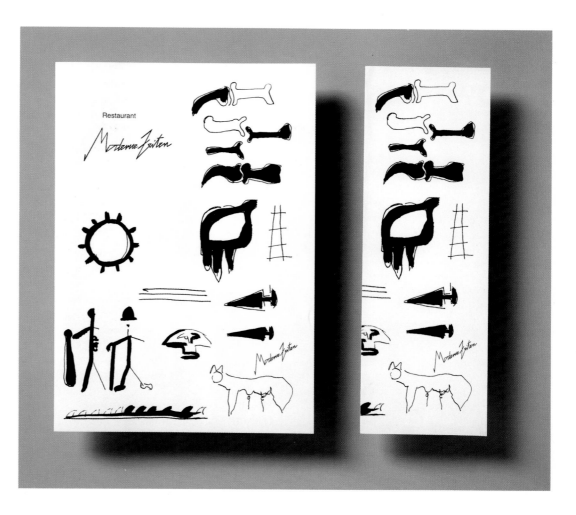

Name:

Moderne Zeiten, Cologne
(Sanssouci Gaststätten, Cologne)

Business type/character:

Mixed conception; bar, café, restaurant. Two stories, restaurant sector on the upper floor. Emphasis upon communication, meeting-point character.

Cards:

Large menu card and beverage list for restaurant, small menu card and beverage list for all other sectors.

Card system:

Restaurant card: simply folded cover, all-in-one. Both sides gloss-foil laminated. Size when closed: 20.5 × 29.5 cm. Outside front cover: full formatted drawing in primitive/archaic style. Logo integrated. Left inside cover food, on the right side beverages on white background. Small card: cover plus eight inside pages, all-in-one. Size when closed: 10 × 29.5 cm. Same cover motif as on large card, spread out over both covers. Selection on white background on the inside.

Special features:

Corporate design approach: card's cover motif also on calling cards and stationery. Play on words: the name "Moderne Zeiten" (modern times) refers to the Chaplin movie of the same name; Chaplin figure features in the cover design. Interrelation between the logo/film title and style as well as illustration theme, which symbolically narrates the development of mankind.

Draft/Design:

The artist CAP (Ingrid Grundheber), Cologne (cover design)/Fabian Charlemagne, Moderne Zeiten

How to adequately communicate the extraordinary

Every specialty promotion subsists upon the aura of it being something extraordinary, unique, overaverage. Its fascination lies in the intensity, with which it directs the spotlight on a certain topic which derives its attraction specifically from its transience: only a few days, a week, a month at the most. This temporarity is what specialty cards have in common with Menus of the Day: they both are principally additive in function and character.

You practically never encounter them alone – they usually complement the regular menu card. Another elementary characteristic feature is that they require a motto, they need a ruling theme. This theme may have all kinds of origin:

* a certain country/region
  – Asian cuisine
  – Mediterranean cooking
  – Saxon specialties

* a group of products, a kind of diet or method of preparation
  – fish and sea food
  – rice
  – Schnitzel
  – wholesome foods
  – Wok cooking

* it could be related to an event
  – which might either be a
  – celebration or
  – public events such as Church conventions, as well as
  – promotion launches for certain products or brands

* it might even be related to a certain person
  – cooking by Witzigmann
  – recipies by Alfons Schuhbeck

Thematical mottos often superimpose or double each other: a goose tastes best in the Advent season; truffle dishes should be served in fall. The combination of certain products with a specific time of the year characterizes the seasonally-founded specialty offer: asparagus season, strawberry season, etc ...

Seasonal specialty offers certainly are the most widespread of all forms of special offers. They probably also are the original version of this marketing instrument stemming from the days when you just couldn't have everything at all times and seasonal availability dictated the course of meals anyway. Today we must ingeniously imitate the formerly natural rythms of availability to recreate this lost exitement.

Consequently, the objective of specialty menu cards is not limited to communicating the offer; it must dramatize this offer with visual means. Seen from a marketing standpoint of view, the purpose of specialty promotions is to increase the attractivity of the offer – and thus of the offerer – and at the same time to underline his or her gastronomical competence.

The economic objective of these actions is to expressly direct the (additional) demand towards the specialty products within the projected period of time. After all, promotional activities require additional expenditures for material, personnel and organizational means – and these have to be neutralized. So if deliberate interference is planned in the decision-making behaviour of customers in favor of a certain product, you had better use a visual hammer! The specialty card, after all, is the most important management instrument available here; and this explicit guidance aspect of demand in a restaurant distinguishes the specialty card by degrees from all other cards.

Signal character is the artistic gist of specialty card design. The idea expressly is not to reproduce the standard designs introduced in the business, but to disregard all limitations in respect of visual design. Its appearance is far, very far away from all ties to the standard card and even to all corporate design norms. Its supreme objective is to attract attention, to deviate from all rules on colors, forms and setting established in everyday gastronomical life.

Space requirement for the presentation of the offer itself usually is quite low; favorable conditions for visual opulence. Creative aspects are more dominant here than for the standard card; the relation between text and picture is far more marketing-oriented than in normal cases – decisively shifted in favor of eyecatching effects.

The specialty theme itself respectively its associative transformation is the ideal stylistic approach. Cost expenditures must be taken into consideration as limiting factor – they must be in proportion to the card's limited usability.

Specialty cards consequently rarely are concepted as independent separate card, but more often as simple loose leaf or as table stand resp. folder. Usually its format is smaller than that of the main card. Table sets are just as well suited for specialty-related promotional purposes – read more about these in the following chapter.

Depiction of the offer itself often has a hand-written resp. script character. This underlines the improvised and spontaneous character of the entire action, which basically also utilizes the idea of daily freshness – not only for season-based promotions. Looked at from this standpoint of view, specialty promotions are nothing else than quotations of the market-kitchen philosophy.

Name:
Churrasco Steakhäuser Schweiz
(Churrasco Steakhouse, Basel/UTC-Gruppe,
Switzerland)

Business type/character:
Steak house concept, multiplied.

Card:
Special summer campaign card (June to August
1991) with additional offers (cocktails, main
courses, desserts) and integrated prize competition.

Card system:
Miscellaneous folded card, both sides entirely
color-illustrated. Varnished with printing lake.
Size when closed: 14.5 × 25.5 cm. Selection on
the insides, reference to prize contest on folded-
in rear page. Design in "colonial style"; nos-
talgic effect achieved by utilization of various
decoration elements, taken from old stock cer-
tificates, cigar bands, copper plate engravings.
Typography of column titles also is reminiscent
of colonial style. The black and white originals
were treated by airbrush.

Special features:
This selection card is part of a promotion package with emphasis upon product promotion in
grocery stores under the Churrasco brand
including prize contest and accompanied by
placard campaigns. Design of the packaging and
advertisement means in the same style as the
card. Objective: synergetic effects through reference to gastronomical experience.

Draft/Design:
Freitag & Partner, Zurich

Name:
Eurest-Betriebsrestaurants
(Eurest Deutschland, Frankfurt/Main)

Business type/character:
Personnel catering: personnel cafeterias operated by Eurest as catering business companies.

Cards:
Two special-campaign cards 1991. Theme of the
year-long campaign: "Enjoy vegetables. Here
and now." The cards depicted here are those for
the spring and fall campaign.

Card system:
Simply folded cover, recycled cardboard, size
when closed: 15 × 21 cm. Outside front cover
with full formatted colored illustration and title
of the campaign, outside back cover yellow respectively red. Cover drawings on both cards
are analogously designed variations of the
theme; vegetables typical for the season on red
and yellow background. Inside sheets blank, offer of the respective business on folded office-
sheet sized insertion sheets or printed-in.

Special features:
Year campaigns are conceptualized centrally;
this cover solution allows flexible and individual
design of the campaign selection according to
the requirements of the individual establishments. Alternating combination of the background color red/yellow underlines kinship but
also independence of the cards. Also used are
posters (42 × 60 cm) as well as expo walls with
the same motif.

Draft/Design:
Internal Eurest workgroup (overall conception)/Agentur Trust, Frankfurt/Main

Name:
Bräustuben Spatenhaus, Munich
(Kuffler-Gruppe, Munich)

Business type/character:
Food-oriented with wide-ranging assortment, traditional local cooking.

Cards:
Ensemble of whole-foods special cards; motifs relating to the four seasons: spring, summer, fall, and winter.

Card system:
Individual insertion sheets for the standard menu card, entirely printed on one side with seasonal decoration. Size: spring: 21 × 32.5 cm, summer: 21 × 29 cm, fall: 21 × 29.5 cm, winter: 21 × 31 cm. Writing by typewriter or PC printer, copied in.

Special features:
Whole-food selection alternating on daily basis as permanent side program. Remarks to the business' whole-food program on the back of the special menu sheets.

Draft/Design:
The artist Ricarda Dietz, Munich

166

AUS UNSERER VOLLWERTKÜCHE
ein gesunder Genuß

Demeter Apfelsaft	0,2l DM 2,50
Demeter Gemüsesaft	0,2l DM 2,80
Brot-Trunk	0,2l DM 2,50
frischgepreßter Orangensaft	0,2l DM 6,--

ROHKOST-SALATTELLER - Salat von Kichererbsen und Gerste,
    verschiedene Keimlinge, Blattsalate, Kohlrabi,
    Zucchini, Karotten, Sellerie, Apfel, Mais,
    Apfel-Meerrettich-Dressing   DM 12,50

    Gemüsegratin mit Tomaten, Champignons, Buchweizen und
        Reisnudeln auf Paprikasauce   DM 12,50

3 Stück GRÜNKERN-KÜCHLEIN mit frischen Rahmpilzen und
    feine Gemüse der Saison   DM 13,50

    Erfrischender Melonensalat mit geraffelten
        Karotten, Wasserkresse, leichte Zitronen-
        marinade   DM 10,50

Natur-Joghurt mit frischen Himbeeren   DM 10,--

Biologische H a f e r c r e m e mit frischen
    Erdbeeren   DM 8,90

Naturbelassen - ungeschält - nicht raffiniert -
ohne künstliche Aroma-und Zusatzstoffe

Grönland-Krevetten
Krabbenfleisch

Westfalen-Schinken
Bündnerfleisch

Geräucherter Fisch:
Lachs, Forelle,
Schwertfisch,
Felchen

Cocktail- und
Senfdillsauce,
Porto, Sherry

**Wählen Sie vom Buffet
umstehende Beilagen
zu Ihren Melonen!**

täglich ab 18.00 h

Buffet à discrétion
(inkl. Dessert) Fr. 28.–

**GALERIE
RESTAURANT**

Gourmet-Teller

Cavaillon-, Cantaloupe-,
Honig- und Wassermelone
Geräucherter Lachs
Krevetten
Westfalen-Schinken
Cocktailsauce,
Meerrettichschaum
Fr. 21.–

Melonien lässt grüssen

Name:

Bahnhof Buffet Bern

Business type/character:

Railroad station gastronomy, wide-spaced range of business types from take-away fast food conception all the way to sophisticated service restaurant.

Cards:

Two special campaign show cards, used in the restaurant "Galerie" (elegant restaurant with local predominantly business clientele): "Melonien lässt grüssen" (approximately: "Hello from melonland") and "Le rendez-vous aux légumes" (vegetable promotion campaign).

Card system:

Vegetable campaign card: simply folded show card, semi-cardboard cover printed white on red on one side. Size when closed: 24 × 16 cm. Text is identical on both show card sides, with differing layout. The card is cut to look like a tomato in the establishment and colored with fluorescent paint. Special card for melons: printed on one side, punched, semi-cardboard folded three times. Can be mounted by insertion into prepunched slits. Size when mounted: 22 × 18.5 cm (maximum). Basic decoration is a slice of melon; text and layout on both show card sides are different. Basic print is two-colored, yellow and orange color subsequently applied with fluorescent marker. The decorative motifs are preprinted, text is subsequently printed in. That allows multiple utilization of the cards.

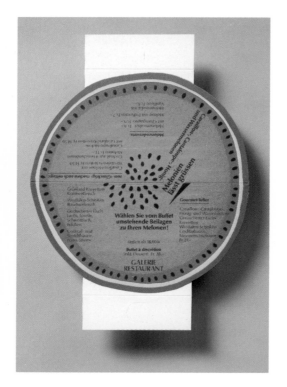

Special features:

Both cards promote the restaurant's regular evening buffet—especially well-suited for special campaigns. Form and color of the show cards emphasize the advertized products even before reading. The melon card's insertion arrangement insures stability without any additional accessories.

Draft/Design:

Hannes Friedli, St. Gallen

Name:

Mövenpick Restaurants Switzerland/Germany (Mövenpick Unternehmungen, Adliswil)

Business type/character:

Emphasis on enjoyment, casualness. Profile emphasis: quality and diversion. Seasonal cuisine. Uniform basic philosophy; appearance and selection vary.

Card:

Special campaign card "The Rolling Kohls" (the rolling cabbages).

Card system:

Card is designed like a double record cover down to the very last detail: folded cover made of double-glued cardboard open on the sides, outside and inside gloss-foil laminated. Size when closed: 31.5 × 31 cm. Continuous background screen: a cook juggling with heads of cabbage. Outside front cover with campaign's (record) title and cabbage photograph. The selection is presented in form of song titles on the left inside cover. A photograph of a long-playing record is depicted on the right inside.

Special features:

Very amusing alienation effect—all the way to naming the campaign dishes, and the allusion to a well-known record label.

Draft/Design:

Mövenpick Werbung Restaurants Schweiz, Adliswil

Die „Pannonische Küche" – eine kulinarische Entdeckung

Es gibt (zum Feinschmecker-Glück!) Regionen, die noch nicht in aller Gourmet-Munde sind. Und wenn man die dann kennenlernt, ist das doppelter Genuß – neue interessante Spezialitäten plus Entdeckerfreude...

Die „Pannonische Küche", die im Burgenland beheimatet ist, gilt hierzulande als ein delikates Neuland: Eine wunderbare historisch gewachsene Mischung aus ungarischer Schärfe, kroatischer Deftigkeit und slowakischer Rustikalität, die jahrhundertelang in der Kaiserstadt Wien verfeinert wurde.

Wir freuen uns, daß wir Sie zu einer derartigen kulinarischen Entdeckungsreise einladen können.

Name:
Restaurant Concorde, Hamburg

Business type/character:
Hotel restaurant in the Airport Hotel, Hamburg

Cards:
Two special cards : Pannonian cooking (1989) and cooking in the time of Czar Peter the Great (1990).

Card system:
Both cards simply folded cover, yellow resp. red cardboard, printed in wine-red resp. black. Size when closed 20 × 37 cm (Pannonian cooking) and 21.5 × 37 cm. Cover outside fronts each with campaign title and tuning-in to the culinary theme. Selection on the inside.

Special features:
The Russian campaign was in context with an exhibition in the hotel gallery. Interesting, atmosphere-creating detail: the campaign title and names of the dishes are also printed in Cyrillic letters. The Pannonian cooking campaign was inspired by the hotel director Valentin Resetarits, who hails from the Burgenland region in Austria.

Draft/Design:
Valentin Resetarits, director Airport Hotel/ Agentur Strategie mit Phantasie, Frankfurt/ Main (Pannonian cooking); Ravindra Ahuja, vice-director Airport Hotel (cooking in the periods of czars)

Name:

Gläsernes Restaurant
(Oikos Okölogisches Handelskontor, Frankfurt/Main)

Business type/character:

Campaign on the occasion of the German Protestant Church Convention, model presented by the Oikos Umweltberatung (Oikos environment consulting). Installation of a complete restaurant open for church convention visitors. Presented for the third time in 1991. Limited selection: one breakfast, appetizer, main course, and dessert on vegetarian basis alternating daily. The objective: to provide ideas for environmentally sound operations in large-scale catering companies.

Cards:

Two examples from the years 1989 (cover) and 1991 (inside).

Card system:

1989 card: simply folded cover made of recycled paper entirely printed on both sides, size when closed: 22.5 × 30.5 cm. Menu of the Day. Outside front cover with two-colored silhouette illustration—symbolic statement: unity of nature and culture. Menu of the Day on left inside cover. Right inside cover: merchandise-knowledge information on the day's product emphasis. The outside back cover features information on objectives and philosophy of the "Gläserne Restaurant." 1991 card: analogue design, however summary overall view on the selection integrated on the cover front page, all

Offers of the Day at a glance on the inside. Highly individualistic text-page layout corresponds with design of an accompanying brochure with detailed information on this model.

Special features:

Cards are multi-functionally conceptualized: as entry card for the restaurant, envelope for the accompanying brochure, recipe booklet to take home. The recipes of the offered dishes are printed on the inside. The 1989 card was awarded a prize in the competition "Grafik-Design Deutschland 89."

Draft/Design:

1989 card: Monika Weiss, Frankfurt/Main (conception)/Karin Altendorfer, Frankfurt/Main (realization); 1991 card: Monika Weiss, Frankfurt/Main

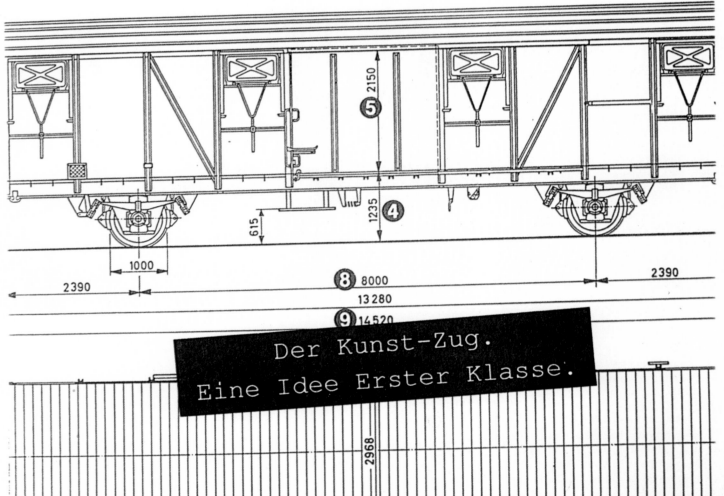

Der Kunst-Zug.
Eine Idee Erster Klasse.

Kulturgüter(speise)wagen.

GETRAENKE		SPEISEN	
Coca Cola, Mineral Chinotto, Schweppes, Rivella, Orangina	Fr. 3.--	**Kalte Küche**	
		Grüner Salat	Fr. 5.--
		Gemischter Salat	Fr. 6.50
		Kleiner hors d'oeuvre	
Jus d'Orange "Michel"	Fr. 4.--	Teller	Fr. 9.50
		Paté Ben (Ben Vautier)	Fr. 10.-
Bier, Hopfenperle	Fr. 4.--	**Warme Küche**	
		Montag, 10. Juni 1991	
		Irish Stew à la Jim Whiting	
		Fr. 14.50	
1/2 Rosé	Fr. 14.--	Dienstag, 11. Juni 1991	
1/2 Merlot, rot	Fr. 12.50	Tripes à la mode de Bernhard	
1/2 Soave, weiss	Fr. 12.50	Luginbühl	
		Fr. 14.50	
2/10 La Côte	Fr. 6.--	Mittwoch, 12. Juni 1991	
2/10 Dôle	Fr. 6.--	Gemüse-Lasagne Hofkunst	
		Fr. 14.50	
Kaffee	Fr. 2.50	Donnerstag, 13. Juni 1991	
		Navarin de boeuf Ben Vautier	
		Fr. 14.50	
		Freitag, 14. Juni 1991	
		Bouillabaisse Eva Aeppli	
		Fr. 14.50	
		Samstag, 15. Juni 1991	
		Boeuf en daube Daniel Spörri	
		Fr. 14.50	
		Sonntag, 16. Juni 1991	
		Moussaka Milena Palakarkina	
		Fr. 14.50	
Geliefert durch den Party Service des		Montag, 17. Juni 1991	
KUNST BAHNHOF KULTUR		Auslauf Jeannot Tinguely	
BUFFET BASEL		Fr. 14.50	
Ⓑ		**Dessert**	
		Zuppa inglese à la Jeannot	
		Fr. 7.50	

Name:
Kulturgüter(speise)wagen
(Bahnhof Buffet Basel)

Business type/character:
Restaurant opened during the art fair "Art 91" in Basel in connection with the "Kunst-Zug" (art-train) exhibited at that occasion, a rolling exhibition with seven coaches designed by renowned object artists; put on the rail by the art gallery owner Klaus Littmann in Basel. Catering was provided by the Bahnhof Buffet Basel's party service.

Card:
Menu card and list of beverages at the occasion of the "Art 91" fair.

Card system:
Simply folded paper cover printed on both sides, size when closed: 10.5 × 29.5 cm. Outside cover: graffiti-type design painted by the late artist Jean Tinguely who participated in the art-train. The names of all participating artists are listed on the rear side. Reproduced by color photocopier. The Kulturgüter(speise)wagen selection is printed on the inside on white background.

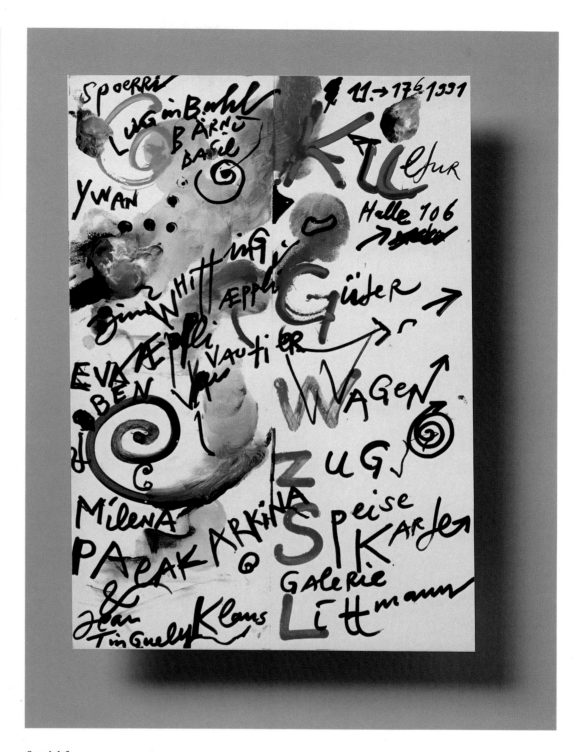

Special features:
Each Menu of the Day card was created by one of the artists participating in the art-train. Today the original cover drawing is exhibited in the Bahnhof Buffet Basel. Coach photograph: title picture of the art-train presentation brochure.

Draft/Design:
The artist Jean Tinguely

Name:
Stockheim-Gastronomie, Düsseldorf

Business type/character:
Various gastronomical conceptions, predominantly at high-volume traffic locations (airports, railroad stations). Party-service.

Card:
Multi-functional special campaign card.

Card system:
Simply folded cover, punched edges, gloss-foil laminated on both sides. Size when closed: 15 × 21 cm. Outside covers entirely covered by photo motif, inside featuring green background with alternating white text print depending upon objective and purpose.

Special features:
Multi-purpose cards for all of the company's establishments. Predominantly used for seasonal campaigns centered around "Freshness"—corresponding to the cover picture's message. Also to be used for special events or as menu card.

Draft/Design:
U.H. Meyer, Düsseldorf (cover photo)

Name:
Mövenpick Restaurants Switzerland/Germany (Mövenpick Unternehmungen, Adliswil)

Business type/character:
Emphasis on enjoyment, casualness. Profile emphasis: quality and diversion. Seasonal cuisine. Uniform basic philosophy; appearance and selection vary.

Card:
Special campaign card for steak tartare.

Card system:
Modified miscellaneous folding: folded-in rear side is narrower. Size when closed: 22.5×34 cm. Full formatted photo illustration on both sides; gloss-foil laminated. Motif on the outside cover shows the basic products on tiled background, campaign title and logo printed on front side. Insides entirely covered with motif on the same background: all campaign dishes are composed on plates. Selection listed on fold-in page in rectangular field. Identification by numbers. Prices are individually added at a later time. Fold-in page on the outside shows the basic product version; analogous design with product photo and text field.

Special features:
Unusual top-view perspective—effective arrangement of products. Product photos have high appetite appeal, which is further increased by dominance of the visual presentation over the text. Card is element of the company's centralized card pool to be used by all Swiss and German restaurants.

Draft/Design:
Mövenpick Werbung Restaurants Schweiz, Adliswil

175

Name:
Mövenpick Restaurants Switzerland/Germany (Mövenpick Unternehmungen, Adliswil)

Business type/character:
Emphasis on enjoyment, casualness. Profile emphasis: quality and diversion. Seasonal cuisine. Uniform basic philosophy; appearance and selection vary.

Cards:
Insertion sheets for promotion campaigns, used for small product-related promotions.

Card system:
Cardboards sized 15 × 29.5 cm, colored photo motif on the top of front cover. Back side blank. The selection is inscribed by the respective restaurant. Motifs consist of product arrangements referring to the promotion theme, predominantly in top-view perspective. In some instances enlivening of background through color stripes.

Special features:
Card is element of the company's centralized card pool to be used by all Swiss and German restaurants. There is a large number of additional motifs available other than those depicted above, as well as numerous table sets in corresponding design.

Draft/Design:
Mövenpick Werbung Restaurants Schweiz, Adliswil

1 GAMBERI «NOILLY PRAT»	2 GAMBERI «ROSE ISLAND»	3 GAMBERI «CURRY»	4 GAMBERI «MAH-MEE»	5 GAMBERI FRITTI	6 GAMBERI «DANIELI»
Con salsa al pesce e alla panna aromatizzata al Noilly Prat, porri, sedano e carote. Con riso.	Saltati su salsa Rose Island, con insalata di mele e ananas. Con pane brioche tostato.	Con mango, peperoni, porri, funghi cinesi e salsa alla panna e al curry. Con riso.	Con porri, carote, funghi cinesi, funghi Shitake e tagliatelle cinesi, affinati con da salsa di sola e curry.	Con insalata di zucchine e finocchi, e salsa alla tartara.	Spiedino arrostito e gratinato con burro Café de Paris. Con spinaci al burro e riso.
Fr. 20.50	Fr. 18.50	Fr. 22.50	Fr. 23.50	Fr. 21.50	Fr. 21.50

Draft/Design:
Mövenpick Werbung Restaurants Schweiz, Adliswil

Name:
Mövenpick Restaurants Switzerland/Germany (Mövenpick Unternehmungen, Adliswil)

Business type/character:
Emphasis on enjoyment, casualness. Profile emphasis: quality and diversion. Seasonal cuisine. Uniform basic philosophy; appearance and selection vary.

Card:
Promotion card for Gamberi (king prawns).

Card system:
Simply folded cover printed on both sides with photographic motifs and gloss-foil laminated. Size when closed 22.5 × 34 cm. Full formatted motif on the outer sides: a minimum of atmosphere-creating accessories on a stone plate. Outside front cover with promotion title on grey background and set-off logo. Cover insides: all promotion dishes composed on plates on the same background. Selection listed at sheet bottom on grey background; identified by numerals.

Special features:
Strong animating effect by top-view perspective. Predominance of the photo motifs creates a high appetite appeal. Card is element of the company's centralized card pool to be used by all Swiss and German restaurants. The offered selection depends upon the location.

178

Card system:
Simply folded cover printed on both sides with photographic motifs and gloss-foil laminated. Size when closed 22.5 × 34 cm. Full formatted motif on the outside covers with vegetables on garden soil. Campaign title and logo on outside front cover. Inside pages: all promotion dishes composed on plates on the soil background. Selection with description and prices listed at sheet bottom; identified by numerals.

Special features:
Top-view perspective creates an impression of product abundance. High appetite appeal through dominance of photo motifs. Background decoration matching the product group image with strong atmospherical effect. Card is element of the company's centralized card pool to be used by all Swiss and German restaurants.

Draft/Design:
Mövenpick Werbung Restaurants Schweiz, Adliswil

Name:
Mövenpick Restaurants Switzerland/Germany (Mövenpick Unternehmungen, Adliswil)

Business type/character:
Emphasis on enjoyment, casualness. Profile emphasis: quality and diversion. Seasonal cuisine. Uniform basic philosophy; appearance and selection vary.

Card:
Promotion card for high-quality whole foods.

ROHKOST-SALAT	SELLERIE-SCHEIBEN	GALETTEN	SHITAKEPILZE UND GEMÜSE	VOLLKORN-SPAGHETTI	SALAT-KOMPOSITION	GEMÜSE-SELEKTION	FRISCHKORN-MÜESLI	ROHKOST-PALETTE	TORTILLA
Richtige Vollwerternährung beginnt bekanntlich mit Rohkost. So empfehlen wir Ihnen als VORSPEISE unseren Rohkost-Salat.	In Vollkornbrösel leicht paniert und gebraten, mit Lauchstreifen auf einer Weisswein-Buttersauce und einem Vollgriess-Gnocchi.	Grünkern- und Vollreis-Galetten mit Basilikum und Thymian gewürzt, in Butter gebraten. Gemischtes Gemüse und Sauce tomates concasses.	Reichhaltiges Gemüse-Pilzgericht mit Soja-Mirin-sauce, fernöstlich gewürzt und mit Vollreis serviert.	Mit Eierschwämmli, kalt gepresstem Olivenöl, frischem Basilikum und gerösteten Pinienkernen.	Wirz- und Stangenselleriesalat an Joghurt-Dressing, rohe Ronden, gekochtes Ei, Apfelschnitze, Sesamsamen und ein Haferflocken-Gerstenbrötli mit Schnittlauchquark.	Eine Auswahl von sieben frischen Gemüsen mit Kürbiskern-Mousseline.	Mit geschrotetem Dinkel, Weizen, Roggen und Hafer. Zubereitet mit Joghurt, frischen Früchten, Honig, Zitronensaft und Rahm. Garniert mit Baumnüssen, Sonnenblumen- und Kürbiskernen.	Rohe Gemüse und Früchte mit Kräuter- und Quark-Dip, gekeimter Linsensalat und geröstete Kürbiskerne.	Flache Omelette mit sautierten Zwiebelstreifen, Gemüse und frischen Eierschwämmli.
Fr. 4.20	Fr. 15.30	Fr. 14.70	Fr. 16.50	Fr. 16.80	Fr. 11.–	Fr. 13.80	Fr. 7.80	Fr. 14.50	Fr. 12.60

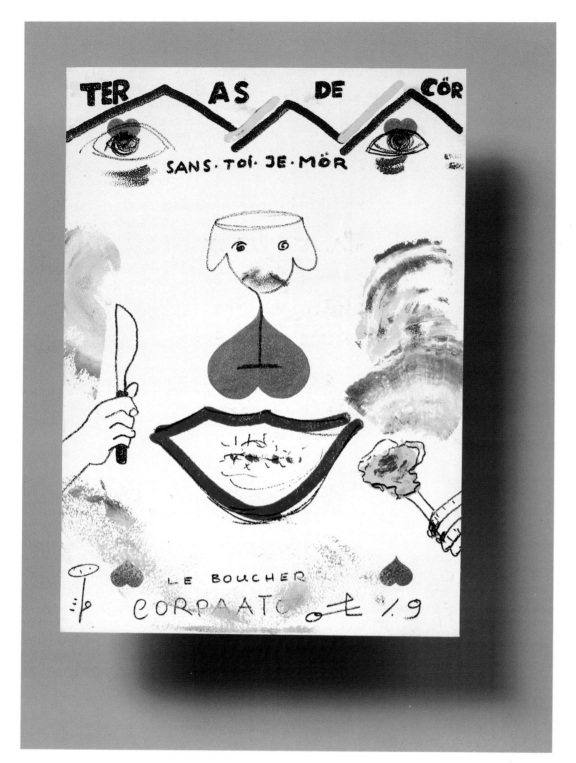

Name:

Golfhotel Les Hauts de Gstaad, Saanenmöser

Business type/character:

Restaurant on the sun deck of the hotel "Ter as de cör."

Cards:

Terrace cards in summer season 1991.

Card system:

Single sheets printed on both sides, sized 15 × 21 cm. The card: the back side is designed like the ace of hearts, front cover without specific motif. Basic decoration is preprinted, the selection is handwritten and subsequently copied in. Each card features a menu proposal or a message for the reader/guest; between six and eight such sheets are held together with clothespins.

Special features:

The cards are the product of an open-house performance in July 1991: the butcher-innkeeper-cook-artist Corpaato painted an oversized (approximately 7 m high) ace-of-hearts card with a knife. The ace-of-heart motif is the result of a Corpaato play on words: "terasse de coeur" sounds similar to "as de coeur" (ace of hearts). The card was honored as most original menu card 1991 by the university of St. Gallen.

Draft/Design:

The artist Corpaato (Jean Pierre Corpataux), Freiburg, Switzerland

DIE GURKE

Name:
Gutsausschank Schloss Vollrads, Oestrich-Winkel

Business type/character:
Restaurant in estate castle, idyllic location, sophisticated country-style cooking.

Cards:
Group of special promotion cards, three product-related topics: strawberries, cucumbers, nettle.

Card system:
Uniform card design: simply folded cover, outside covers illustrated and gloss-foil laminated, left inside features information on the promoted product, the selection is listed on the right side. Each front outside cover with a product-related picture motif, a visual reference to the estate castle. The promoted product is stated below the picture. The rear cover side features an artistic variation on the topic.

182

Special features:

The promotion cards are used on a yearly basis depending upon season. The humorous character of the illustrations generates a sympathetic effect. The brochure with the recipes for the offered dishes is on sale with each special card; the brochure has the same cover illustration and size. Guests are informed about the brochure in the promotion card.

Draft/Design:

The artist Michael Apitz, Geisenheim (illustrations)

DIE ERDBEERE

DIE BRENNESSEL

Playground for creative forms of expression

Actually the idea of table and tray sets was born in a very functional environment: in the world of fast-food restaurants as it emerged a few decades ago. It had to come up with a substitute – in concentrated form – for both table cloth and menu card. The goal was for the result to be both aesthetically pleasing and communicative in nature. The beginnings were in essence very rational efforts, typically to be found in self-service restaurants.

Today, we also frequently find table and tray sets in restaurants with a service-concept, and only rarely do they serve as an alternative to menu cards. The use as the single visual signal of significance (as in Maredo steakhouses during their first years) has also gone out of fashion; today the set is generally used as an additional supporting medium.

Relieved of the burden of being singly responsible for communicating the services offered, they could now become a totally new carrier of information; suddenly these pieces of paper became a playground for new possibilities in design and aesthetics. In comparison to regular menu-cards they now achieve less and more at the same time. With growing emancipation from the information-objective, the sets could now be used as a marketing-instrument: the emphasis shifted to advertisement.

Today, the set's scale of function by far surpasses the merchandizing possibilities of classical cards. Beginning with

* the emphasis on information – analogous to the menu-card – over to
* a combination of information and stimulation all the way to
* a purely decorative, animating effect.

The set is especially interesting because a customer will have it right in front of his eyes during his entire stay in a restaurant – much different than a menu-card. This is quite a chance for marketing coaches to put to use more differentiated marketing strategies.

The stimulating effect of the set helps to underline certain articles or groups of articles, and to influence the frequency of sales. Character and design in this case reflect the self-image of the particular concept: the emphasis is either on the financially attractive or the emotionally charged aspect.

Wording and illustration set the desired effects – the stronger the visual stimulation, the stronger the effect measurable in sales. Whether the offers are listed with price included or suggestive 'food' photography speaks for itself – this depends on the amount of influence desired and on the general concept.

This of course is only the case in service-concept restaurants; here a set is advertisement at the 'point of sale'. The customer's attention can directly or indirectly be directed to certain products/groups of products before he makes up his mind.

This is different in self-service-concepts: here the set will underline the sale directly. The influencing effect looses importance. Instead: brandname, image presentation, and emotional reminders set signals to motivate a return visit.

The great forte of table and tray sets is their versatility. They lend themselves in an exceptional way to create visual accents: to stimulate sales in certain product-segments, for various special attractions and promotions, and for additional sales and testing new products. But there are also purely aesthetically pleasing possibilities to emphasize an image – with no ties to any particular product.

The lines between product and image advertisement are of course very softly drawn. A pleasing presentation always expresses a statement about the establishment's self-image. Care needs to be taken where a concrete offer is realistically pictured. The limiting factor in this case is having to stay very close to reality. It is okay to opt for visual attraction, but any idealization is damaging to credibility. Any awakened expectation needs to be redeemable.

No doubt – Mövenpick has distinguished itself in this discipline among the gastronomical systems in Central Europe: their use of table sets has been extraordinarily creative. This Swiss enterprise offers ample evidence of how to completely free the set-visuals from delivering product information. The sheer aesthetic enjoyment, not burdened by any literal reference to the product sold, becomes a subtle but effective mood-setter.

In general, Swiss gastronomical industry has contributed many innovative ideas to this theme. One should take the chance to be inspired by the multitude of design ideas.

Almost all examples document the change in set design, with the trend going to to pure imagery – in some cases at an almost artistic level. Nowhere else is there so much freedom in communicating with the customer, the possibilities are nearly unlimited. They go all the way to exclusive artist's designs – a very effective contribution to corporate culture.

In this conception as design and marketing playground, the table or tray set of course by far surpasses the menu-card function. This is just the strongpoint of this discipline – it sets impulses in design and strongly influences all 'neighbouring' means of communication in a restaurant.

At the same time, there are many possibilities of integrating the set into the corporate design. Visual and thematic references, playing with quotations – all elements of visual presentation can be tied into a harmonious whole. Or even further: set series matching in design, or bringing into the game a supplier or sponsor.

This last example could also be a possibility for individual restaurants in order to work with table or tray sets. It is true, that up to almost only multiplied systems have used this creative, versatile medium. It would be unwise, though, to put it down as an aesthetic luxury article: it is loaded with marketing potential!

Name:

Cindy Restaurants Switzerland
(Mövenpick Unternehmungen, Adliswil)

Business type/character:

Fast-food conception, counter service, profile products: burgers and pizza. Primarily targeted at the young and youthful. Multiplied.

Sets:

Two tray sets in cartoon style, resembling pop-art à la Roy Lichtenstein. Size: 36×26 cm (I love you), and 37×26 cm (take-away comic strip). Image advertising and overall promotion for pizza respectively take-away.

Special features:

The tray sets are elements of a comprehensive advertisement means package: posters, stickers, T-shirts printed with analogous topics, take-away folders. Recurring motifs/figures. Predominantly used for communication of prize contest and other join-in campaigns to strengthen guest affiliation and increase of brand's sympathy value. Pop art design and direct address—"Pick up a pizza"—is targeted at young clientele.

Draft/Design:

Klaus Winckler, Agentur Winckler, Frankfurt/ Main (illustrations)/Cindy

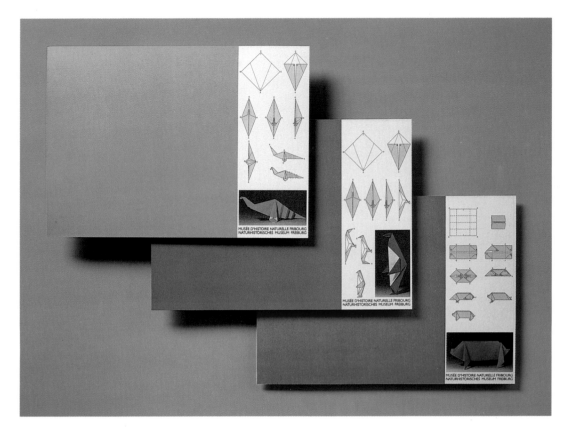

Name:
Naturhistorisches Museum Freiburg, Switzerland (natural historical museum)

Sets:
Four-part table set series, each set conceptualized as Origami folding game with instructions to fold animal figures. Size: 39 × 28 cm, perforated. External employment for advertisement for museum: the sets predominantly were made available to school cafeterias and other restaurants owned by public institutions in the Canton Freiburg (100,000 copies).

Special features:
Beautiful thematic reference to the museum. Awarded a gold medal and the jury's special prize in the Swiss table set design competition 1990 (patronage: Bruhin Druckerei, Freienbach).

Draft/Design:
Natural historical museum (idea)/Hannes Saxer, Bern (finished art work)/Agentur Conception Realisation, Communication Visuelle Roland Diacon, Berlin

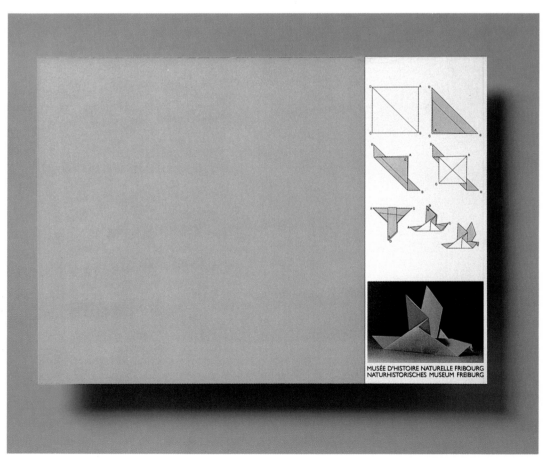

Name:
Romeo! Romeo!, Cologne
(Up to 1991; Spitz-Gruppe, Cologne)

Business type/character:
Italian bar. Mixed conception: café/bistro, emphasis on fun and communication. Contemporary style. Elegant positioning, small exquisite snacks.

Sets:
Two table set versions with purely atmospheric character. Printed in color. Size: 34 × 24 cm. Illustrations: artistic interpretations of the logo — the name plus waiter outline, the original in turquoise/red.

Special features:
The style of the color drawings implies identity statement: unconventional, modern, design-conscious. Unobtrusive inclusion of sponsors. Calling card ready for adding to address file. Universal utilization of the word-image logo for all other communication and advertisement means.

Draft/Design:
Agentur Axis, Cologne

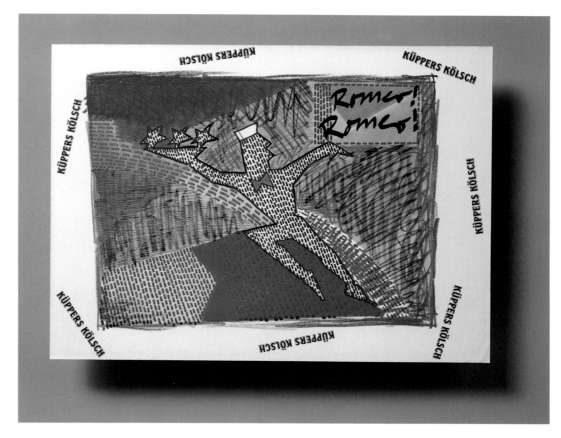

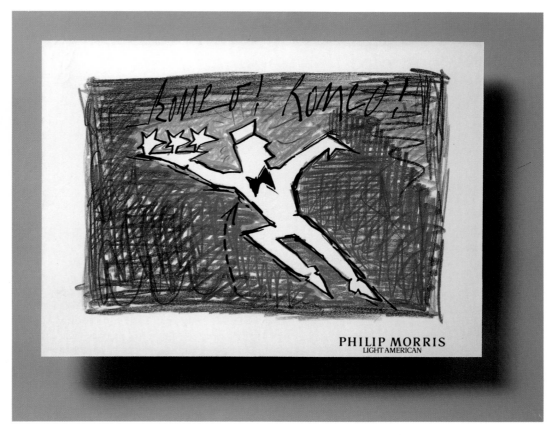

189

Name:
Wienerwald-Restaurants Germany
(Wigast, Vienna)

Business type/character:
Poultry specialties, multiplied.

Sets:
Two table sets in related design. Size: 34 × 24
cm. Chicken breast filet motif is employed in the
scope of a special sales drive (product test), supplementary to the menu card. This campaign offer is not listed in the standard menu card.
Supporting poster with analogous motif. Duck
table set for promotion of duck campaign. Employed supplementary to the menu card, this
product was also not listed in the standard card
at the time.

Special features:
Duck table set is part of a comprehensive sales
promotion package. Other advertisement means
in the restaurants: window posters, table show
cards, ceiling hangers, buttons for employees,
napkins with imprinted action symbols for duck
(see table set), small flags for sticking into the
grilled duck. Folder for distribution in take-
away sale. Small clay ducks as gift and sympathy
winners for guests.

Draft/Design:
Wienerwald Deutschland (conception)/Hild-
mann & Schneider, Düsseldorf

Frisch aus der Pfanne:
3 Medaillons
Schweinemedaillons
„Flandern"

in Champignonrahmsauce,
dazu Rosenkohl, in Speck
und Zwiebeln geschwenkt
und Kartoffelkroketten

11.⁹⁵

Familientag für 25 Mark:
2 Schnitzel nach Wahl
und 2 Kinderschnitzel „Bob der Bär".
Echt stark für 6 Mark:
Ab 15 Uhr servieren wir Ihnen Schnitzel auf Toast:
Schnitzeltoast Baden, Hawaii, Puszta und Jäger Art.

Genußideen im Restaurant-Café. **KAUfHOF.**

In bester Gesellschaft…
Spargel & Puter
Riesenportion

Stangenspargel mit Putenschnitzel im
Eimantel gebacken, dazu Sauce Hollandaise
und Petersilienkartoffeln.

12.⁹⁵

Familientag für 25 Mark:
2 Schnitzel nach Wahl
und 2 Kinderschnitzel „Bob der Bär".
Echt stark für 6 Mark:
Ab 15 Uhr servieren wir Ihnen Schnitzel auf Toast:
Schnitzeltoast Baden, Hawaii, Puszta und Jäger Art.

Genußideen im Restaurant-Café. **KAUfHOF.**

Name:
Kaufhof-Gastronomie
(KGSG Kaufhof Gastronomie Service Gesellschaft, Cologne)

Business type/character:
Restaurants in Kaufhof department stores; wide-ranged selection and target group approach.

Sets:
Series of three sets sized at 40 × 28 cm, used as table sets in service restaurants and as tray set in self-service establishments. Supplementary to menu card: targeted promotion of one special product not listed in standard card. At the same time used as promotion medium for the product group "Schnitzel."

Special features:
High degree of animation through large-formatted product photographs.

Draft/Design:
Agentur Hessel, Solingen

Goldrichtig gewählt:
3 Medaillons
mit Folienkartoffel

3 Schweinemedaillons mit würziger
Kräuterbutter, dazu eine
Folienkartoffel mit
Schnittlauchquark gefüllt

11.⁵⁰

Genußideen im Restaurant-Café. KA

Name:

Kartoffel mit…(Potatoes with…), Hamburg (Deutsche Service-Gesellschaft der Bahn, Frankfurt/Main)

Business type/character:

Potato specialties, developed for market halls, railroad station stands, etc. This location: colonnade at Hamburg's central railroad station. Fast-food conception, limited selection. Look-in kitchen with round-about counter.

Sets:

Table resp. counter set with menu card function. Size: 41.5 × 29.5 cm. Food and beverage selection at a glance. Menu of the Day communicated via show boards. The set's coloring fits the product in earthy colors with vigorous color accents in the typography.

Special features:

The table set's specific communication objective: easy-to-understand explanation of the combination principle with three basic products and progressive price rates depending upon the group of ingredients.

Draft/Design:

Hamburger Bahnhofsgaststätten Gesellschaft (DSG, Frankfurt/Main)

Name:
Spaghetti Factory, Switzerland
(Bindella Unternehmungen, Zurich)

Business type/character:
Young specialty conception with product emphasis upon spaghetti; profile basis: the Italo-American spaghetti culture. Multiplied.

Sets:
Two table set versions: breakfast set and standard set. Size: 39 × 28.5 cm. Coloring varies the logo's two colors. Both sets also have menu card function; the breakfast selection as well as the basic spaghetti assortment are exclusively communicated via sets. Supplementary special cards employed for promotion of the fringed assortment groups also listed on the standard set.

Special features:
The set is designed to resemble the Stars and Stripes. This underlines the conception's foundation in the American, esp. Californian way of life. This approach is maintained all the way to naming the offered dishes. Corporate design conception; logo and stripe motif also used for merchandise products and other communication means. The spaghetti photo is taken from the current image brochure.

Draft/Design:
Werbeatelier Gerhard Brauchle, Thal/Lesch & Frei Werbeagentur, Zurich (logo, table sets)

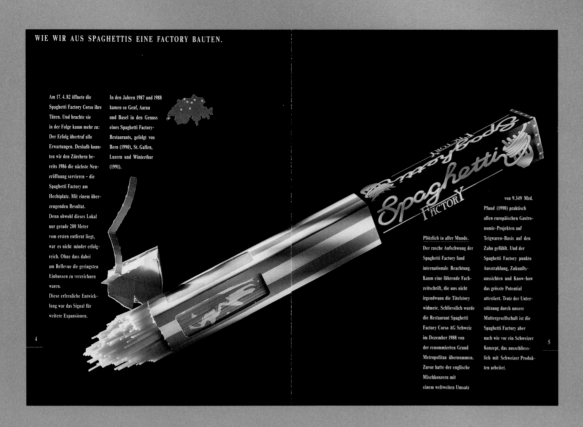

Name:
Orion Restaurants und Kongresszentrum, Zurich
(until spring 1990: Kramer Restaurationsbetriebe, Uitikon-Waldegg)

Business type/character:
Restaurant complex with day-time restaurant
and gourmet restaurant (Orion Le Gourmet),
congress capacities.

Sets:
Table set series with four motifs, used in the
day-time restaurant. No menu card function;
decorative-atmospherical background and advertisement for the congress center and gourmet restaurant. Size: 40 × 28 cm.

Special features:
The table sets' photo motifs and layouts repeat
the motifs on the Le Gourmet menu card. Alternating promotion text. Awarded a gold medal
and the jury's special prize in the Swiss table set
design competition 1988 (patronage: Bruhin
Druckerei, Freienbach).

Draft/Design:
Agentur Marty, Köniz (Bern)

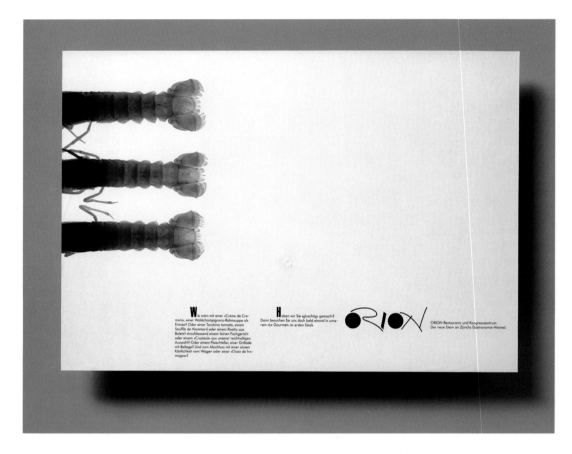

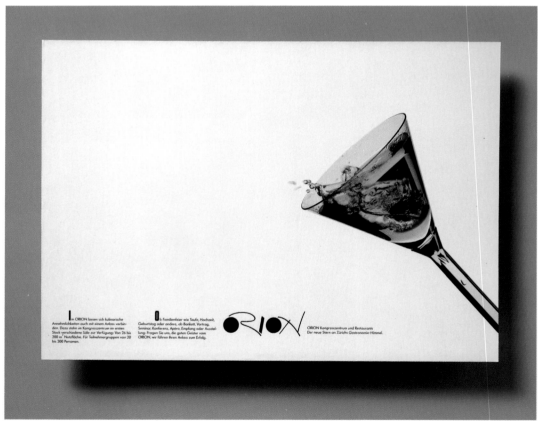

Kennen Sie unser «Le Gourmet» im ersten Stock? Nein? Dann schauen Sie doch mal herein. Kommen Sie die Treppe hoch und lassen Sie sich überraschen. Von der imposanten Präsentation der frischen Tagesangebote auf dem mit Crushed-Ice gefüllten Buffet. Von der Innenarchitektur und der Ambiance.

Lassen Sie sich vom Chef-de-Service die Karte zeigen oder gleich einen Tisch reservieren. Für heute abend. Oder für morgen. Für ein Tête-à-tête, eine Familienfeier oder ein geschäftliches Treffen. Ganz wie Sie wünschen – wir sind für Sie da.

ORION Restaurants und Kongresszentrum: Der neue Stern an Zürichs Gastronomie-Himmel.

Die ORION Restaurants bieten mehr. Wer das «Le Gourmet» im ersten Stock besucht, weiss, wovon wir sprechen: Von einem kulinarischen Erlebnis erster Güte.

Sehen die fantastische Präsentation der frischen Tagesspezialitäten auf dem mit Crushed-Ice gefüllten Buffet lässt Gutes ahnen. Das Versprechen wird eingelöst: Von einer Küchenbrigade, die ihren Beruf als Berufung versteht. Von Servicemitarbeitern, denen es Freude macht, Gäste zu verwöhnen.

ORION Restaurants und Kongresszentrum: Der neue Stern an Zürichs Gastronomie-Himmel.

Name:
Merkur-Restaurants, Switzerland
(Merkur, Bern)

Business type/character:
Approximately 30 restaurants in shopping centers and highly frequented urban locations. Oriented towards families and stop-and-go eating.

Sets:
Table set ensemble with four seasonal motifs, matching the respective season's menu card and beverage list. Size: 39×28 cm. Exclusively menu-card-accompanying atmospherical function. The sets' layout utilizes individual elements taken from the title collages of the cards on white background; a short illustrative text in addition.

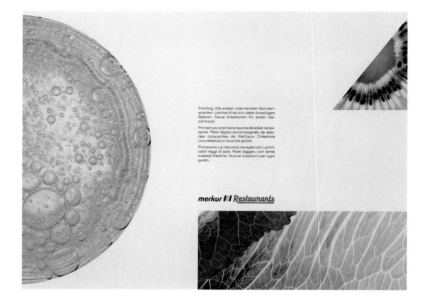

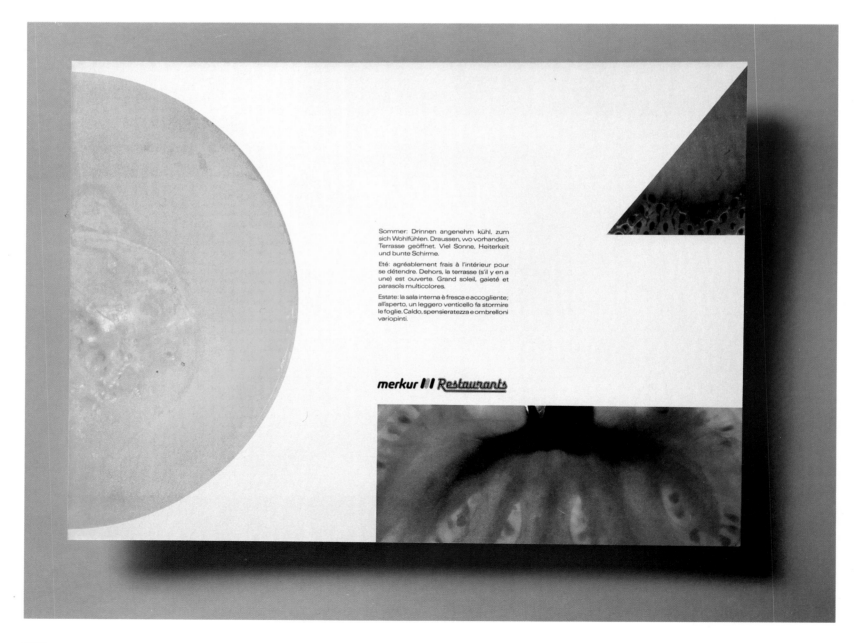

Herbst: Erntezeit. Die Natur bietet ihre Gaben an; vielfältig und reichhaltig. Warme Farben verbreiten ihre wohltuende Wirkung.

Automne: les récoltes battent leur plein. La nature se révèle dans toute sa générosité et sa variété. Les teintes chaudes dispensent leur rayonnement apaisant.

Autunno: tempo di vendemmia; la natura è prodiga di doni, ricchi e preziosi. I colori diventano più sfumati, riempiono l'animo di dolci sensazioni.

merkur ||| Restaurants

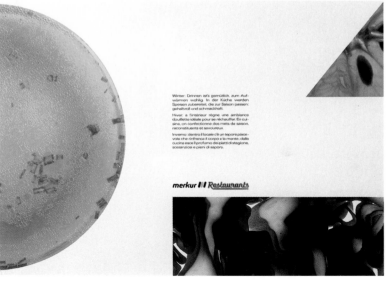

Winter: Drinnen ist's gemütlich, zum Aufwärmen wohlig. In der Küche werden Speisen zubereitet, die zur Saison passen: gehaltvoll und schmackhaft.

Hiver: à l'intérieur règne une ambiance douillette idéale pour se réchauffer. En cuisine, on confectionne des mets de saison, reconstituants et savoureux.

Inverno: dentro il locale c'è un tepore piacevole che rinfranca il corpo e la mente; dalla cucina esce il profumo dei piatti di stagione, sostanziosi e pieni di sapore.

merkur ||| Restaurants

Special features:
An example for the complete emancipation of the table set apart from the selection communication/product-related sales promotion. Instead: image promotion, atmospheric impulses.

Draft/Design:
Agentur Marty, Köniz (Bern)

199

Name:
Mövenpick-Restaurants Switzerland/Germany (Mövenpick Unternehmungen, Adliswil)

Business type/character:
Emphasis on enjoyment, casualness. Profile emphasis: quality and diversion. Seasonal cuisine. Uniform basic philosophy; appearance and selection vary.

Sets:
Selection of 18 motifs from the company's extensive central table set pool, principally usable by all Swiss and German businesses. Size: 40 × 30 cm. Employed parallel to product-related actions but strictly detached from actual offer communication. Exclusively atmosphere supporting, animating and at the same time image supporting function. Appetite appeal as focus point.

Special features:
Three examples of the table set series in uniform basic layout. Typical: colored background bars with transparent effect, the depicted items seem to float. The sets serve to visually support pasta, oyster, and salad campaigns. The salad and pasta motifs were awarded a bronze medal in the Swiss table set design competition 1990 (patronage: Bruhin Druckerei, Freienbach).

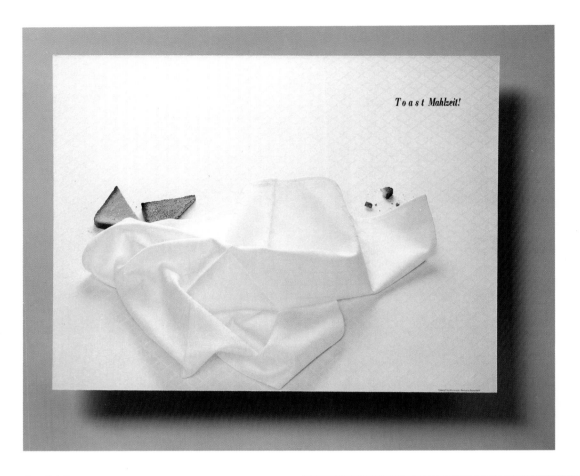

Special features:

Shrimps and toast table set: minimalistic design. Typical: the top-view perspective preferred by Mövenpick.

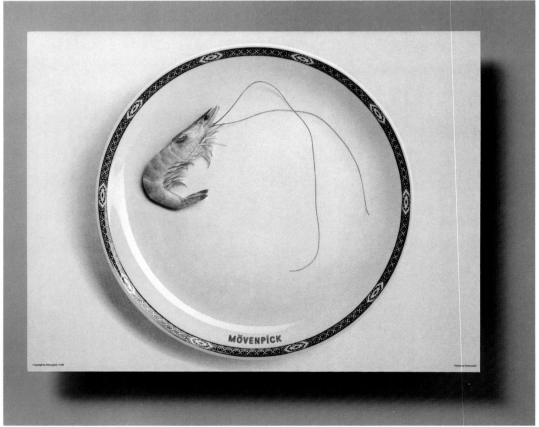

Printed in Switzerland, Copyright by Mövenpick

Special features:
Three examples for visual "origin marketing": soil, grain, high-quality food. Depiction of the promoted products/product group in its natural, "live" surroundings. Matching earthy, warm, harmonious colors.

Special features:

Three table set examples with related layout conception: apples, artichokes, avocados. Typical: a fruit cut open in front of many fruits. Original idea for apple set (and rare deviation from the principle of pure food photography): the table set inside the table set.

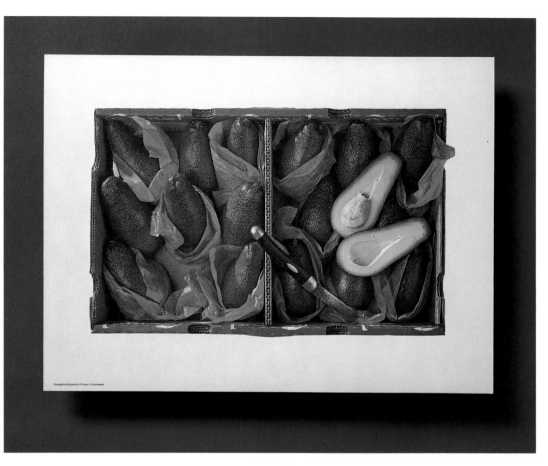

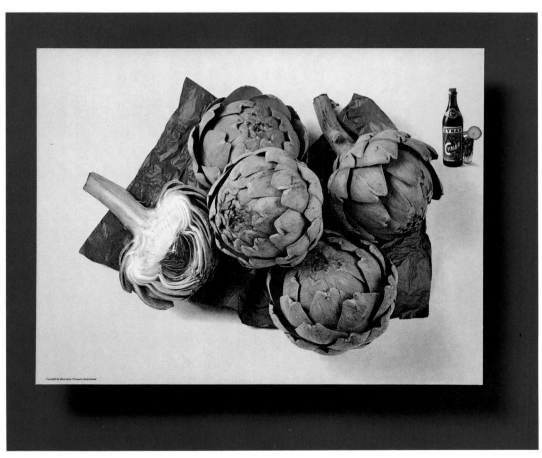

Special features:

Four examples for table sets; melon/asparagus
in frontal perspective, lobster/curry in top-view
perspective. Perspective determines the drama-
turgic structure of the motifs.

Draft/Design:
Mövenpick Werbung Restaurants Schweiz,
Adliswil

209

Name:
Sais, Zurich

Business type/character:
Up-stream industry company; convenience producer.

Sets:
Table set series in uniform layout with four illustration motifs on the topic "dessert," size: 38 × 27 cm. Humorous cartoons with text bubbles and punch line: "A meal without dessert is like…" No menu card function; purely product-group promotion.

Special features:
Table set series was made available to Swiss restaurant operators as service article for promotion purposes. Awarded the bronze medal in the Swiss table set design competition 1988 (patronage: Bruhin Druckerei, Freienbach).

Draft/Design:
Troxler & Hunziker, Zurich

**Ein Essen ohne Dessert
ist wie ein Kavalier ohne Rosen!**

**Ein Essen ohne Dessert
ist wie ein Liebesfilm ohne Happy-End!**

Nestlé-Foodservice, 4007 Basel ©   la chasse est ouverte.   A.P.Perrot 88

Nestlé-Foodservice, 4007 Basel ©   Le grand buffet   A.P.Perrot 88

Name:
Nestlé Foodservice, Basel

Business type/character:
Up-stream industry company; convenience producer.

Sets:
"L'humour gourmand": table set series with four illustration motifs making fun of culinary topics: "Le grand buffet," "Nouvelle cuisine," "Catering aèrien," "La chasse est ouverte." Size: 39 × 28 cm. Purely atmosphere-related function. Produced in fall 1990 for a fixed period of time in the course of a sales-promotion campaign; table sets as promotion product for clients from the gastronomy business.

Special features:
Awarded the gold medal in the Swiss table set design competition 1991 (patronage: Bruhin Druckerei, Freienbach).

Draft/Design:
A.P.Peret (drawings)/Nestlé

Name:
Pizzeria/Trattoria mamma mia, Rorschach

Business type/character:
Typical Italian pizza parlor, popular, uncomplicated.

Sets:
Selection from a series of altogether eight table sets published at the occasion of the restaurant's tenth anniversary. Exclusively atmospheric function. All sets in same layout and with identical text. Alternating color illustration in sketch technique with improvised appearance. Food motif—typical local products. Size: 39 × 28 cm.

Special features:
The illustrations have an amusing delightful effect. The table set series was awarded a gold medal in the Swiss table set designer competition 1990 (Patronat: Bruhin Druckerei, Freienbach).

Draft/Design:
Didi Bischof, Grub SG (Illustration)/Rutishauser Werbung & Design, Grub SB

Name:
SSG Schweizerische Speisewagen-Gesellschaft, Olten

Business type/character:
Traffic-oriented gastronomy; on-board catering (catering in dining coach, mobile mini-bars), railroad-station buffets, motorway restaurants.

Set:
Christmas table set, used in all SSG dining coaches and restaurant businesses in the pre-Christmas season 1991. Size 29.5 × 21.5 cm. Exclusively atmosphere creating and image supporting function.

Special features:
Atmospheric and at the same time modern design, courting kitsch but softening this effect by layout and light effects. Awarded a gold medal and the jury prize in the Swiss table set design competition 1991 (patronage: Bruhin Druckerei, Freienbach).

Draft/Design:
SSG (idea)/Angelica Hiltmann, Wettswil (creation)/Agire Advertising Gritti & Schaffhuser, Luzern (layout).

Name:
Bahnhof Buffet Basel

Business type/character:
Gastronomical service in the Basel SBB train station. Various business types; large centralized service center: Brasserie. High proportion of guests from the surrounding urban environment.

Sets:
Table set art: selection of four motifs from a series with approximately 20 subjects, each picture designed for the Bahnhof Buffet Basel from locally and internationally renowned artists. Used in the period of time between 1975 and 1984—an average of two new motifs per year. No menu card function; atmospheric, image designing momentum. The only prerequisite imposed upon the artists was the size—all sets: 40 × 29.5 cm. The majority of the b/w motifs show interpretations of the themes "railway station/train" and "gastronomy."

Special features:
The table set art was initiated by the then railroad restaurant's operator Emil Wartmann; the basic idea was to provide delight in art for everyone. The sets quickly advanced to collector's items. A limited edition of original graphics was printed for each motif. Today many of the originals are exhibited in the Bahnhof Buffet.

Draft/Design:
The artists Helen Sager, Romolo Esposito, Mario Grasser, Ben Vautier (and many others: illustrations/Bahnhof Buffet Basel (technical realization)

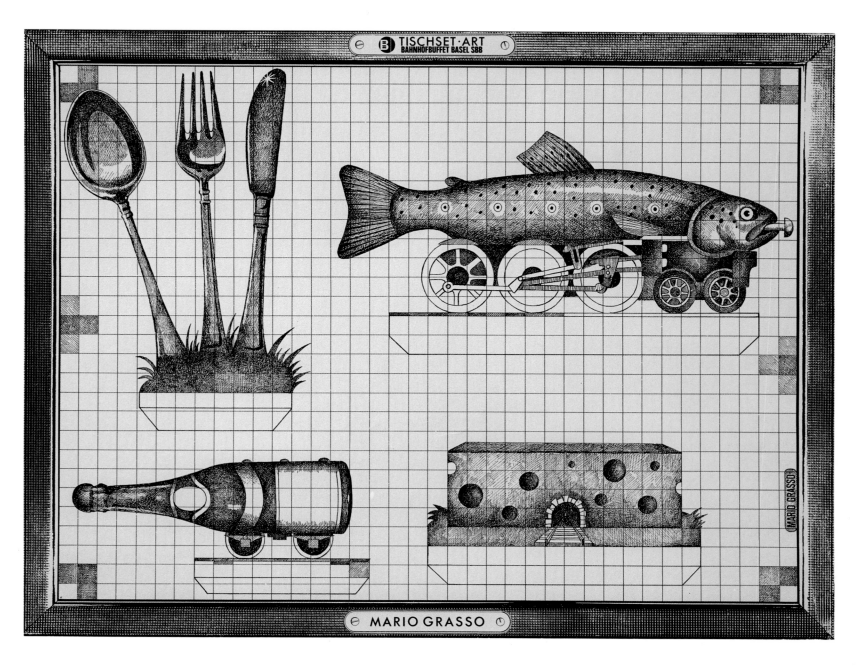

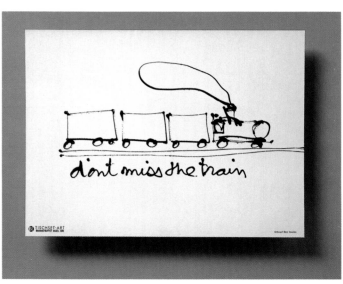

Focus on the promise of pleasure

To be stuck with the last place in the menu's natural hierarchy isn't exactly comfortable. The sweet little extra, the highlight of a culinary experience, has a much harder time finding its way onto your plate than its predecessors. It's really too annoying – a guest who has already worked his way through appetizers, a main course, and maybe even side-dishes has probably lost most of his appetite for more. And it's a rare customer who comes to a restaurant only to have a dessert!

So that's the situation – and the marketing objective is to pass precisely this hurdle.

Separating the dessert items from the other fare and giving them their own menu card is one strategic step in this concept. Having their own 'special appearance' releases the sweet products from being 'last in line'; presented in a separate card, a certain choice of desserts receives a lot more attention.

It is true, though, that dessert cards are to a very large degree pure ice cream cards. It is certain that the rise in popularity of ice cream in the restaurant business was instrumental in helping this independent form of presention for the last sweet course on its way. A dessert card comprised of only traditional desserts is harder to find, this can be easily explained in terms of marketing politics. Traditional desserts often involve quite an expenditure of labor, especially in the kitchen – so any restaurant's list of home-made desserts is probably going to be small. When offering ice creams, though,

it is comparatively easy to realize a wide variety of dishes.

But: together with the advantage of bringing special attention to this segment of products comes the disadvantage: special ice cream and dessert cards calls for increased expenditures. Special care needs to be given by the staff. In so far the strategy of isolating dessert is not without opponents.

If the concept of separate presentation is chosen, though, then it is necessary to stick to certain guidelines. Ice cream and dessert are very close to being impulse sales items, so to achieve a higher turnover in this segment, strong visual stimulation needs to be used. The only sales help here is the 'appetite appeal', so desserts should be shown off in a manner not to be overlooked. There could be no more rewarding theme for a food-stylist: after all, what could be more photogenic than a scrumptious dessert? Colorful, vibrant, sensuous – it's easy to come up with a whole list of attributes of visual lust.

Like no other product, these speciality cards, in particular ice cream cards, rely on photography to catch the eye. Modern examples show a trend away from simply depicting the product and towards developing a whole world of experience around the items offered.

A favourite theme in this context is the world of vacation and leisure; increasingly popular are very suggestive images which immediately bring to mind the joy of living, light-heartedness, exuberance: summer, sun, seaside and sports, lushy exotic nature. If people are depicted, they are young, beautiful, happy and dynamic. A world of images full of sensuality and pleasure, very often spiced with an erotic touch.

There are extreme cases in which the presentation of the product steps back completely behind the visual mise-en-scène of the joy to be alive. The attraction behind this kind of imagery – this we know very well from advertisement on TV and in cinemas – lies in the stimulation of the non-cog-

nitive parts of our consciousness. The objective is to charge the product with a wealth of meanings that promise much more than simply a delicious taste.

Coding and decoding of this image-symbolism is of course to a large degree dependent upon convention, fashion and lifestyle. In one word: zeitgeist. And really, ice cream and dessert cards are very visibly coloured by certain lifestyles. This also means: the visual appearance can go out-of-date relatively fast.

Ideally, the character of the sweet card correlates with the other cards used in a particular establishment. But this is no hard and fast rule: as in the case of specialty-cards, the ties of corporate design can be left behind. Creating a desire to have dessert in any case involves special, more psychological concepts.

This is why it is so convenient for a restaurant-proprietor to simply rely on the large assortment of menu cards the ice-cream industry holds in store for him. These companies have invested a lot to come up with attractive merchandizing-concepts and have significantly changed the overall style of dessert presentation.

Generally, dessert and ice-cream cards use a smaller format than the basic menu cards – but they make up for what they lack in size by using full fledged visual impact. Often this signal character is heightened even more by the use of high-gloss material. The most important rule is visual opulence. The temptation has to be simply irresistible!

Name:
Fröhlicher Rheinfelder Hof, Basel

Business type/character:
Hotel-gastronomy; two restaurants. Characterized by the close ties to carneval club activities centered around the Basel Carneval.

Card:
"Vacation in Basel": ice-cream dessert card, used in both restaurants.

Card system:
Miscellaneous folded card, size when closed: 14 × 30 cm. Illustrated on both sides in cheerful colored design, matching the basic cards' appearance. Inside and outside each with full-format motifs with numerous charming details. Cheerful alienation keeping in line with the product group: the Basel cathedral is transferred into a vacation beach landscape. Both motifs integrate the company's logo. The selection on the inner sides and folded-in back page is printed in preprinted background motif.

Special features:
Example for an animating graphic solution. Integrated into the corporate design conception in spite of an independent appearance.

Draft/Design:
The artist Däge, Däge Design, Basel

Name:
Gelateria della bella Puppa, Ingolstadt (up to late 1991)

Business type/character:
Ice cream café with Italian ambiance, classical ice cream café selection: ice cream specialties, drinks. Modern ambiance, primarily targeted at the young and youthful.

Card:
Selection card.

Card system:
Simple folded cover, asymmetrically punched. Maximum size: 21.5 × 37 cm. Gloss-foil laminated on both sides. Front cover page: logo and colorful illustration on black background, inside and back cover page with colorful typography on grey-white background.

Special features:
Modern appearance provided by cover motif, background decoration, and angled headlines respectively text blocks. The prime colors pink and mint are analogue to the interior colors.

Draft/Design:
Martin Mayer, Gelateria della bella Puppa/creativ display, Ingolstadt

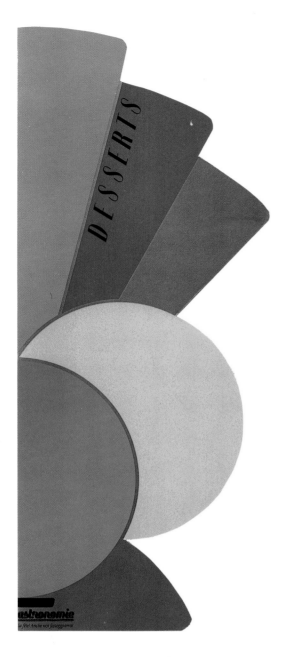

Name:
Merkur-Gastronomie, Switzerland
(Merkur, Bern)

Business type/character:
Approximately 30 restaurants in shopping-centers and urban high volume traffic locations, approximately 30 cafés, approximately 25 buffet/snack-bars and other business types.

Card:
Dessert card, employed with no reserves as to concept in restaurants, cafés, and a number of buffet-bars, altogether about 70 catering units.

Card system:
Cover plus eight inside pages, stapled. The maximum size when closed is 16×38 cm. Entirely gloss-foil laminated. Cover front and back pages featuring color collages with different colors. Selection with product photos on the inside, with various geometrical forms enlivening the picture.

Special features:
Cards appearance is relatively independent in comparison with the basic cards of the respective business types; the kinship is indicated by the collage technique on the cover.

Draft/Design:
Agentur Marty, Köniz (Bern)

Name:
Hard Rock Café, Frankfurt/Main

Business type/character:
Music pub, emphasis on drinks, with meeting-point character. Designed in lofthouse style.

Card:
Ice cream card with detailed information on the ice cream selection featured in the standard card.

Card system:
Simply folded cover, gloss-foil laminated on both sides, size when closed: 12 × 30 cm. On the outside colorful illustration in Zeitgeist-Design. Front cover page with classical Hard Rock logo. Selection on the inside, additional colors green and pink matching the colors on the basic card.

Special features:
The ice cream card's visual appearance is more colorful, more turbulent, more sensual than the basic card; it underlines the pleasure-oriented product group profile.

Draft/Design:
Gerd Baumann, CAW Werbung, Frankfurt/Main

HONEY MOON	
Vanilleeis, Maple walnut, Chocolat chip, heiße Honig-Schokoladensauce, Sahne	8,50

N. Y. HARLEM	
Schokoeis und Schokosauce auf Bourbon	8,50

CARAMELLO	
Caramelita, Maple walnut, Schoko- und Caramelsauce, Krokant und Sahne	6,50

Hard Rock CUP	
sechs verschiedene Sorten mit Baileys überzogen und Sahne	12,50

PINA COLADA	
Choco-Coconut, Vanille, Ananas und Pistazienstreusel	6,50

WAIKIKI BEACH CUP	
Coco-Nut, Erdbeer-Sorbet, Macadamia-Nuss, Früchte und ein Schuß karibischer Rum	7,50

BLACK MUSIC	
Choco-Coconut, Pistazie, Vanille, Caramelsauce, Sahne	7,50

HOT SUMMER NIGHT	
Apricotcreme, Stracciatella, Macadamia-Nuss, Espresso Croquant	8,50

COCO NUT	
Choco-Coconut, Eierlikör und Sahne	6,–

ROCKY MOUNTAIN	
Chocolat Chip, Espresso croquant, Pistazie, dipped in chocolat	7,50

Hard Rock HOT COFFEE	
heißer Kaffee mit Vanilleeis und Schuß	7,50

STRAWBERRY SENSATION	
ein Berg frischer Erdbeeren, Bourbon-Vanille, Stracciatella, Erdbeersorbet (saisonbedingt)	7,–

TARTUFO	
…bella italia!	4,–

CREAMSHAKES	
MAPLE WALNUT	4,50
CARAMEL	4,50
CHOCOLAT	4,50
COCOS	4,50
VANILLA	4,50
STRAWBERRY	4,50
UNSERE EISSCHOKOLADE …mit einem Hauch Tia Maria	4,50

TROPICAL FLOATS	
APERITIVO Zitronen-Sorbet mit Campari-Soda aufgefüllt	6,50
SUNSHINE FLOAT Vanilleeis mit Orangensaft	4,50
LEMON-FLOAT Zitroneneis mit Sprite	3,50

SORBETS	
ZITRONEN SORBET Zitroneneis mit Sekt	6,50
CHAMPAGNER-ANANAS-SORBET	6,50

STELLEN SIE IHREN EISBECHER
ZUSAMMEN AUS DEN SORTEN

Apricotcreme, Macadamia-Nuss, Stracciatella, Vanille, Pistazie, Zitronen-Sorbet, Chocolat Chip, Erdbeer-Sorbet, Cream-Erdbeere, Maple walnut, Espresso Croquant, Caramelita, Coco-Nut

DIE RIESENKUGEL	1,80
SCHLAGSAHNE	1,–

Name:
Churrasco Steakrestaurants Deutschland
(Whitbread Restaurants Holding Deutschland,
Düsseldorf/Whitbread-Gruppe, Great Britain)

Business type/character:
Steakhouse conception, multiplied.

Card:
Dessert card.

Card system:
Simply folded cover, printed on both sides,
gloss-foil laminated. Size when closed: 17.5 ×
29 cm. Visual appearance matching the basic
cards: cover with "floating" ingredients and
logo, inside with unattached "floating" depictions of the selection. Inserted text fields with
white background, typography black with red
initials; a reference to the logo colored white,
black and red.

Special features:
Easy-going, casual appearance of the dessert
card through light-colored background: matching product.

Draft/Design:
Churrasco Steakrestaurants Germany

Name:
Mövenpick Restaurants Schweiz/Deutschland
(Mövenpick Unternehmungen, Adliswil)

Business type/character:
Emphasis on enjoyment, casualness. Profile emphasis: quality and diversion. Seasonal cuisine.
Uniform basic philosophy; appearance and selection vary.

Card:
Summer collection: Mövenpick ice cream card
summer 1987.

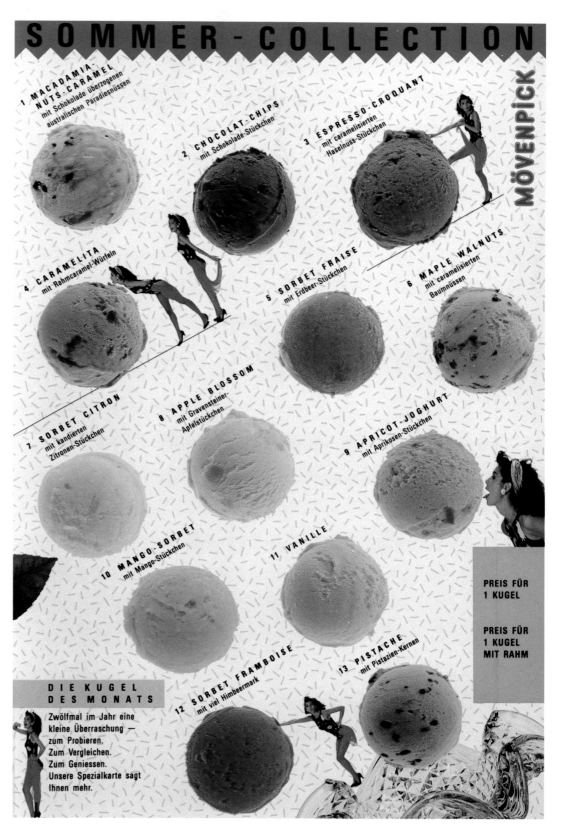

Card system:

Accordion-type folding, four-part, entirely printed on both sides, gloss-foil laminated. Size when closed: 20.5 × 31 cm. Front cover sheet with card title and logo. All selections including the different kinds of ice are depicted as balls; "floating" in front of slightly structured background. The back cover with background decoration is only for individual additional offers.

Special features:

Effective designer's idea: scantily clad girls in miniature format between the ice cream photographs. Witty alienation in the style of "Alice in Wonderland"; at the same time product-group-adequate charging of card with sensuality and joy of life.

Draft/Design:

Mövenpick Werbung Restaurants Schweiz/ Adliswil

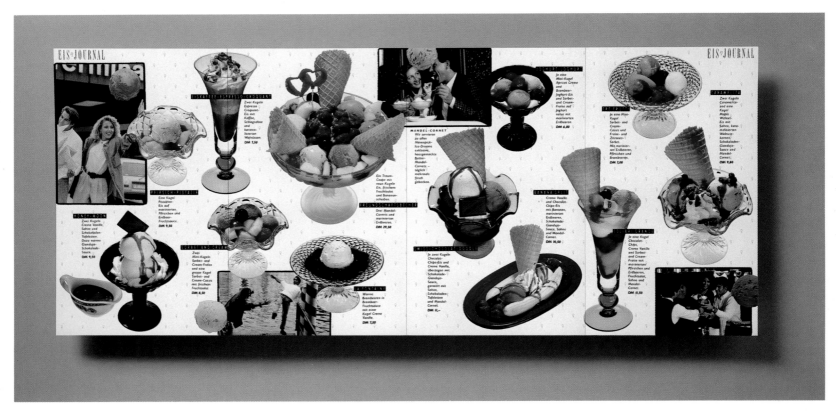

Name:
Mövenpick Restaurants Schweiz/Deutschland
(Mövenpick Unternehmungen, Adliswil)

Business type/character:
Emphasis on enjoyment, casualness. Profile emphasis: quality and diversion. Seasonal cuisine. Uniform basic philosophy; appearance and selection vary.

Card:
Eis-Journal: Mövenpick ice cream card 1989.

Card system:
Altar-like folding, entirely printed on both sides, gloss-foil laminated. Size when closed: 20.5 × 33 cm. Front cover sheet with card title and logo. Overall background decoration: tiny ice cream cones. Folded-in rear sides and inside with "floating" illustration of the offer. Ice drinks on the back side.

Special features:
The black and white photographs on the cover and selection pages boost the product group's pleasure appeal. The displayed motif combines joy of life and joy of ice. The design makes use of the transfer effect of strong meaningful pictures; the suggestive force emitted by utilization of human "performers" and spheres of experience is quite remarkable.

Draft/Design:
Mövenpick Werbung Restaurants Schweiz, Adliswil

Name:
Mövenpick Restaurants Schweiz/Deutschland
(Mövenpick Unternehmungen, Adliswil)

Business type/character:
Emphasis on enjoyment, casualness. Profile emphasis: quality and diversion. Seasonal cuisine. Uniform basic philosophy; appearance and selection vary.

Card:
Dreams of Ice Cream: Mövenpick ice cream card 1991.

Card system:
Cover plus four inside pages, folded, stapled. Entirely gloss-foil laminated. Round punched corners, size when closed: 23.5×37 cm. Unusual: staggered cross-format of the individual pages (width: $9/14/19/23.5$). When closed, the cards frontal view shows a lily; the motif is completed on the inside, partially highlighted as background decoration. Inside with "floating" depiction of the selection, ice drinks on back page.

Special features:
Picture motif (lily-blossoms with dew drops) stands for freshness and sensual-aesthetic experience. The card features an animating introductory text to each topic in addition to the product description.

Draft/Design:
Mövenpick Werbung Restaurants Schweiz, Adliswil

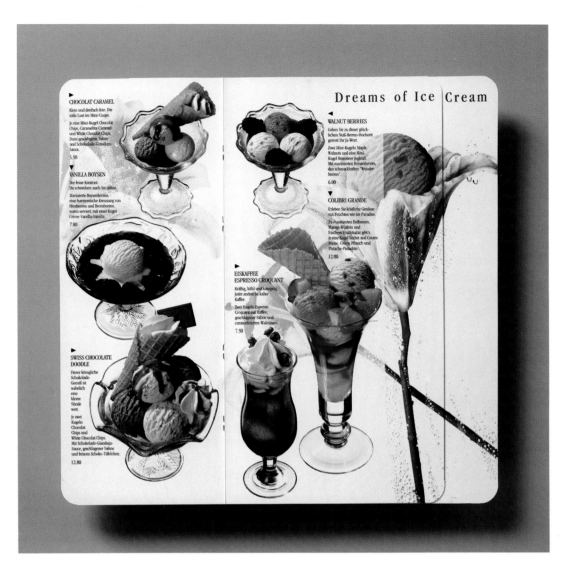

A different kind of design – suited for children

It's a well-known fact that today's children are tomorrow's target-group – but few restaurant operators have drawn as many marketing-consequences out of this insight as McDonald's. The restaurant world as a whole is not very well adapted to children and their special needs – easy to see why. But still it's impossible to completely ignore them: parents will just bring them along. And not only to fast-food restaurants.

This is where a far-sighted entrepreneur should call to mind: the little ones tend to remember very well where they have been made to feel welcome, which restaurants provided children's corners, comfortable high-chairs and funny, entertaining menues made just for them. There is no question they will make themselves heard the next time the family is debating on where to go for dinner. Even much later, the former child, now a parent him or herself, will fondly remember the places which courted their favors so long ago …

Where the young guests are concerned, menu-card design is a totally different game. To them the information which dishes are specially prepared for them is not of primary importance. The actual number of items may even be very small; we all know that kids' culinary expectations tend to be modest. Their list of requirements is led by other desires.

The first demand on children's menu-cards is that they be entertaining. A well-made card keeps them occupied until their parents have finished eating. So this is what counts: keep them busy! Help them to pass the time with imagination and creativity.

That is why children's menu cards have become a favorite designer object. This is where they can put to use their most outrageous and playful ideas. Creativity may flow in wider channels – forget about corporate design, image and profile.

The objective is to give children something to play with, something that is familiar to their imaginative world. The best examples offer more that just consuming entertainment: be it in the shape of coloring books, cut-out masks or other objects, or participation in a contest or sweepstake – the important thing is to be active; to do, instead of just passively sitting.

Good children's menu cards involve the child – actually their function is that of a toy. And of course they should be allowed to take home the result of their creativity. Children's menu cards of this kind are one-time items not designed for re-using.

Even though it seems that children's menu cards do not meet a grown-up's requirements, they are to a very large degree addressed to the adult clientele. They signalize:

* This restaurant cares about the – often difficult! – young customers.
* It provides a special service so that parents may relax and enjoy their own culinary experience.

By meeting these expectations the children's menu card fulfils quite a marketing task. It draws the young clientele and impresses adults as a positive image-segment. In the minds of stress-plagued parents, having their children feel comfortable is very often a deciding factor for a return-visit.

Design suited for children, this generally means colorful and figurative. Inspiration is often drawn from the world of comic-strips and fairytales, also very popular are animal cartoons with humanized features. To use already familiar and well-known comic-strip motives creates a certain synergetic effect; whereas inventing a new symbol, especially if one manages to create a close connection to the gastronomical products, can cause positive brand-name-association at a very early stage.

Consequently, in the visual art of children's menu cards, the presentation of foods and beverages is not the primary objective. Since it is not what children are interested in, the seemingly most important function of a card – presentation of food and drink – is reduced to practically nil.

Instead of reproducing an adult's hierarchy of values, a designer of children's menu cards has to think himself back to childhood, down to the language he uses to communicate the offered items. Children require different consideration in the way of addressing them, choice of words and even script choosen for printing.

Card system:
Miscellaneous folded card, size when closed: 17.5 × 29.5 cm. Front and back covers entirely illustrated. Colored front cover drawing with identification figure "Pedro Churrasco." Inside b/w with additional color red: comic-strip with Pedro as protagonist. May be colored by children. Food and beverage selection very unobtrusive: inserted in red squares. The dishes' names are centered around the comic-figure: Pedro Power Portion, etc.

Special features:
A prime example for development of a child-related "in-house"-identification and symbol figure for the gastronomical brand. Requires some explanations; text on the folded-in back cover. Conceptualized as continuing comic series: an additional attraction and entertainment moment.

Name:
Churrasco Steakrestaurants Germany (Whitbread Restaurants Holding Deutschland, Düsseldorf/Whitbread-Gruppe, Great Britain)

Business type/character:
Steakhouse conception, multiplied.

Card:
Children's menu card, designed as cartoon.

Draft/Design:
Detlef von der Weiden, Cologne (illustrations)/ Churrasco Steakrestaurants Deutschland

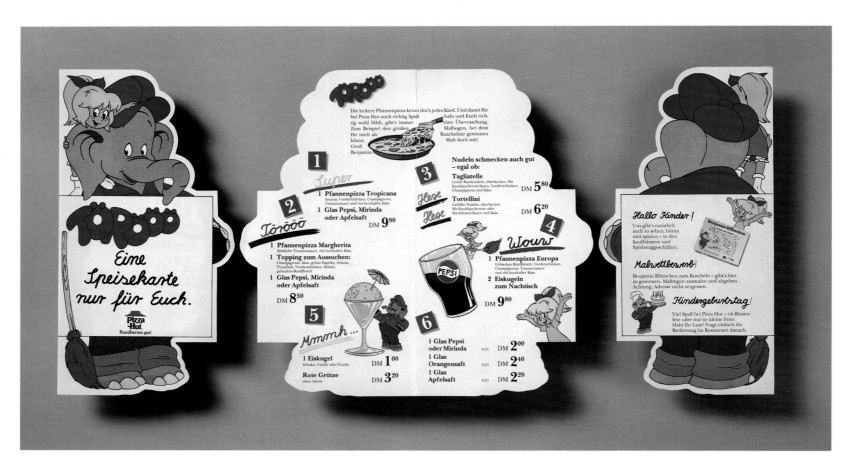

Name:

Pizza Hut Restaurants Deutschland (Pizza Hut Restaurationsgesellschaft, Mühlheim a.d. Ruhr/ PepsiCo-Guppe, USA)

Business type/character:

Pizza parlor, family-oriented. Product approach founded in US pizza culture. Multiplied.

Card:

Children's menu.

Card system:

Simply folded cover, paper, printed on both sides and punched. Size when closed: 15×27.5 cm (maximum). The card's shape correlates with cover motif: two popular cartoon-figures—Benjamin Blümchen and Bibi Blocksberg. Both figures also feature in the card's inside (selection of food and beverages). Outside back cover with information on drawing competition and birthday-party arrangements.

Special features:

Sympathy transfer by employment of cartoonfigures extremely popular among children. Extensive employment also on table-sets (35×25 cm) with product promotion: menu for children and adults, children promotion coupons as well as other sales promotion means. Especially for children: a small Benjamin-figurine, which is fastened to the spatular handle for children's pizza, paint-and-cut-out sheets.

Draft/Design:

Pizza Hut (Idea)/MTB Werbeagentur, Mühlheim a.d. Ruhr (realization)

Name:
Wienerwald-Restaurants Österreich/Deutschland_ (Wigast, Vienna)

Business type/character:
Poultry specialties, multiplied.

Card:
"Iss mit!" (Eat along!): children's menu.

Card system:
Simply folded cover, color print on both sides. Size when closed: 21 × 24 cm. Color drawing on outside front cover, insides b/w-motifs on blue background to be colored by children. Children's menu selection on small stripe running the length of both pages at the bottom. Two picture puzzles on the outside back cover.

Special features:
Emphasis on pastime and entertainment aspects; selection communication is secondary. The card is expressly designed for the children to take home. Card is used in Austria and Germany with varying menu offers.

Draft/Design:
RSCG Jasch & Schramm, Vienna (today: Euro RSCG)

Name:
Stockheim-Gastronomie, Düsseldorf

Business type/character:
Various gastronomical conceptions, predominantly at locations characterized by high traffic volume (airports, railroad stations).

Card:
Children's menu, used until 1990 in the airport restaurants at Cologne and Düsseldorf.

Card system:
Simply folded cover printed on both sides, size when closed: 14.5 × 21 cm. Outside front cover in full color, inside and back cover with illustrations to be colored by children. Small menu selection on the inside.

Special features:
Two slits for inserting crayons are punched into the right side of the card.

Draft/Design:
Stockheim Public Relations

Name:
Mövenpick Restaurants Schweiz/Deutschland
(Mövenpick Unternehmungen, Adliswil)

Business type/character:
Emphasis on enjoyment, casualness. Profile emphasis: quality and diversion. Seasonal cuisine. Uniform basic philosophy; appearance and selection vary.

Masks:
No menu cards, exclusively designed as toys for children. Three examples from a large selection of motifs. Each motif color printed on one side, punched, and with openings for eyes, nose, and ears. Size: approximately 36×25 cm (maximum).

Special features:
The masks are taken from the company's extensive menu card pool, principally usable by all Swiss and German businesses.

Draft/Design:
Mövenpick Werbung Restaurants Schweiz, Adliswil

Name:
Restaurant "Lord Nelson," Hamburg

Business type/character:
Hotel restaurant in the Holiday Inn Crowne Plaza, Hamburg.

Card:
"Was magst Du am liebsten" (what is your favorite dish); children's menu.

Card system:
Simply folded cover, color print on the outside, inside b/w. Size when closed: 25 × 25 cm. Front cover with punched circle, allowing view of the illustration on the inside. Cover illustration in relatively modern style. Bilingual: cover text as well as menu selection on the inside in German and English.

Special features:
The offered dishes' fantasy names are taken from the fairy tale, comic, and movie world. The card can be colored and taken along.

Draft/Design:
Adapted from an affiliated hotel in Munich

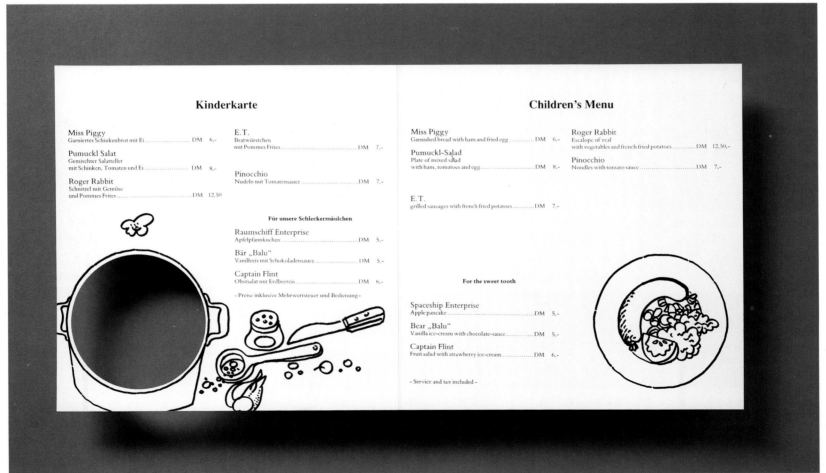

Kinderkarte

Miss Piggy
Garniertes Schinkenbrot mit Ei .... DM 6,-

Pumuckl Salat
Gemischter Salatteller
mit Schinken, Tomaten und Ei .... DM 8,-

Roger Rabbit
Schnitzel mit Gemüse
und Pommes Frites .... DM 12,50

E.T.
Bratwürstchen
mit Pommes Frites .... DM 7,-

Pinocchio
Nudeln mit Tomatensauce .... DM 7,-

Für unsere Schleckermäulchen

Raumschiff Enterprise
Apfelpfannkuchen .... DM 5,-

Bär „Balu"
Vanilleeis mit Schokoladensauce .... DM 5,-

Captain Flint
Obstsalat mit Erdbeereis .... DM 6,-

- Preise inklusive Mehrwertsteuer und Bedienung -

Children's Menu

Miss Piggy
Garnished bread with ham and fried egg .... DM 6,-

Pumuckl-Salad
Plate of mixed salad
with ham, tomatoes and egg .... DM 8,-

E.T.
grilled sausages with french fried potatoes .... DM 7,-

Roger Rabbit
Escalope of veal
with vegetables and french fried potatoes .... DM 12,50,-

Pinocchio
Noodles with tomato sauce .... DM 7,-

For the sweet tooth

Spaceship Enterprise
Apple pancake .... DM 5,-

Bear „Balu"
Vanilla ice-cream with chocolate-sauce .... DM 5,-

Captain Flint
Fruit salad with strawberry ice-cream .... DM 6,-

- Service and tax included -

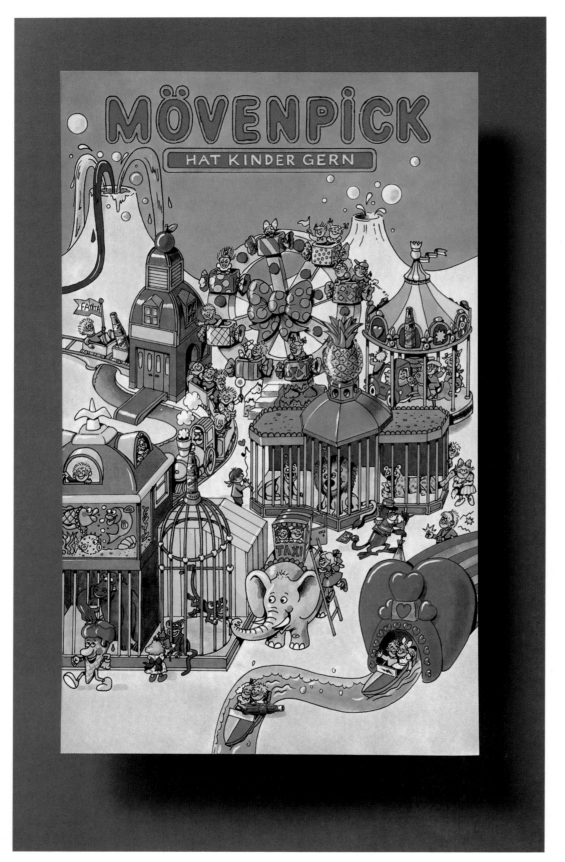

Name:
Mövenpick Restaurants Schweiz/Deutschland (Mövenpick Unternehmungen, Adliswil)

Business type/character:
Emphasis on enjoyment, casualness. Profile emphasis: quality and diversion. Seasonal cuisine. Uniform basic philosophy; appearance and selection vary.

Card:
Children's menu: "Mövenpick hat Kinder gern" (Mövenpick is fond of children).

Card system:
Simply folded cover, colorprinted on both sides, gloss-foil laminated. Size when closed: 24.5 × 40 cm. Outside front covers with full-format colorful illustrations; idealized children's adventure world with zoo, fun-fair, and wonderland motifs. Inside pages also illustrated, the right side with blank square for posting the individual menu selection sheets.

Special features:
Integrated into the card: picture puzzle with on-the-spot prize awarding. Keeping-the-children-occupied and richness in detail are two elements of the exemplary realization of a children's menu pastime function. The card is taken from the company's extensive menu card pool, principally usable by all Swiss and German businesses.

Draft/Design:
Mövenpick Werbung Restaurants Schweiz, Adliswil

Within the image:
Rosenberger
Restaurants
Die Kinderfreundlichen

Besuchen Sie unsere Restaurants
an Österreichs Autobahnen
Großram   St. Pölten
Strengberg   St. Valentin
Haag   Gralla Ost
Ansfelden-Nord   Innsbruck-Ampaß
                 Angath
Copyright by Rosenberger

Speisenangebote
siehe Rückseite

Name:
Rosenberger-Gruppe, St. Pölten

Business type/character:
Hotel and motorway restaurants; restaurants in urban hot spots. A wide range of business types ranging from service restaurants to market restaurant. Currently a total of 22 hotels and restaurants in Austria (with partners).

Card:
Children's menu card, designed as punch-out paper farm. Employed in all businesses.

Card system:
Cardboard printed on both sides, size: 29.5 × 21 cm. Outside front cover color illustrated with farmyard figures. The motifs' contours are perforated, they can be punched out and mounted right on the table. Outside back cover green/white with menu und beverage selection (children's menus).

Special features:
Prices are not stated in Schilling, but in Groschen (equivalent to pennies). The entire card is primarily intended for playing purposes. Children cards change every six to nine months; they're used simultaneously in the entire group.

Draft/Design:
Rosenberger-Gruppe

Name:
Mövenpick Restaurants Schweiz/Deutschland
(Mövenpick Unternehmungen, Adliswil)

Business type/character:
Emphasis on enjoyment, casualness. Profile emphasis: quality and diversion. Seasonal cuisine. Uniform basic philosophy; appearance and selection vary.

Set:
Children's table set sized at 40 × 30 cm. Its black and white illustrations can be colored by children; exclusively conceptualized for entertainment and pastime purposes.

Special features:
The card is taken from the company's extensive menu card pool, principally usable by all Swiss and German businesses.

Draft/Design:
Mövenpick Werbung Restaurants Schweiz, Adliswil

Für jede ausgemalte Karte gibt's eine kleine Überraschung! Schreib Deinen Namen, Deine Adresse und Dein Alter auf die Rückseite und wirf die Karte in den Sonder-briefkasten neben der Tür.
Die schönsten Karten werden übrigens aufgehängt.

Sollest Du mit dem Ausmalen
nicht fertig werden, dann
nimm die Karte mit nach
Haus und schick sie uns.

Restaurant Chili's
Boznerplatz 6
6020 Innsbruck

Name
_____

Adresse
_____

_____

Alter
_____

Name:
Chili's, Innsbruck (System-Gastronomie, Innsbruck)

Business type/character:
Tex-Mex restaurant, product emphasis on Mexican specialties, steaks, burgers. Strong in atmosphere.

Card:
Children's menu card with integrated drawing competition.

Card system:
Cardboard printed on both sides with gable punching and folding groove. Size when closed/folded: 21×15 cm; b/w with additional color bordeaux. On the outside front cover scrawled motifs for drawing; children's selection inserted in black field. Back cover: address field and explanations concerning the drawing competition on the part of the back cover to be folded forward. The folded card looks like an envelope.

Special features:
Emphasis on fun and pastime; selection communication is relatively secondary. Nice idea: the best drawings are exhibited in the restaurant.

Draft/Design:
System-Gastronomie, Innsbruck

Maiskolben am Grill goldbraun gebraten	26.-
Mini (Hamm) Burger mit Pommes Frites	56.-
Hühnerbrüstchen gebraten, mit kleinem Baked Potato	56.-
Mini-Steak mit Maisgemüse und Knoblauchbrot	78.-